CONTENTS

Basics

The skills of brick laying, mixing and laying concrete, outdoor plumbing and simple woodwork are the basics for every handyman working in the garden. This section has information on all these techniques.

BRICKS & MORTAR

When you look around you will see there is an enormous variety of bricks available – but the most common type has an orange-brown colour and is extensively used for houses, garages and garden walls. These are called 'flettons', because they are made from fletton clay, but are generally known as 'commons'.

Facing bricks are the only other type used extensively for domestic purposes. These are also made of fletton clay but have a more decorative appearance, formed by burning mineral granules or coarse sand into the clay. Facing bricks can be obtained with all-round decorative faces or with just three.

Bricks are manufactured in one size only – $225 \times 112.5 \times 75$mm ($9 \times 4\frac{1}{2} \times 3$ in) – but the actual size is 10mm (or $\frac{3}{8}$ in) less all round. The reason for this is quite simple: since mortar is used to join the bricks, the thickness of each joint – a built-in allowance of 10mm ($\frac{3}{8}$ in) – is added to all three dimensions. This makes it much easier to calculate accurately the number of bricks required.

The V-shaped indentation in one face – called a frog – allows plenty of mortar to lie in the brick, giving a firmer bond to the flat surface of the brick that will be laid above.

Second-hand bricks

Builders' merchants not only sell new bricks but some also supply second-hand ones obtained from local demolition sites. In many areas you are positively welcome at demolition sites to buy old materials; and if you buy from such a site, you have a good chance of getting bricks to match the existing ones in your own property.

The other obvious advantage of second-hand bricks is they are cheaper; but you must select them carefully. Choose bricks which have the least mortar on them, because this has to be chipped off with a bolster chisel and club hammer before the bricks can be used. Try to get those where the mortar looks sandy because this will crumble off easily with the help of a wire brush. Reject any cracked bricks and ones with very porous faces.

The right mortar

Mortar for general bricklaying is made by mixing one part Portland cement, one part hydrated lime and six parts clean builder's sand. If you want a stronger mix – for a garden wall, for example, which has to withstand more extreme elements – a mix of one part Portland cement to three parts sand should be used. This mortar will be more workable if a small amount of liquid plasticizer, available from builders' merchants, is added to the mix. Then use just sufficient clean water to make the mortar workable.

Estimating how much mortar to mix depends on how quickly you can lay bricks. This is important because mortar becomes useless within a couple of hours. So start by mixing small batches. Do not add water to setting mortar because the mix will become too weak to support the weight of the bricks.

Professional bricklayers use a different system, which is worth following once you have gained enough experience. Soak the lime in water overnight. In the morning pour off the surplus water and mix the lime with sand in the proportions given earlier. Use only a small amount of water so a stiff consistency is achieved. The resultant mix is known as 'coarse stuff'. During a day's work you can add cement – in the proportion of 1:6 – to the 'coarse stuff' to give you small batches of mortar quickly as and when you need them. The 'coarse stuff' will stiffen from time to time, but if you sprinkle on some water and turn the mix over, it will keep it fresh.

Ready-mix

Many people doing a job requiring only a couple of hundred bricks prefer to use one of the proprietary mortar mixes. These are supplied in large bags and contain all the necessary ingredients: all you have to do is empty the bag and mix in water according to the instructions. A 20 kilogram (or 44 lb) bag contains enough mortar for about 80 bricks. The only disadvantage is that for large jobs the cost is far greater than buying and mixing your own ingredients.

Below: When estimating what quantity of bricks you require for a particular job, remember the stated size of the brick includes an allowance for the mortar on all sides; there is no need to calculate this yourself
Bottom: Before using second-hand bricks, chip off any old mortar with a hammer and chisel

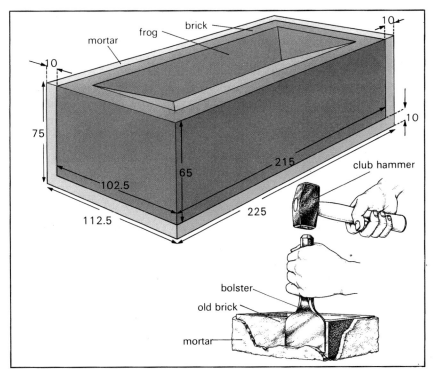

BASIC BRICKBUILDING

Accurate bricklaying on the correct foundations is vital for a professional finish – and a job that's permanent.

To ensure long-lasting brickwork pay particular attention to the foundations. If these are not adequate, in time the bricks may crack and the wall collapse. To support a brick wall you will need to make a level concrete strip foundation of a suitable depth and width for the proposed height of the wall. There are building regulations specifying the width, depth, thickness and reinforcements necessary for foundations, so consult your local building inspector for advice.

To make a concrete strip foundation first cut a trench in firm, previously undug ground. For a foundation which requires 225mm (or 9 in) thick concrete and one course of 75mm (or 3 in) thick brickwork below ground level you will need to dig a trench at least 300mm (or 12 in) deep. If at this depth you have not reached a really firm surface, you will have to dig on until you do: then fill the extra depth to the trench bottom with well compacted hardcore (broken brick and concrete). If you dig to a depth of 600mm (or 24 in), for example, you should have 300mm (or 12 in) of hardcore at the bottom, then 225mm (or 9 in) of concrete and finally 75mm (or 3 in) of brickwork. For a single brick wall 1m (39 in) high you will need a strip foundation of 100mm (or 4 in) thick concrete, 300mm (or 12 in) wide, in a trench of the same dimensions.

Preparing trench Using a builder's square to get accurate right-angles, set out the width and length of the trenches with lines fixed to pegs around each proposed corner and mark out the exact length at the corners with pins. To avoid having to cut bricks later it is worth

positioning a row to make sure they fit exactly within the proposed length of the trench. Replace the pegs with profile boards supported by wood pegs driven into the ground. Use low grade timber to make the boards which should be about 25mm (or 1 in) thick, 100–175mm (or 4–7 in) deep and 450mm (or 17 in) long. Cut four notches into the top edge of each board: two outer notches

Above: When the wall is finally up, put the finishing touches to it by pointing the mortar joints
Left: No wall will stand up properly unless built on the right foundations
1a *For a 225mm (9 in) thick wall you must lay 225mm (9 in) of concrete and one brick course in a trench at least 300mm (12 in) deep*
1b *If the base of the trench is not really firm, you must dig deeper and fill the extra depth with hardcore*
1c *With a single brick wall you need only lay 100mm (4 in) of concrete up to ground level*

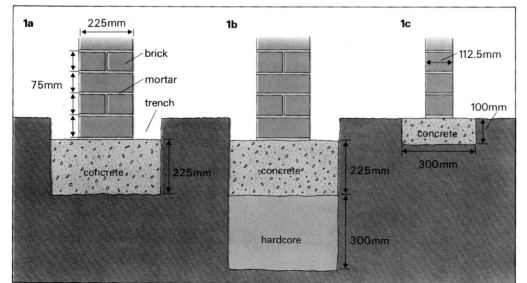

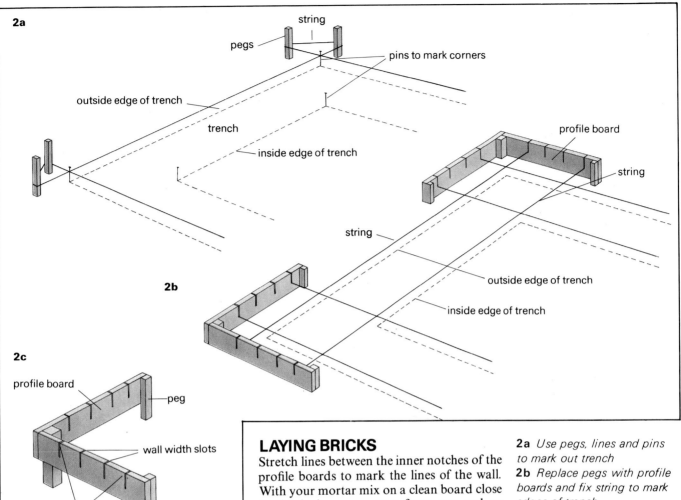

2a

string

pegs

pins to mark corners

outside edge of trench

trench

inside edge of trench

profile board

string

string

outside edge of trench

inside edge of trench

2b

2c

profile board

peg

wall width slots

trench width slots

to mark the width of the foundations and two inner notches to mark the thickness of the wall. Make sure the profile boards are level and of the same height and that they are set well back from the edge of the trench. Measure the diagonals to check they are of equal length to ensure the corners are true right-angles. Stretch lines between the outer notches of the boards; you can then dig the trench.

Laying concrete

Once the trench is dug to the required depth, drive a series of flat wood pegs into the trench so the tops of each are set at the proposed level of the finished concrete. This makes the final levelling of the concrete a lot easier. The length of the pegs required will depend on the depth of the trench and an extra 100–150mm (4–6 in) should be allowed for driving into the soil. Place any hardcore required around the pegs and across the trench, compacting each section thoroughly. Take care not to move any pegs out of level as you work. Then pour the concrete, which should be on the dry side, and pack it down firmly to peg top level. Let the surface harden before laying any bricks.

LAYING BRICKS

Stretch lines between the inner notches of the profile boards to mark the lines of the wall. With your mortar mix on a clean board close to the laying area, start from one end or corner and spread the mortar with a bricklayer's trowel. The mortar should form a bed about 16mm (or $\frac{5}{8}$ in) thick, trowelled as level as possible, and should cover the greater part of the concrete with a clear border on each side. Using the line indicating the outer side of the wall as a guide, mark its position onto the mortar bed at suitable intervals using a spirit level vertically. Use the point of the trowel to score a line between these marks in the soft mortar to provide a guide for setting down the first course of bricks. Remove the profile lines and start building the corners of the walls.

The simplest method of joining or bonding

2a *Use pegs, lines and pins to mark out trench*
2b *Replace pegs with profile boards and fix string to mark edges of trench*
2c *Profile boards must be notched to indicate widths of trench and wall*
3a & 3b *Use pegs as guide to mark final concrete level*
4a *Use a string for outside of wall as guide to mark mortar with spirit level; score line*
4b *Remove string and start building corners*
4c *Check corners are square*
4d *Check depth of each course with gauge rod*
4e *Use pins and line as guide to lay infill bricks*

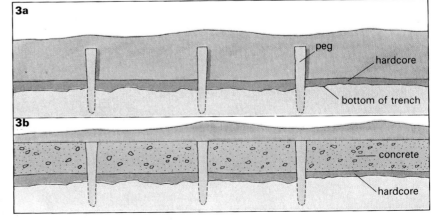

3a

peg

hardcore

bottom of trench

3b

concrete

hardcore

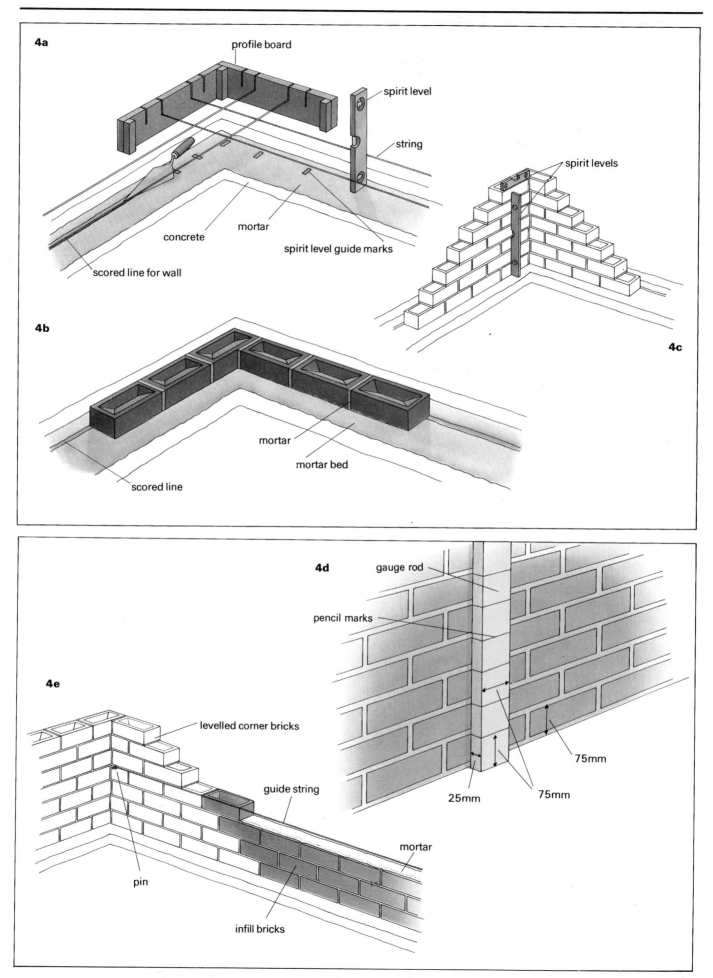

4a

profile board

spirit level

string

spirit levels

concrete

mortar

spirit level guide marks

scored line for wall

4b

mortar

mortar bed

scored line

4c

4d

gauge rod

pencil marks

75mm

25mm

75mm

4e

levelled corner bricks

guide string

mortar

pin

infill bricks

bricks is called stretcher bonding. By this method every brick in a wall is laid lengthwise so the vertical joint between two bricks in one course lies in the centre of a brick in the courses above and below. To make corners in single thickness walls using this method you will not need to cut bricks, provided there are four corners.

Build up the corners to about six or seven courses high. Check with the spirit level to make sure each corner is a true vertical and place a gauge rod against it as each brick is added to check the thickness of your mortar bed. You can make a gauge rod from a piece of 75 × 25mm (3 × 1 in) timber about 1m (39 in) long. Mark clear lines across the face at 75mm (3 in) intervals using a try square.

For accurate positioning of infill bricks (those bricks linking up the corners) you will need a fine string line and two steel pins. Push the pins into the mortar bed at each end directly above the line of bricks to be laid. With the string held taut by the pins, you will have a straight, level line against which to set the bricks. Move the pins and line up course by course until the corner height levels have been reached.

Trowelling mortar

Mix the mortar so it slides easily off the trowel but keeps its form when in place. Lift a small amount of mortar at a time and spread it as evenly as possible. Aim to spread it along a line from the centre of the bricks.

Spread one end of each brick with mortar and place that end close to the brick previously laid, trying to keep an even mortar line to match the horizontal beds. Remember the recessed part of the brick, known as the frog, is placed face upwards. Use the handle

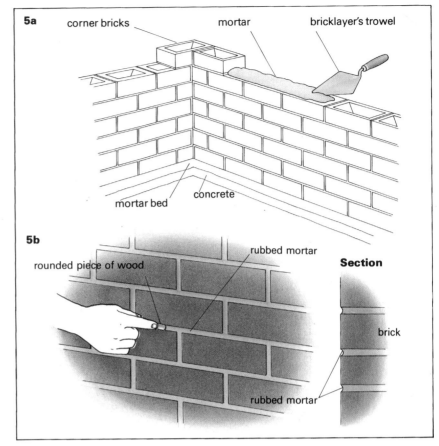

5a Spread even line of mortar along centre of bricks when infilling courses
5b Simplest joint made by running round piece of metal or wood along mortar
6a Split bricks by tapping firmly with bolster and hammer
6b You can break bricks with edge of trowel

end of the trowel to tap the brick into the mortar for any slight adjustment. Until you gain experience, it is best to use a spirit level at intervals to check the line both along and across the bricks. Remove surplus mortar by drawing the edge of the trowel along the bottom edge of the bricks, then use a rounded piece of metal or wood to form a rubbed joint between the bricks. This is the easiest finish.

CUTTING BRICKS

When a single brick wall exceeds 2.5m (or 8 ft) in length, you will have to build piers into it. These consist of a double thickness of bricks which have to be bonded correctly to give the maximum support strength to the wall. This means cutting bricks in half and three-quarter lengths.

Clearly mark the cutting line and use a brick bolster and club hammer to tap a surface cut along the line on all sides of the brick. (To sharpen a blunt bolster, file the edge at an angle from either side of the blade until a keen cutting edge is produced.) Once the groove has been cut, turn the brick (frog down) on a flat surface. Place the bolster into the groove on the flat underside of the brick and use the club hammer with a little more force. A clean break should result. As you gain experience, you will find you can cut most bricks by bringing down the side of the trowel with some force on each side in turn.

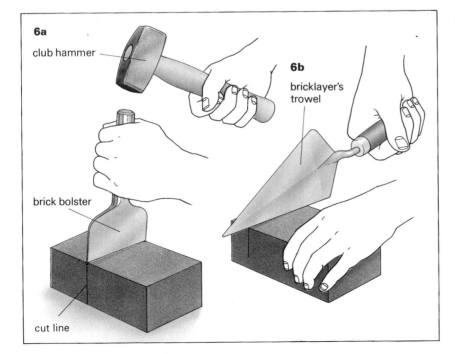

11

MIXING CONCRETE

Concrete is widely used in both the home and garden; you can buy it in pre-packed dry-mix form for small jobs, mix your own ingredients for medium size work or have ready-mixed concrete delivered in bulk, ready to lay, when tackling large areas. The basic concrete mix is Portland cement, sand, stones and water. The cement is normally grey but other colours, including white, are available for decorative work, although all are more expensive than the standard grey. If using colouring, you may have difficulty achieving a uniform effect.

The sand and stones (called aggregate) are bonded by the cement as it reacts with water to form a mineral glue which, helped by the aggregate, gains in strength as it hardens. Only sharp, washed sand should be used; soft sand is mainly used for mortar when laying bricks. The type of aggregate varies according to the type of job. For foundations or other large jobs, use a coarse aggregate: gravel, crushed gravel or crushed stone between 5 and 20mm ($\frac{3}{16}-\frac{3}{4}$ in) in diameter. For finer jobs, such as making window sills or slabs, use a coarse sand or a mix of sand and fine shingle not more than 10mm ($\frac{3}{8}$ in) in diameter. Coarse aggregate mixed with sand (known as a combined aggregate or ballast) is generally the most convenient way of buying the material from a builders' merchant – but make sure you are sold washed ballast.

Water Always use clean tap water and add only enough to make the concrete workable, usually about half a bucket for each bucket of cement. If you add too much water, the mix will be sloppy and will shrink on drying; too little and the mix will be difficult to work and small air pockets will appear in the finished work. Both of these defects cause weakening of the finished concrete. Mixing becomes easier if you add a proprietary wetting agent or some washing-up liquid to each bucket of water.

Above right: Keep materials separate and store cement bags clear of the ground
Right: Use our graph to estimate what quantity of concrete you will need. Find the area to be concreted on the vertical scale; read across the lines of the graph until you reach the desired thickness and then down to the horizontal scale to find the volume of concrete. You will find how much of each ingredient you need for the different volumes by reading across the bottom scales. The shaded area indicates when ready-mix concrete is more economical

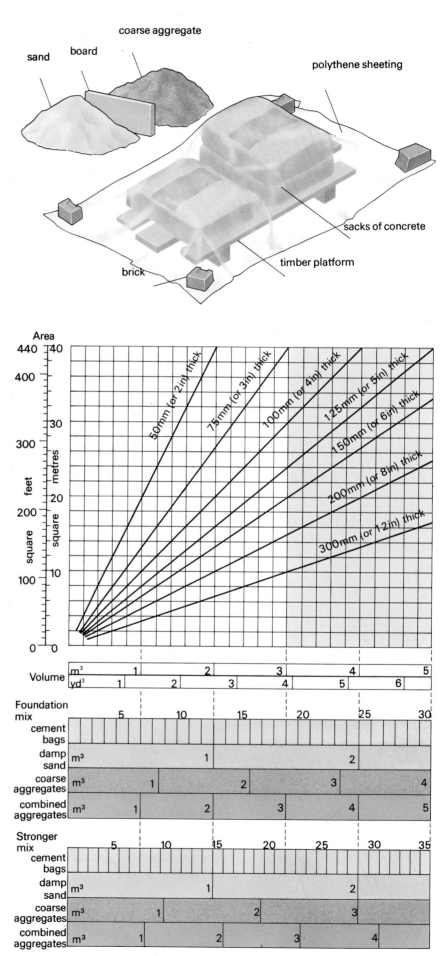

Lime A handful of hydrated lime added to each mix will slow the setting time and the concrete will be less likely to shrink and crack.

PVA The mixing becomes smoother if you add PVA (builders' merchants stock several proprietary brands) to the water; this also helps to reduce the dust when the concrete has set. Neat PVA brushed onto existing concrete helps to bond a fresh layer.

Ready-mix concrete

There are several companies who will deliver ready-mixed concrete to your home and will advise you on the best mix for a particular job. Before you order, decide whether the site is accessible, if you can get the preparatory work done by your delivery date and whether you can organize enough volunteer labour among your friends to help you lay the concrete before it becomes unworkable. The smallest economic load is about 3 cu m (4 cu yds).

Pre-packed concrete

Bagged in various sizes and grades, pre-packed mixes are an expensive way of buying concrete for anything other than small jobs –

but, if storage is a problem they are useful and do save time in proportioning materials.

Storing materials

If you are storing cement outdoors, keep the bags clear of the ground and cover them with waterproof sheeting. Bagged aggregate is easier to store than loose material, but is more expensive. If you are storing more than one type of loose aggregate, you must put a board between each one to keep them separate. Never store materials on earth.

Warning If you are leaving materials overnight in the road outside your house, you must place red warning lamps alongside and should not obstruct the pavement.

Estimating quantities

Using our easy-to-check graph decide how much concrete you want for each task and how much of each material you need. Wastage is not allowed for, but add an extra ten percent for cement and round up your aggregate requirements to the next half or whole cubic measurement.

First work out the area you are concreting and relate this to the desired thickness of concrete; this gives you the volume you

1 *When mixing concrete by hand, tip the ingredients into a neat pile*
2 *Make a crater in the middle, pour in water and turn in material from the outside*
3 *Add more water as necessary, using a watering can to regulate the amount*
4 *Turn the pile with a shovel to mix the materials thoroughly*

Normal strength blockwork and rendering mortar is made from one part cement, one part lime and six parts soft (builder's) sand. For lightweight blockwork use one part cement, two parts lime and nine parts soft sand. Bedding mortar consists of one part cement to five parts sharp (concreting) sand.

Most supplies of sand and aggregate will be delivered damp due to washing at the quarry or being left uncovered. If in hot weather your supplies are delivered dry, you will need to reduce your sand or ballast content and increase the water content accordingly. After a little experience you will get the feel of the right texture for each mix and should not have any problems achieving the correct balance every time.

Mixing the concrete
If you are mixing the concrete yourself, you can do it by hand – using a shovel, buckets and a watering can – or you can hire a cement mixer. The mixers run on either petrol or mains electricity; some can be powered by an electric drill. Also available is a manual roller mixer which turns the concrete as you roll it along. Bear in mind petrol-driven machines are noisy; if you are using one for prolonged periods, you may disturb the neighbours.

If concreting is likely to take some weeks, it may be worth buying a second-hand mixer and selling it when you have finished.

Because concrete hardens quickly, you should not mix more than you can lay while it remains workable. Never allow concrete to harden in a mixer; wash the mixer out with water and a stiff brush before it sets, otherwise you will have to spend a lot of time with a hammer and chisel before you can return the mixer to the hire firm or use it again.
Mixing by hand Work on a firm, dry surface. Using buckets, measure out the sand and the aggregate and form it into a compact heap with a crater in the middle. Add the cement and turn the heap until the materials are uniform in colour. If using a pre-packed mix, turn the materials over until the colour is consistent.

Pour water into the crater and turn in dry material from the outside; keep mixing and adding water until the whole pile is of a consistent form and colour.
Machine mixing Make sure the machine is level. Place half the aggregate and half the water in the machine and mix them for a short time. Add the cement and the remainder of the aggregate and water until you achieve the correct consistency. Mix for about two minutes, but not for much longer. The concrete should fall cleanly off the blades in the drum without being too soupy.
Warning Don't wash surplus cement into drains since it will set at the bottom and cause a blockage.

5 *When using a machine, mix half the water with half the aggregate, then add the cement and the remainder of the water and aggregate*
6 *After a few minutes the concrete will be of workable consistency and is ready for use*

require, so you can establish the quantities of each ingredient. Determining the area of a rectangle (one side multiplied by the adjacent side) is simple, so is a triangle (half one side multiplied by the perpendicular height from that side). For other areas with straight sides, break them down into squares, rectangles and triangles and add them together.

Basic mixes
There are four basic mixes. For foundations etc. where the thickness of the concrete is 75mm (3 in) or more, you need one part cement, two and a half parts damp sand and four parts coarse aggregate. A stronger mix more suited to small units or thin sections will be made from one part cement, two parts damp sand and three parts coarse aggregate.

LAYING A SLAB OF CONCRETE

The principles of laying concrete are the same whether you are working on large or small areas. We describe here the techniques necessary for laying a concrete slab, such as might form the base for a garden shed or garage. As with all concrete, the right preparation is vital.

Site conditions and the finished thickness of your concrete base determine the depth of subsoil you must remove and the amount of hardcore to be rammed in before you lay any concrete. For a small job a base of 75mm (3 in) deep is usually sufficient, unless the soil is very soft clay when the thickness should be 100mm (4 in). The subsoil should be firm and fairly level and if you are digging into a well-compacted subsoil you should stop approximately 125–150mm (5–6 in) below the finishing level of the concrete. If you are working on recently laid topsoil, dig out to a depth of at least 225mm (9 in) and then compact the soil with the back of a shovel or a punner or ramming tool.

Warning You must dig out topsoil, vegetation and roots over an area that extends 150mm (6 in) on all sides of the planned base.

Making formwork
Now make a formwork to the required level and dimensions of your base. Use 25mm (1in) thick timber of the same width as the depth of your intended finished base, with lengths cut to the appropriate size. Sharpen one end of each of the timber pegs to a point and drive the pegs partway into the ground about 1m (or 39 in) apart. Check each corner for squareness with a builder's square and drive the pegs into the ground until the proper level is reached. Nail the outer edges of the timber to the pegs, with the tops of the pegs flush with the top of the edging timber.

Planning drainage
If a drainage slope is required, a fall of 1:60 is usually sufficient, as long as the surface of the concrete is flat and smooth. You can achieve this drop by gently hammering one end of the formwork deeper into the ground than its opposite end. To check whether you have the right fall, place a board across the formwork in the direction of the required slope and a 15mm ($\frac{5}{8}$ in) shim under the lower end of a 900mm (3ft) spirit level. When the bubble shows dead centre, you will have achieved the correct fall. Make the test at both sides and in the middle of the formwork.

Making hardcore base
Spread coarse hardcore inside the formwork on top of the firm subsoil base. Broken brick, broken concrete or stonework is ideal. Keep the smaller grade hardcore or clinker and spread this between the larger pieces to bring up the level to the bottom edges of the formwork. Tread it down firmly or force it down with a ramming tool or punner.

Damp proofing
Concrete is a porous material and will allow moisture to rise through it from the base. If you want a dry concrete floor, in a shed for example, place a damp proof membrane of plastic sheeting over the base before laying the concrete.

Make sure the base is well compacted and level off sharp corners of the hardcore to prevent it ripping the membrane; for added

Above: Successful concreting depends on the right base, of which hardcore is an essential ingredient
1 Make sure your site is firm and level and clear an extra 150mm all round
2 Set out the formwork, using a builder's square to ensure the corners are at right-angles
3 If you need a slope for drainage, hammer one side of the formwork further into the ground. To check the fall is accurate, place a spirit level on a board across the formwork in the direction of the required slope and put the correct size of shim under one end of the level. When the bubble is dead centre, you will have the right fall

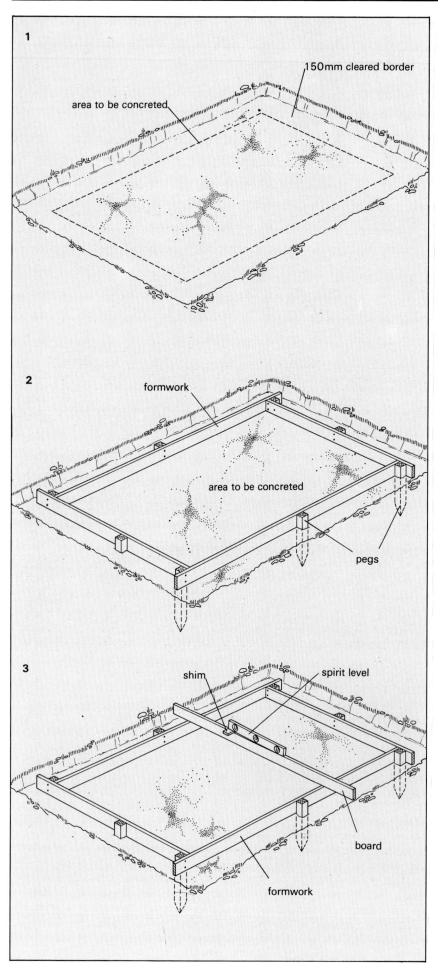

1

area to be concreted

150mm cleared border

2

formwork

area to be concreted

pegs

3

shim

spirit level

board

formwork

protection, place sharp sand on top of the base and level it carefully. Lay a sheet of 1000-gauge plastic sheeting over the sand, turning it up the sides of the formwork. If necessary, overlap the sheets by at least 150mm (6 in). Then lay concrete on top.

Laying concrete

Now the concrete can be spread on top of the hardcore. Mix your concrete as near to the base as possible to reduce the distance you have to carry the heavy wet mix. Make sure you have a firm, clean mixing surface – a solid path is ideal since this can be washed down after the mixing is finished. If this is any distance away from the site, use a wheelbarrow to transport the wet mix.

Wheelbarrow plank It might be necessary to carry concrete down steps. You can overcome this hazard by laying a builder's deal plank, which should never be less than 32mm ($1\frac{1}{4}$ in) thick, across the steps. Spike the top end in place and hammer in pegs each side at the bottom to prevent it moving sideways. This type of plank should never span more than 2m (6 ft 6 in) unsupported. The alternative is to use a builder's bucket and carry the wet mix to the site, depositing it in mounds within the formwork.

Use the rake to spread the concrete level and about 10–15mm ($\frac{3}{8}$–$\frac{5}{8}$ in) above the edges of the formwork.

Finishing methods

The concrete is now ready for compacting. This is an important stage which will give the finished job strength and durability. Any small voids in the mix are closed and the air is expelled by tamping down the surface with the edge of a timber plank – or a timber tamping board if you have help, with one person on each side of the formwork.

Tamping involves a chopping action and you should move the timber along the concrete, about half the thickness of the timber each time. Do this twice and any high or low spots will show. These surface deviations should be eliminated when you make one final pass along the entire surface with a sawing motion that will leave the surface ready for the finishing operation. If any low spots remain, add extra concrete and make another sawing pass. Various finishes can be applied to the surface, although the rippled effect left by the final sawing action is ideal for a drive or an incline where a grip might be required in icy conditions. This finish is generally too coarse for a floor base and is difficult to sweep.

Brushed finish A light brushing with a soft broom will remove the rippled effect and produce a smoother finish. The effect will vary, depending on how long the concrete is allowed to set before you start brushing. Test a small area at various stages until the desired

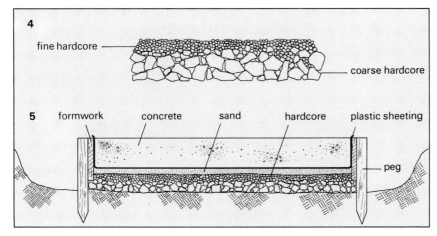

4 fine hardcore — coarse hardcore

5 formwork | concrete | sand | hardcore | plastic sheeting | peg

finish is achieved, then complete the entire area.

If you leave the brushed effect until the concrete is quite firm, you can make another light brushing, having sprinkled water on the concrete through a fine rose on a watering can. This will expose the aggregate, giving a smooth but stony effect to the surface. Timing is crucial as the aggregate can be washed out if the water is applied too soon – and the surface will be ruined.

Wood float finish A lightly textured finish can be achieved by rubbing a wood float (using a light circular motion) across the surface soon after tamping down.

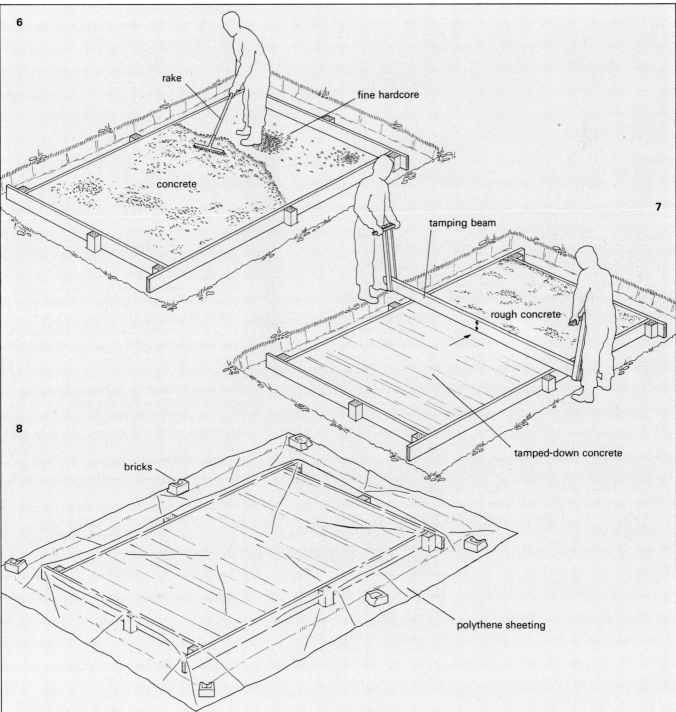

6 rake | fine hardcore | concrete

7 tamping beam | rough concrete | tamped-down concrete

8 bricks | polythene sheeting

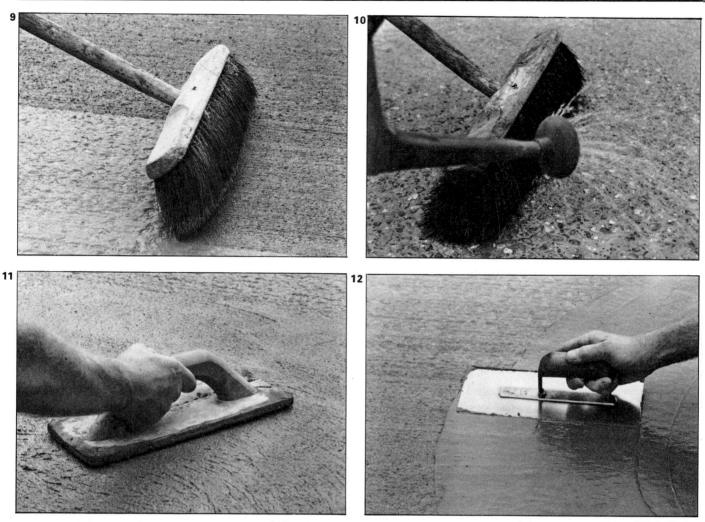

4 *Lay large grade hardcore packed with smaller pieces*
5 *Before laying a damp proof course, place sand over the hardcore*
6 *Rake the concrete level*
7 *Compact the concrete with a tamping beam*
8 *Cover finished concrete with polythene sheeting*
9–12 *Finishing techniques*
9 *Brush out ripples*
10 *Lightly dampen the surface for a smoother finish*
11 *Make a lightly textured finish with a wood float*
12 *For a really smooth finish, use a steel float*

Steel float finish After the wood float has been applied, a steel float will polish out the texture left by the wood float and provide a really durable finish. Don't use the steel float too soon after tamping or it may cut into the concrete. Wait long enough for the concrete to begin to harden at the top before working on the finish.

Curing concrete

When you are satisfied with the concrete finish, it is important you cure the concrete properly. This is one reason why you are advised against laying concrete in frosty conditions, since frost is concrete's biggest enemy. If frosts are likely (and they can occur even in May), protect the surface with a thick layer of straw under a sheet of polythene. If this is not available, cover the surface with a thick layer of sand or earth once the concrete is firm.

The concrete must be prevented from drying too quickly in hot weather. This can be done by covering the surface with sheet polythene or dampened hessian or sacking. Weight down the covering along the edges to prevent the wind lifting it. If sacking is used, keep it dampened for up to four days before removing it. In normal weather concrete takes a week to cure (ten days in cold weather), during which time the covers should be retained. The floor can be used as soon as the curing period is over.

Take precautions to keep children and animals off the new surface, since footprints and pawmarks are difficult to remove from a hardening surface.

Removing formwork Once the concrete is cured, you can uncover the surface and lever the formwork out of the ground. Dismantle the timber carefully, remove the nails from the board and pegs and store the timber in a dry place for future use.

For formwork
timber 25mm (1in) thick, 75 or 100mm (3 or 4in) wide
timber pegs 50 × 50mm (2 × 2in)
builder's square
measuring tape
spirit level, wood shim
club hammer
50mm (2in) galvanized wire nails

For finish
rake, tamping beam
punner or ramming tool
soft brush, wood and steel floats
polythene sheeting, hessian or sacking, straw (for protection)

equipment

FITTING AN OUTSIDE TAP

An outside tap, with a hose connector, is virtually essential for the gardener or car owner. It saves connecting a hose to the tap over the kitchen sink, which can involve an inconvenient suspension of other kitchen activities and, by creating back pressure within the tap, may lead to early gland failure – indicated by water round the spindle.

Fitting an outside tap is a job you can easily do yourself, particularly if you use a proprietary garden tap kit – you should be able to obtain one of these from your local builders' merchant or DIY stockist. Before you begin work you should get in touch with your local water authority to find out whether, and under what conditions, they will permit the connection of an outside tap to the rising main. Normally this will be allowed, but the authority will probably make an extra charge on the water rate for the use of the tap.

Preparing for installation

Drill a 25mm (1 in) diameter hole through the external wall to within 350mm (or 14 in) of the rising main and about 75mm (3 in) above the level at which the tap will be fitted. You can use a cold chisel and club hammer to make the hole, but an electric drill with a 25 mm (1 in) bit will, of course, make the job easier – particularly if the drill has a hammer action.

Turn off the main stopcock and drain the rising main from the tap over the kitchen sink –·if there is a draincock immediately above the stopcock, .drain from this as well. Use a hacksaw to cut a 19mm ($\frac{3}{4}$ in) piece out of the rising main at the same distance from the floor as the hole which you have cut through the wall. Make sure your cuts are made squarely and remove any burr from the pipe ends with a file.

Carrying out installation

Unscrew the cap nuts and olives from the two ends of the crosspiece or run of the tee junction supplied with the kit. Smear the pipe ends with boss white and slip first a cap nut and then an olive over one of the cut ends of the pipe. Smear the olive with boss white. To make fitting easier the tee junction has no pipe stop at one end; pull out the pipe end and slip this end of the tee over it. Push the olive up to the tee and loosely screw on the cap nut – don't tighten it. Fit the cap nut and olive

An outside tap is a useful addition to the home's plumbing system since it will ease the demand on the kitchen tap when watering the garden or washing the car. You will also be saved the inconvenience of wet feet messing up the floor, buckets slopping water or hose pipe trailing over the kitchen sink

over the other pipe and apply boss white as before, then push the tee up over this pipe end until the pipe end is firmly against the pipe stop. Move the olive up to the tee and screw on the cap nut. Make sure the outlet of the tee is directed, parallel to the wall, towards the hole you have cut in the wall. Hold the body of the tee with an adjustable wrench and tighten the cap nuts with a spanner – this will help prevent overtightening.

Screw-down stopcock Although not included in the garden tap kit, you should fit a screw-down stopcock into the length of pipe inside the kitchen. During winter this can be turned off and the outside tap opened to preclude any risk of frost damage. Fitting this stopcock will also reduce the time the rest of the plumbing system is not in action; once it is in positon – and turned off – the main stopcock can be opened so water flows through the rising main and all the domestic plumbing fittings can be brought back into use. This

means you can take your time over fitting the outside tap and avoid possible mistakes from trying to get the job done too quickly.

Cut a 200mm (or 8 in) length from the 330mm (13 in) pipe without elbow; fit one end of this into the tee in the rising main using a compression joint (cap nut, olive and boss white) in the same way as for fitting the tee. Attach the free end of the pipe to the inlet side of the stopcock, again using a compression joint. Take the 330mm (13 in) length of 15mm ($\frac{1}{2}$ in) copper tube with elbow attached and push it through the hole in the wall, from the inside, so the fixed connection of the elbow is inside the wall. Carefully measure the distance between the outlet of the screw-down stopcock and the outside end of this elbow and allow extra length for the pipe which will be within the fittings. Using a hacksaw, cut the remaining piece of copper tube without elbow to the required length and connect the two ends to the elbow and the outlet of the

Making the tee junction:
1a *Fit the cap nut and olive over the pipe end;*
1b *Push the body of the tee junction over the end of the pipe coated with boss white;*
1c *Fit the bottom pipe into the other end of the tee;*
1d *Tighten the cap nuts with a spanner, holding the body of the tee with an adjustable spanner*

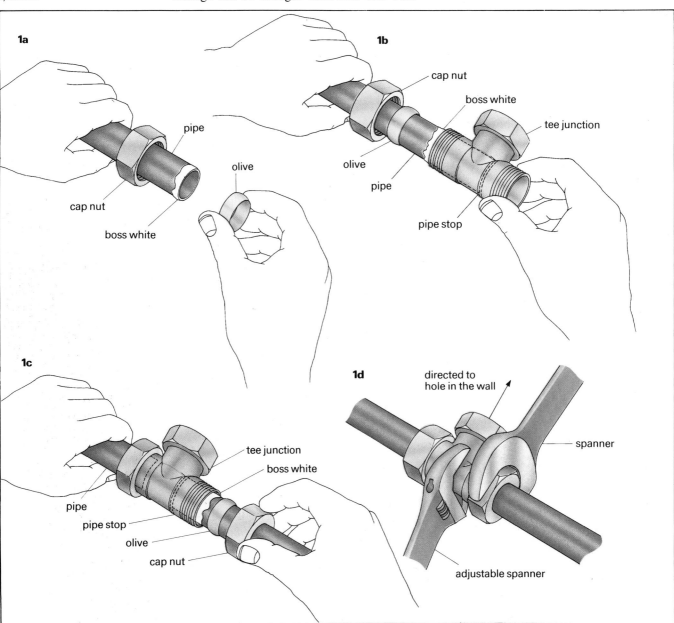

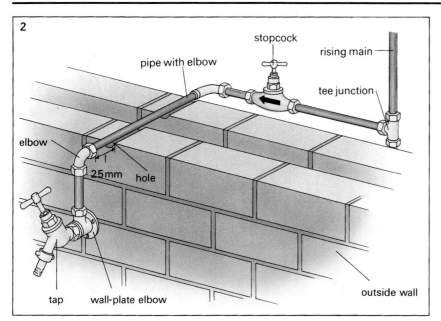

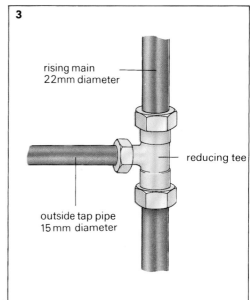

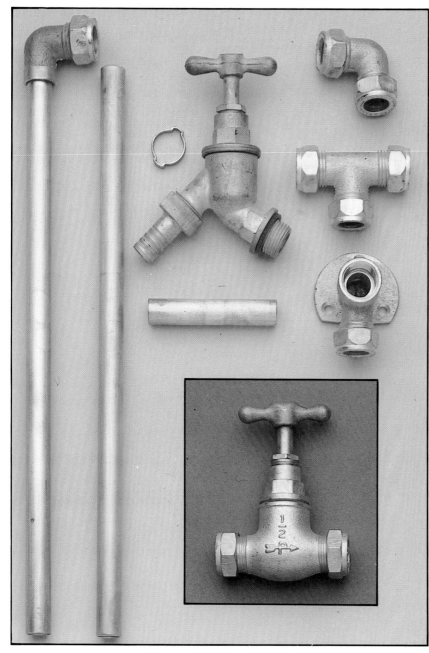

stopcock with compression joints as before.
Finishing off Outside the house, cut the pipe end so 25mm (1 in) is projecting from the hole in the wall. Connect the elbow joint to this pipe end so the outlet of the elbow points downward to the position at which you want to fix the outside tap. Place the wall-plate elbow against the wall, mark the screw positions and drill and plug the wall. Cut the short piece of copper tube to length, if necessary, and connect the outlet of the elbow projecting from the wall to the inlet of the wall-plate. Then screw the wall-plate to the wall. To ensure a watertight joint, bind PFTE thread sealing tape round the tail of the tap and screw the tap into the wall-plate elbow. If, when it is first screwed home, the tap is not upright, add washers to the tail until it comes to the right position. The tap handle will be angled away from the wall so you can turn it without grazing your fingers. Use an exterior grade filler to repair the hole in the wall.

Warning These instructions for fitting an outside tap apply only to houses with a 15mm ($\frac{1}{2}$ in) copper or stainless steel rising main. Some houses, where water pressure is low, may have a 22mm ($\frac{3}{4}$ in) rising main and a reducing tee will be needed; this is fitted in the same way as an ordinary tee. Also, in older houses there may be a lead or heavy galvanized steel rising main. To connect an outside tap to a main of this kind, you should seek professional help – at least for fitting the tee junction to the rising main.

2 *Section through wall showing connections at the rising main, the stopcock inside and the outside tap fittings*
3 *Reducing tee connection in rising main*
Left: A garden plumbing kit and optional screw-down stopcock (inset)

MAKE A SIMPLE TOOL RACK

Gardening tools are notoriously difficult to keep tidy anywhere. They often finish up as a bundle of dangerous prongs and blades. The answer to all this confusion lies in a neat, purpose-made tool rack.

Tools

carpenter's brace and 25mm (1 in) drill bit (to match dowel hook diameter)
drill and bit, *for wall-fixing screw-holes*
tenon saw
mallet, or hammer

Materials

1m (3 ft) length of 25mm (1 in) diameter hardwood dowel
two 50mm (2 in) No 10 woodworking screws, *for wall-fixing*
1m (3 ft) length 100 × 25mm (4 × 1 in) softwood board (or backing strip)
woodworking glue
1 sheet medium glasspaper

The main point of any rack of this type is that it should be easy to use; if not, it will quickly be discarded and the tools will be relegated once again to a heap on the floor. Our rack was designed with this in mind and it is quite simple to construct with the aid of a few elementary carpentry tools.

We show the rack in use carrying the normal range of gardening equipment, all of which can be quickly and securely stored by simply hooking in position.

The rack is built to fit in our 'tuck-away' tool shed, for which we give building instructions, pages 93–98, but its overall length can be adjusted as needed for use in other locations. Spacing and length of dowelling pegs were gauged after checking the storage requirements of a wide range of items. However, where there are specialized storage problems, spacings, dowel lengths and diameters can easily be modified as required.

Construction

Begin by marking the main softwood backing strip with the dowel-centre locations. Draw a line centrally along the length of the piece and then mark off the holes at 100mm (4 in) spacings.

Lay the backing firmly on a piece of scrap timber and then carefully bore the dowel holes about 18mm (¾ in), giving a 10 degree bias toward one side in order to slope fixed dowels slightly upwards (see diagram). When boring holes, remember that the centre lead screw of the

bit should pierce completely through the rear face of the backing to prevent glue-pressure building up as the dowels are tapped into position.

Cut the dowels to length and glass-paper away all sharp edges. Run some woodworking glue into each hole and then gently tap the dowels in position with a mallet or hammer. If you use a hammer, hold a piece of scrap timber between hammer and dowel to prevent damage to the dowel end. Any slight inaccuracy in the angle at which the holes

have been bored can be corrected at this stage by tapping the dowels into alignment before the glue sets.

As the original rack was made to fit our 'tuck-away' tool shed we arranged the fixing screw-holes to coincide with vertical timber frame members, thus securing the wall mounting. This method of fixing is suitable for most timber and similar sheds. Where you are mounting the rack on a masonry wall, you must use purpose-made plastic or fibre wall plugs to take fixing screws.

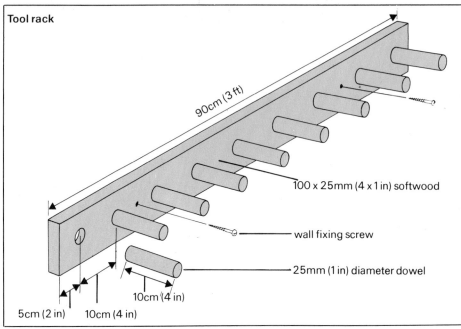

Tool rack

90cm (3 ft)

100 x 25mm (4 x 1 in) softwood

wall fixing screw

25mm (1 in) diameter dowel

10cm (4 in)

5cm (2 in)   10cm (4 in)

MAKE A TOOL TROLLEY

Another answer to the problem of tidy, safe storage for garden tools is to make a completely portable tool rack trolley on which a wide range of tools and other equipment can be permanently housed.

Tools
bench or table, preferably fitted with vice
tenon saw
hammer; screwdriver
rule; set square
hand or electric drill with an assortment of bits

Materials
Timber:
7m (24 ft) of 50 × 25mm (2 × 1 in) planed softwood
12m (40 ft) of 75 × 25mm (3 × 1 in) planed softwood
2·5m (8 ft) of 25mm (1 in) dowel

Fixings and accessories:
seventy 45mm ($1\frac{3}{4}$ in) × No 8 sheradized countersunk wood screws
100g ($3\frac{1}{2}$ oz) of 40mm ($1\frac{1}{2}$ in) sheradized panel pins
waterproof wood glue
two 180mm (6 in) diameter wheels with suitable steel rod axle 760mm (30 in) long
four 3mm ($\frac{1}{8}$ in) diameter split pins
2 bicycle hand grips
6 large spring tool clips with fixing screws
4 brass screw eye hooks
two 600mm (24 in) bungee elastic straps (available in motoring accessory shops)
hardboard sheet 860 × 250mm ($34\frac{1}{2}$ × 10 in)

At the start of a gardening session all that is required is for seed, plants, fertilizer and other necessary items to be loaded and then the trolley, complete with tools, can be wheeled to the work site. As tools are used and finished with, they are replaced tidily on the trolley and at the end of the day the complete unit can simply be wheeled away.

The trolley includes such useful features as a shelf top, that can be used for on-site potting and similar work, and storage space for bags of seed, fertilizer and so on. Built-in tool clips can be added to hold small hand tools. Even when fully loaded the trolley is completely stable and easily manoeuvrable.

Use this grid drawing to mark cutting lines **E** *and* **F** *(see diagram overleaf)*

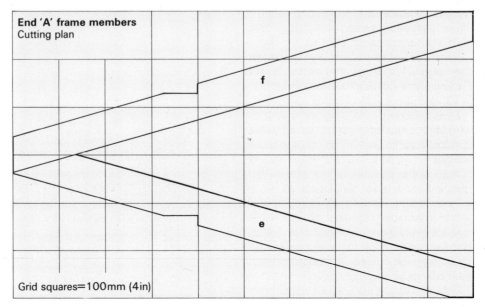

End 'A' frame members
Cutting plan

f

e

Grid squares=100mm (4 in)

Construction

Start by building the base platform. Cut parts **A** and **B** to length and then pin and glue together as shown in the exploded diagram at right and in picture **1**. Check the assembly for squareness as work proceeds. Next drill and screw pilot holes to all perimeter joints and drive home the reinforcing screws, **2**.

Use the grid drawing overleaf to mark cutting lines on parts **E** and **F** and then assemble as in **3**, using a temporary 600mm (24 in) spacer batten at the extreme lower edge. The simple scarf type joint used at the apex of the frame is secured by screws as shown.

Stand the base platform on end and screw and glue the end frames in position, as shown in **4**. Next add the top main member part **H** by glueing and screwing through the end frames, **5**.

Cut the handle support members, parts **G**, to length and drill for the dowelling cross members. To ensure accuracy both members should be drilled in one operation, see **6**. Fix these two members to the end frame notches using screws and glue. Ensure that the pieces are fitted as a pair and drilled so that the dowel holes align accurately. Push the cross-member dowels into position, **7**, centralize, and then glue and pin together.

Prepare the steel axle by drilling 3mm ($\frac{1}{8}$ in) diameter holes, so that split pins may be fitted either side of the wheel. The precise location of these holes will depend upon the make and type of wheels used.

Cut the axle retaining blocks, parts **D**, to length and then cut a channel across the centre as a tight fit to the steel axle. These blocks are fitted over the axle and to either side of the main platform, see **8**, each being clamped firmly in position with four screws. The wheels are added and retained by split pins, as in **9–10**.

Cut and fit the legs, parts **C**, driving the fixing screws directly onto the base platform rear corners, **11**.

Turn the trolley upright and cut and fit shelf supports, parts **J**, to the inner face of the end frames. Cut a hardboard shelf, as in **12**, and slip it into position.

Give the completed structure a coat of wood preservative, ensuring that all under surfaces and end grain of the wood are well soaked.

Add screw eyes to either end of the handle supports so that an elastic strap may be fitted to retain long-handled tools when manoeuvring the trolley over uneven surfaces. Spring and other purpose-made clips to hold small hand tools may be added to the top main members as you need them.

Timber cutting list is given right.

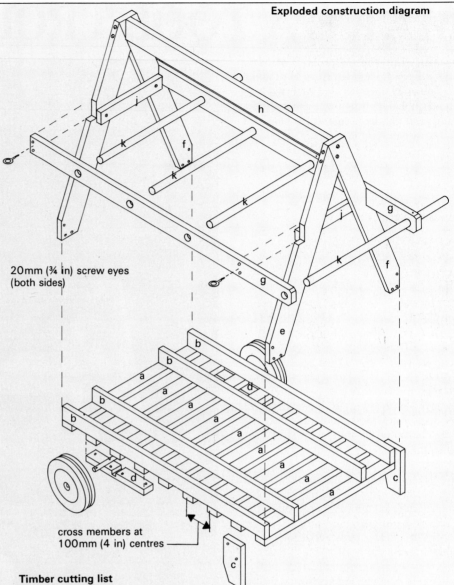

Exploded construction diagram

20mm (¾ in) screw eyes (both sides)

cross members at 100mm (4 in) centres

Timber cutting list

Code	No. Req'd	Length	Material	Location
A	9	600mm (24 in) of 50 x 25mm (2 x 1 in)	Softwood	Base platform cross members
B	4	860mm (34½ in) of 75 x 25mm (3 x 1 in)	Softwood	Base platform top members
C	2	165mm (6½ in) of 75 x 25mm (3 x 1 in)	Softwood	Legs
D	2	250mm (10 in) of 50 x 25mm (2 x 1 in)	Softwood	Axle retaining blocks
E	2	1060mm (42½ in) of 75 x 25mm (3 x 1 in)	Softwood	End 'A' frame members – see grid drawing
F	2	1060mm (42½ in) of 75 x 25mm (3 x 1 in)	Softwood	End 'A' frame members see grid drawing
G	2	1110mm (44½ in) of 75 x 25mm (3 x 1 in)	Softwood	Handle supports
H	1	860mm (34½ in) of 75 x 25mm (3 x 1 in)	Softwood	Top main member
J	2	250mm (10 in) of 50 x 25mm (2 x 1 in)	Softwood	Top shelf supports
K	4	530mm (21 in) of 25mm (1 in) dia.	Dowel	Top shelf cross members and handle

Boundaries

Gardens and smaller areas within the garden all need boundaries. Whether you build a wall or put up a fence you will find ideas and techniques here. We also give instructions for hanging a gate and for repairing existing fences and gates.

GARDEN WALLS

The kind of garden wall you build will depend on the type and size of the area involved. The wall can be high or low, solid or partially open, and it can be constructed from a variety of materials.

Brick walls

The material most commonly used for constructing garden walls is brick.

For any wall over 1.4m (4½ ft) high, 229mm (9 in) thick brickwork will usually be required, though 114mm (4½ in) thick brickwork can occasionally be used; this will, however, need buttressing at frequent intervals. For walls over 2m (6½ ft) high, 343mm (13½ in) brickwork will be most suitable. If a wall adjoins a house which has brick walls, it is worth trying to match the bricks used in the garden wall with those used in the house; if your house is a listed building or you live in a conservation area, there may be a legal requirement to use sympathetic materials. In any event a garden wall more than 2m (6½ft) high usually requires planning permission.

If you are unable to obtain bricks which match exactly the bricks in the house walls, the weather will often rapidly mellow the new wall. To accelerate this process you can paint on a solution of liquid fertilizer to encourage the growth of mosses and lichens.

Coping For the coping or finish along the top of the wall it is usually best to keep to a straightforward design; bricks on edge placed side by side in a continuous line are most suitable for a 229mm (9 in) thick wall. To make certain of weather protection you can use a 'creasing' course of staggered tiles below the bricks laid on edge.

A good finish for a 114mm (4½ in) thick wall is either to omit a coping altogether – and use a top course of a harder engineering brick instead – or to use cut headers; these are bricks cut in half to measure 114mm (4½ in) and laid on edge to form the coping.

Brick patterns You can use brick in complicated patterns and designs but on the whole these tend to detract from the beauty of the material. A possible exception is a simple honeycomb wall which is 114mm (4½ in) thick and uses a simple stretcher bond with a gap left between each brick to produce a lattice effect. This gives a partial view and incomplete shelter from wind, but it can form an attractive screen within a garden by defining an area without cutting it off completely.

Concrete walls

Walls can be built from concrete blocks which are available in a wide range of sizes and textures. Walls using 229 × 229 × 457mm

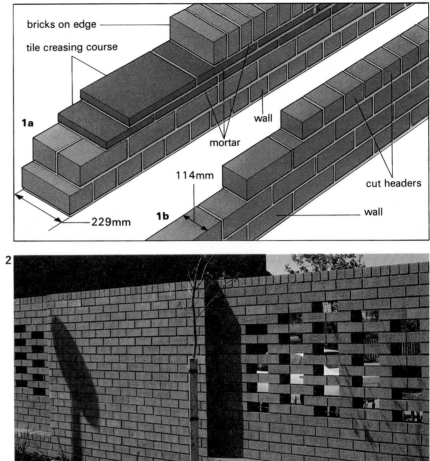

(9 × 9 × 18 in) blocks are capable of carrying substantial loads and therefore make ideal bases for pergolas, barbecues and built-in seating. Bricks on edge are commonly used for coping on walls of this type, but simply detailed aluminium or other types of metal coping can also look most effective. You could make maximum use of a concrete block wall by using it to enclose a sitting area on one side and put up a lean-to greenhouse or a carport on the other side. Concrete blocks do not require rendering since they are quite weatherproof when coped; a simple application of a stone paint can make them very attractive in appearance.

Decorative walling Concrete blocks are commonly used in a wide range of decorative walling. Screen blocks are a familiar sight in many gardens, but be careful if you intend using these since they have an inherently busy pattern and a surfeit can quickly become boring. A single run gives a better effect than being enclosed on all four sides by walls of this type. Planting can be used to good effect to soften their rather mechanical looking outline; for example, a screen block wall

1a Brick wall with staggered tiles laid below the brick coping to give extra protection against the weather
1b Single thickness brick wall with a coping of cut headers
2 By incorporating a honeycomb bond into a brick wall you can provide an attractive screen within the garden without cutting off the view completely

showing through the foliage of a willow tree could be most effective.

The 'landscape bloc' is a well-designed and practical material which has recently become available. It has a flattened 'U' shape and can be put together in a variety of ways to make walls and screens with differing characteristics. It is sufficiently adaptable to be used to form raised beds, seats and tables as well as retaining walls and steps.

Precast concrete slabs Paving slabs, which can be used in certain situations for walling, are usually cut in half to conserve material. In design terms they provide a useful link between the surface used in a terrace or patio and a low retaining wall. Paving slabs can be used as coping on a low wall – a row of 600 × 600mm (2 × 2 ft) slabs provides a useful long seat at minimal cost.

Concrete cast on site Rather than buying individual modules, you may decide to cast the concrete on site; this method is particularly suitable for low and retaining walls. You can finish off the surface in a variety of ways – for example with attractive board marking used in the shuttering, or with various exposed aggregates.

Stone walls

You may decide to use stone, a traditional walling material which is now relatively expensive. As a general rule you should try to use local stone; the wall will not look out of place and you will avoid the cost of long distance haulage.

Walls in the country are often built dry with the stones placed one on top of another and no mortar between the joints; this operation requires considerable skill. Or stone can be teamed with rammed earth to form a combination of a wall and a bank with the stone acting as a weatherproof face.

Rectangular blocks These are far easier to lay than random shape ones and the resulting wall will look less rural and more archi-

tectural, a point worth bearing in mind in an urban situation where a link between house and garden is important. Sawn blocks look the most architectural but they are expensive.

Small stones In some areas small stones such as cobbles and flints are used as a decorative feature within a framework of some other material such as brick. Flint-knapping is a highly skilled craft; a wall finished with flints in this way can be an excellent feature if it is in keeping with its surroundings.

Building foundations

The foundation or footing you build will depend upon the site conditions. The main object of the footing is to carry the wall above without movement or subsidence; this means the footing will have to be taken down to a point where there is no frost penetration or movement due to the water in the ground. Where there are shrinkable clays, ground movement due to a fluctuating water table is common; if there are young fast-growing trees such as willows or poplars in the vicinity, the problem can be aggravated. Mature trees which have reached their adult proportions will rarely be a problem close to a wall or building since their root system will

3a Garden wall with a bitumen damp proof course which is stepped to suit the sloping site
3b To give a wall in an exposed position greater strength, two layers of engineering bricks can be used as a damp proof course
3c Alternatively the damp proof course can consist of two staggered layers of slate with mortar in between

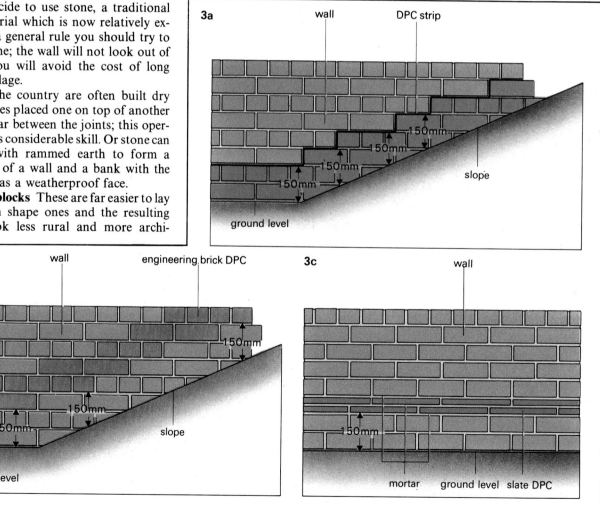

3a wall   DPC strip   150mm   150mm   150mm   150mm   slope   ground level

3b wall   engineering brick DPC   150mm   150mm   150mm   slope   ground level

3c wall   150mm   mortar   ground level   slate DPC

have become established and little further development is likely. In poor ground or conditions it may be appropriate to excavate to a depth of 1m (3 ft) to make sure a wall has the best possible chance of stability. As a general rule a free-standing wall is less prone to damage due to settlement than a wall which is an integral part of a larger structure.

In most garden situations a footing depth of 600mm (2 ft), 450mm (1½ ft) or even less is usually quite adequate. For a 229mm (9 in) thick brick or concrete block wall approximately 1.8m (6 ft) in height a concrete foundation mix of one part sand to two parts cement and five parts aggregate is suitable; the dimensions of the footings will be between 450mm (1½ ft) and 600mm (2 ft) wide and between 150mm (6 in) and 600mm (2 ft) in depth. As a guide, the minimum width of the footings should normally be twice the width of the finished wall. If you are dealing with a sloping site, remember the footings will have to be stepped.

Keeping out weather
You will have to prevent weather penetrating the wall at the top and bottom.
Damp proof courses A horizontal dpc should be laid 150mm (6 in) above ground level; if you are working on a sloping site, this should be stepped with the fall. In very exposed situations a wall can become weakened along the line of a horizontal dpc so the whole structure is liable to be blown over. In this case a dpc consisting of two courses of engineering bricks laid 150mm (6 in) above ground level is suitable. Other types of dpc can be constructed from lead, copper or at least two courses of slate laid to a breaking, or staggered, bond with each slate bedded in a mortar mix of three parts sand to one part cement. Mastic asphalt or bitumen roll can also be used.

Installing copings Coping will keep the weather out of the top of the wall as well as shedding water off its face. Copings can either be flush with the wall, when some streaking of the surface is likely from drip down, or they can project from each side, so the drips fall clear to the ground. With a projecting coping a shadow will be cast and this can give an attractive and definite end to the vertical wall line.

Some copings are constructed from the same material as the rest of the wall, or sometimes a different material is used.

Limestone and slates are easier to work than other types of stone and are therefore particularly suitable for use as coping materials. Sandstone can undergo shrinkage and thus open up the joints between the stones. To ensure a completely weatherproof seal, a dpc is often inserted under a stone coping although in the case of slate, which gives a particularly crisp finish, there is no need for this since it is virtually impervious.

Precast concrete copings are available in a wide range of finishes and sizes and can provide an ideal finish for a reasonable price. If they overhang the wall, it is worth including a throating to keep drips clear of the wall. Copings can be flat or weathered so they

4 *A screen block wall gives some privacy and provides support for climbing plants, while simulated stone blocks and concrete coping make an attractive raised bed*
Types of coping
5a *Metal sheet*
5b *Bull-nosed bricks*
5c *Stone or concrete*
5d *Precast concrete with drip channels*
5e *Precast concrete slabs*

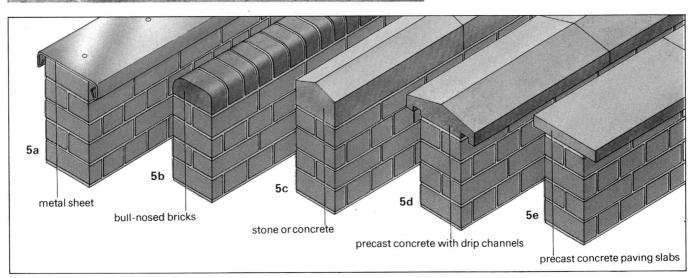

5a metal sheet

5b bull-nosed bricks

5c stone or concrete

5d precast concrete with drip channels

5e precast concrete paving slabs

slope downwards in one direction or on both sides.

If you are using a tile 'creasing' course with a coping of bricks on edge, it should consist of two courses of plain tiles laid to a breaking bond. There is no need for the tiles to project beyond the face of the wall.

Metal copings can often give a very precise finish to a wall. They are impervious to water and you can extend the line of a metal roof by using a similar material to that used in the roof for the coping of the garden wall. The three metals most commonly used are copper and aluminium, which are expensive but long-lasting, and zinc, which is considerably cheaper but will not last as long.

Apart from metal copings which are usually screwed or clipped into position, all the other types can normally be bedded on a mortar mix of three parts sand to one part cement. Make sure the mortar layer is not too thick, particularly where a dpc is used; as a guide, a layer of the same thickness as the joints used in the general construction of the wall will be suitable.

Building retaining walls

Walls over 1m (3ft) high are often used for retaining levels on sloping sites. They require considerable strength and complicated construction work, although a wide variety of materials can be used. Since the back of the wall will be permanently wet, there is little point in incorporating a horizontal dpc; the back of the wall could, however, be protected with a water-proofing compound. To relieve pressure from ground water you should leave an open vertical joint between the brick or blockwork at 1m (3ft) intervals along the length of the wall. This joint should be one course above ground level since if it is any lower it is likely to become blocked by dirt and weed growth. On very wet sites, sections of land drainpipe may be built into the wall.

Building concrete walls

For garden walling, concrete blocks measuring $229 \times 229 \times 457$mm ($9 \times 9 \times 18$ in) are generally the most suitable size to use. They are usually available with hollow cores which can be filled with concrete and strengthened with steel reinforcing rods tied into the footings; with a wall less than 1.8m (6ft) high, however, this is not usually necessary. Each block constitutes the thickness of the wall so you can use a simple stretcher bond and cut the blocks to form the ends of each course.

Using screen blocks These blocks, which are more delicate in appearance and strength, are usually 114mm ($4\frac{1}{2}$in) thick. Short runs of walling are built between specifically detailed pilasters and corners which have a keyway into which the blocks can be built. The pilasters and corners are hollow and can be built round steel reinforcing rods which have been bedded into the footings of the wall in the same way as for concrete block walling. As work progresses concrete is poured into the pilasters around the rods to provide strength and support for the wall as a whole. There is usually a purpose-made coping available for this type of wall. Since the wall is pierced, there is less wind resistance than with a solid wall of the same dimensions; so although the wall is only 114mm ($4\frac{1}{2}$in) thick, it has reasonable mechanical strength.

Building stone walls

These tend to be expensive and difficult to lay and construction is often best left to a local craftsman. Rubble walls, which are most commonly seen, can be of a number of different types. Regular and irregular courses can be used where the stones are rough-faced and roughly rectangular. With irregular courses, several stones can make up the depth of a course. In walls built of random rubble, there are no courses; each stone is selected to interlock with its neighbour.

Traditionally, all these types of stone walls were laid dry, but using mortar makes construction easier. If you are using this technique, make sure you keep the joints as small as possible so the mortar does not mar the appearance of the wall.

Most stone walls are laid to a batter so the wall is wider at the bottom than the top to give the wall stability and strength. Coping is usually traditional and it is best to copy coping used on stone walls in your area. This may be stones on edge or flat; some walls have no coping at all. In areas where stone is used for building, there is often a layer of rock just beneath the surface so foundations can be kept to a minimum; if there is a layer of soil, you will have to excavate for foundations.

6 To give a stone wall stability and strength, lay it to a batter or angle; use large stones at the bottom and smaller ones on top
7 A natural stone wall can double as a planting ground and is ideal in rural situations

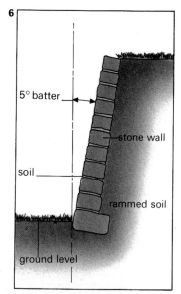

6

5° batter
stone wall
soil
rammed soil
ground level

7

BUILDING FENCES: 1

You can build any type of fencing on flat ground or ground which has only a slight gradient; on steeper ground you should build a fence which uses horizontal boards. There are two ways of coping with the problem of sloping ground. The first way is usually ruled out because of the extra work; it involves shaping boards, posts and panels so each bay of the fence will be horizontal. The second method is more practical; you step each fence bay an equal amount throughout the run of the fence to give it a uniform appearance.

On a slight slope you should be able to lay several bays to one level forming a step and fixing the remaining bays at another. On a steep slope you will need longer posts because every bay may need to be stepped. Make sure you maintain uniform steps; to do this you may need to dig out some areas so the panels are clear of the ground as they are fitted to the posts. Conversely, if the gap between the bottom and the ground is too large, you may need to build up the ground.

If the ground level in your neighbour's garden is higher than that in your own, one side of the fence will be in contact with the ground. Even if you apply preservative, rotting is inevitable; if you leave a bank between the soil and the fence, the soil will probably subside. The answer is to build a retaining wall with the timber fence placed on top; bed in 50mm (2 in) thick paving slabs so they stand vertically for a bank of 450mm (18 in) of soil or less. For higher banks, build a small brick wall and leave a gap for drainage and for the posts, which should be inserted on concrete spurs.

FITTING TIMBER POSTS

If you intend building a new timber fence on the site of an old one, the greatest problem is in removing the old fence posts which may have become stumps in the ground. The old posts could well have been set into concrete and rubble and you will have to excavate around them to break up the buried material before removing them. Individual posts may not prove to be too much trouble; if you have a series of old damaged posts, it is probably worth considering an alternative posting arrangement.

When building a fence on a slope, always take horizontal measurements between posts
1a For steep slope, raise each bay above previous one
1b For shallow slope, form step with several bays
1c Alternatively landscape ground to form stepped levels and build retaining walls

When ground is higher on one side of fence, build wall to support bank (page 30)
2a If difference in levels is no more than 450mm (18 in), use paving slabs set in concrete
2b If difference is more than 450mm (18 in), build brick wall

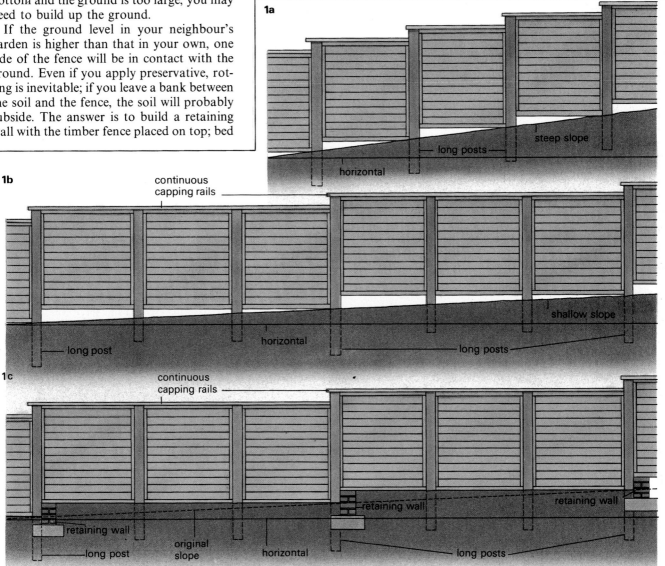

1a

steep slope

long posts

horizontal

1b

continuous capping rails

shallow slope

long post

horizontal

long posts

1c

continuous capping rails

retaining wall

retaining wall

retaining wall

long post

original slope

horizontal

long posts

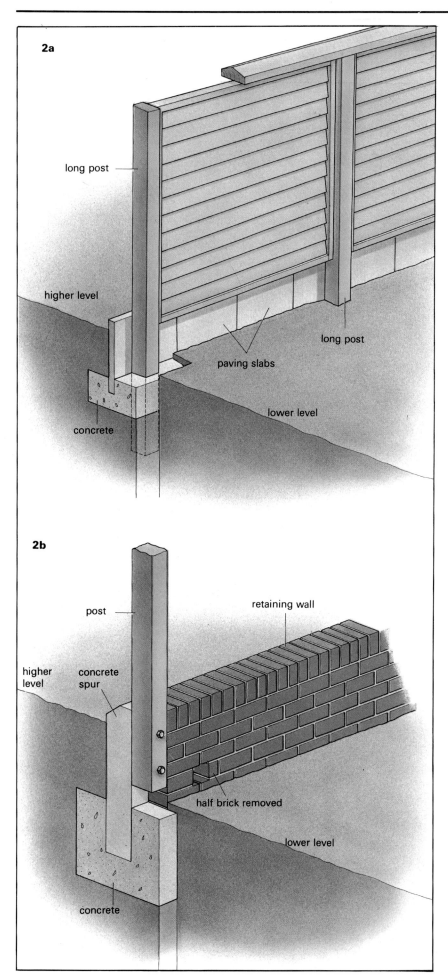

2a

long post

higher level

long post

paving slabs

concrete

lower level

2b

post

retaining wall

higher level

concrete spur

half brick removed

lower level

concrete

Short panel If the new posts have to be placed near or at the position of the old ones, which is quite likely since the standard panel width is 1.8m (6ft), you may find it impossible to dig through the old hardcore to make the new post holes. Consider fitting a shorter panel at the start of the fence; this will ensure the other posts fall midway between the old posts and so avoid the hardcore. Many fence panel manufacturers will supply shorter panels.

Paving slabs Another problem you may encounter is if you have to set a post into the base of a long patio, especially if the neighbouring house has one as well. If it is made of paving slabs laid on a base of sand, it may be a simple matter of lifting the appropriate slabs and digging down. But if the patio is made of concrete, you will have to hire a rotary action demolition hammer to break it up.

Tree roots These can also pose problems and a shorter fence panel may be the answer. Make sure you excavate all the post positions before ordering your fence to see if an odd size could help avoid the roots.

Concrete If you are faced with a layer of thick concrete across the proposed fence post position, you may be able to excavate about 450mm (18in) and strengthen the post by drilling through it and bolting it to the adjacent concrete; the technique is similar to bolting a post to a wall, as described below. Once concrete and rubble have been placed around the post and the concrete repaired, you should have a solid fixing. To ensure a post clears the edge of a concrete base or patio, you can screw a piece of timber to the previous post; the timber must be thick enough so the next panel ends clear of the concrete. The next post can then be fitted away from the concrete.

Preventing rotting and sagging

You can protect timber posts from rotting or sagging by fixing each one to a concrete spur buried in the ground and set in concrete. Bury the spur and push a nail through the holes to mark their positions on the post; drill right through the posts and secure them to the spurs with galvanized steel bolts. Make sure the bolts are long enough to pass through both spur and post for a secure fixing.

Putting in metposts

A metpost is essentially a 900mm (36in) long steel spike with a steel cup; it will save you digging post holes because the spike is simply driven into the ground. Bury about 750mm (30in) of the spike and leave 150mm (6in) of square steel cup projecting; tap the post onto the cup – a 1mm (or $\frac{1}{24}$in) gap is allowable – and secure it with screws inserted through the predrilled holes in the cup. Problems of rotting are minimized because the post itself

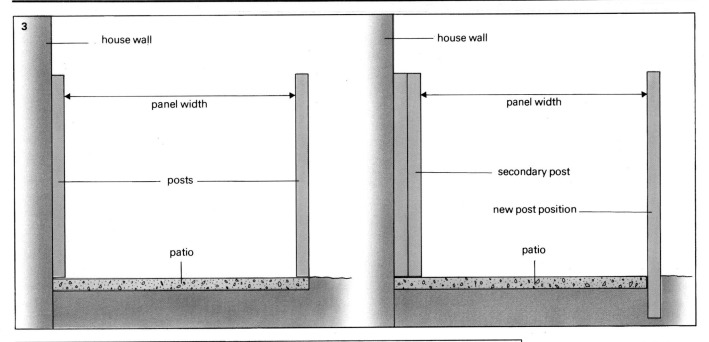

3

house wall

panel width

posts

patio

house wall

panel width

secondary post

new post position

patio

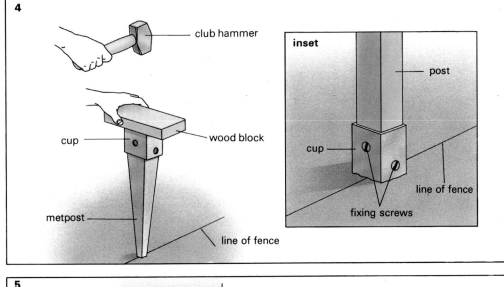

4

club hammer

cup

wood block

metpost

line of fence

inset

post

cup

fixing screws

line of fence

3 *If post position coincides with edge of concrete patio, screw secondary timber post to first post to take fence panel clear of obstruction*
4 *Metpost is driven into ground with club hammer and block; secure base of post to metpost with fixing screws (inset)*
5 *Post can be securely fixed to wall with screw bolts; for extra strength cut fork in end of screw bolt before cementing into wall (inset)*

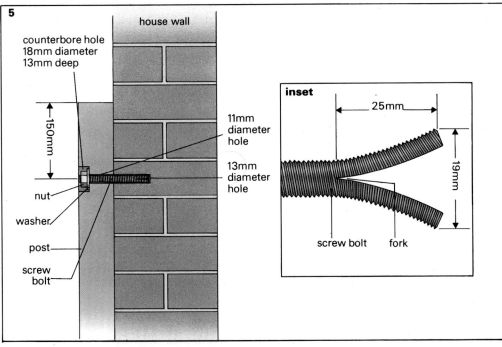

5

house wall

counterbore hole
18mm diameter
13mm deep

150mm

11mm
diameter
hole

13mm
diameter
hole

nut

washer

post

screw
bolt

inset

25mm

19mm

screw bolt   fork

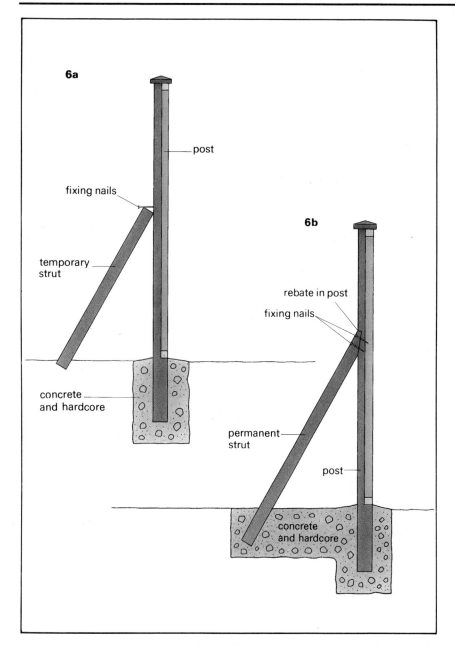

6a

post

fixing nails

temporary
strut

concrete
and hardcore

6b

rebate in post

fixing nails

permanent
strut

post

concrete
and hardcore

*6a Fit temporary struts to
post until concrete has set;
use nails driven into post to
support strut*

*6b For extra support in
exposed areas, fit permanent
struts; bed in concrete and
form rebate in post to accept
strut*

is not in contact with the ground; any rainwater will eventually drain out through a hole
in the base of the spike. Manufacturers claim
the metpost will not move once driven firmly
into the ground, even in areas with high
winds. When fitting posts near to obstruc-
tions, you only need to dig a small hole. One
company will supply these posts in a package
with their panel fances; the cup will only
accept 75×62mm ($3 \times 2\frac{1}{2}$ in) posts, but you
can obtain 75mm (3 in) square cups from
builders' merchants. Larger posts can only be
used if you taper the lower portions to fit the
standard size cups.

When calculating costs, remember to offset
the cost of metposts against the lower cost of
shorter posts; you do not need to bury
450–750mm (18–30 in) of post into the
ground. They require no concreting, maintenance costs are less, labour is less and the
cost of hiring or buying a post hole boring
tool is eliminated.

Fitting post to wall

The key to a stable fence is well-anchored
posts – and one of the best ways to fix a post
soundly is to secure it to a house wall; if your
screw fixings are weak, wind pressure could
rock the post loose until the fence is separated
from the wall. You could use expansion bolts
to give a secure fixing, but screw bolts with
nuts and washers (available in various
lengths and diameters) are more economical.
For a 75mm (3 in) square post you will need
three bolts about 137mm ($5\frac{1}{2}$ in) long; if the
post is less than 120mm (48 in) high, you will
need only two. If you have 100×75mm
(4×3 in) posts, with the 75mm (3 in) face
fixed to the wall, use 160mm ($6\frac{1}{2}$ in) bolts.
Bury about 75mm (3 in) of the bolt into the
wall after 'forking' the end; hold it between
padding in a vice, saw down about 25mm
(1 in) with a hacksaw and bend the fork open
to about 19mm ($\frac{3}{4}$ in). You may find it
ecomonical to buy a long length of narrow
screw bolt and saw lengths off as you require
them; usually about 9mm ($\frac{3}{8}$ in) will be
sufficient.

The wall post will usually be shorter than
the others which stand in the ground. Drill
three 11mm ($\frac{7}{16}$ in) holes through the post –
about 150mm (6 in) from each end and one in
the middle. Use an 18mm ($\frac{3}{4}$ in) bit to counterbore these holes by 13–19mm ($\frac{1}{2}$–$\frac{3}{4}$ in) on one
face of the post. Hold the post in position and
check it is vertical with a spirit level or plumb
line and bob; mark the drilling positions with
a nail onto the wall. Remove the post and use
a 13mm ($\frac{1}{2}$ in) masonry bit to drill 75mm (3 in)
holes into the wall. Fit the bolts, forked end
first, into the wall by squeezing the fork
together and tapping with a mallet protected
by a wood block; fill with a cement mix or
wall filler. Locate the post over the bolts once
the filler has set hard, making sure the bolts
are level so the post holes fit over them
squarely. Put the washers and nuts onto the
bolts and tighten with a ring spanner. Because the end of the bolt is split inside the
wall, the fixing creates extra anchorage to
restrict post movement.

Fixing posts in ground

You can either fix each post as you build the
fence or fix them all beforehand, in which
case make sure your measurements are precise and use a spacer batten to ensure the
posts are the correct distance apart. Once you
have dug out each hole, fit the post and fill
with alternate layers of hardcore and concrete. Use a weak concrete mix (one part
cement, three parts coarse sand and six parts
stone or broken brick); if the posts do rot,
you will find it easier to remove them. Finish
with a collar of concrete, about 25mm (1 in)
higher than ground level, and round it off
away from the post to ensure rainwater flows
away from the base of the post. You can also

place a half brick in the bottom of the post hole before you fit the post to prevent the end grain coming into contact with the ground. Fix struts by driving two nails through them into the post, making sure the post is vertical first. Allow about a week for the concrete to harden before removing the struts.

Shrinkage The concrete may shrink slightly as it dries, resulting in a small gap between the post and concrete through which water could enter and rot the post. Regular treatment with preservative could help counter this problem.

Fitting permanent struts
In weak ground you really have no alternative to bedding posts in concrete, except if you are able to use a metpost. In strong ground, hardcore plus a mix of soil and gravel can be adequate for certain types of fence, such as a low boundary fence in a sheltered position. If you fix a high close-boarded fence in an exposed position where it will be buffeted by wind, you will probably need extra support in the form of permanent struts.

It is best to nail the struts to the posts and concrete both into the ground; this means you will have to dig a short trench from the post to the base of the strut. Remember to treat the struts with preservative before fixing them; they should also be treated regularly afterwards. Always support end posts with

struts, except if you are able to bolt them to walls. Support of the intermediate posts depends on the height and length of your fence. Generally, if the fence is 1500mm (60 in) tall, you should support every third post; but fences of 1200mm (48 in) or under will require support at every fourth post. The supporting struts are not attractive, but they are insurance against future fence failure.

Capping
You will need to protect the tops of timber posts from rainwater which soaks into the end grain. Some manufacturers provide timber caps which you nail into place or you can saw off the tops to a bevel or add a capping piece.

ERECTING A PANEL FENCE
You will need someone to help you if you want to build a tall fence; low panel fences, however, can be easily built by one person. First stretch a string line at ground level between two stakes to mark the position of the proposed fence. Cut a timber batten to the length of the panels you are using and mark off the positions of the posts with pieces of brick; it is important to make these measurements correctly to avoid problems of joining the panels later. Dig out the holes to the required depth; you could use a spade or buy or hire a post-boring tool, which works like a large corkscrew.

Fixing posts
Once the holes have been bored you can fit the posts. To prevent the base of the post rotting from the end grain, place a half brick in the hole before fitting the post. Check the post is upright with a spirit level and stabilize it as you pack the rubble round its base; wedge two struts of timber under nails temporarily driven into the post.

7a With slotted concrete fence posts, panels simply slide in
7b With recessed type of concrete post, straight, end and corner brackets hold panels
Building timber panel fence using slotted concrete posts (see next page):
8 Digging post hole
9 Checking post is vertical with spirit level
10 Using straight-edge and spirit level to check posts are set at same height
11 Placing temporary struts to hold fence while concrete sets
12 Concreting post into ground
13 Fitting panel into slot in post

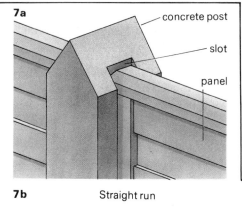

7a
concrete post
slot
panel

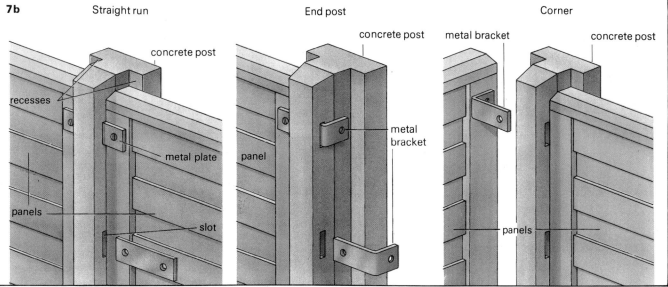

7b
Straight run
recesses
concrete post
panels
metal plate
slot

End post
concrete post
panel
metal bracket

Corner
metal bracket
concrete post
panels

Fixing panels

Hold the panel against the post and leave a 75–100mm (3–4 in) gap between its base and the ground by supporting both ends of the panel on bricks. Use aluminium alloy or galvanized nails about 62mm ($2\frac{1}{2}$ in) long to secure the panel to the post; fix three nails on both sides of the panel (six per panel end in total). The relatively thin timber at the end of the panel may split as you drive in the nails; if this happens, drill pilot holes through the panels or blunt the end of the nails with pincers before using them.

You can eliminate the need to level each panel (or post) as it is built by fitting a string line at the height of the fence; stretch the line between two posts driven firmly into the ground at each end of the proposed fence. This may not be possible on sloping ground where you will need to have one or more steps in the fence. Nail the free end of the panel to the second post as before, checking the panel is horizontal. The post can now be supported with temporary struts and you can pack the hole with concrete and hardcore as already described. Fix the remaining posts and panels in the same way.

Fixing capping rail

Fence panels are normally fixed so 50 or 75mm (2 or 3 in) of post projects above the panels; this should improve the appearance of the fence as well as enable the post tops to be capped or bevelled. A useful way of protecting and strengthening a panel fence is to run a continuous capping rail across the posts and panels. Cut the posts or build them so they are flush with the panels; if the panels have fitted capping rails, you can prise them off and remove them. Make sure the panels are in line before you nail the capping strips back so each one spans a post top and most of the adjoining panel. You will need an extra length of capping rail, shaped to match, to make up the difference lost by covering the posts. If the strip is not wide enough to cover the posts completely, first fix a metal capping to the posts or shape to a bevel the portion of the post top which will be exposed.

Using concrete posts

For fence panels, the assembly methods are basically similar whether you use timber or concrete posts; the difference is each panel is fitted to the concrete post according to the manufacturer's instructions. The most common concrete posts have slots running down their sides to accept the edges of the panels. Hold the post upright and push the panel firmly into the slot; the panel is held by its own weight. Another system uses galvanized plates and screws; this allows you to remove each panel easily for repairs or for access through the fence – if you want to site a caravan for example.

BUILDING FENCES: 2

There are several types of fence you can build yourself, apart from the timber panel type. Choose between arris rail, chain link, wire, plastic, palings or post and rail. The methods of dealing with sloping ground and positioning posts are the same as for the panel type.

ARRIS RAIL FENCE

This fence can be built using the same basic methods as for a timber panel fence: two or three arris rails can be put up, depending on the height you require. If you buy prefabricated timber posts for the job, they will have preformed mortises to accept the arris rails; other types of post will have to be shaped on site. If you use concrete posts, their mortises may be wedge-shaped: you will have to cut the rails to match. This also applies to any rails which have square sawn ends.

Concrete posts These may have preformed grooves to accept gravel boards; if they do not, and you require gravel boards, you will have to set vertical battens into the ground alongside the posts and concrete them in with the posts. Make sure you treat the battens with preservative before fixing them. Concrete posts are heavy – a 2m (or 7ft) post weighs about 45kg (or 100lb) – and therefore not easy to handle; but they are long-lasting.

Putting up posts

Fit the post and check it is vertical; make sure you keep it supported as you fit the rails. Normally the tenon is inserted half-way into the post so there is an equal amount of mortise available for the next rail's tenon. This distance is not important for the first and last posts; with these you can allow for the full width of the post as long as you allow for the extra rail length when ordering or cutting them.

Make sure someone holds the second post steady as you insert the opposite ends of the rails. Use a hammer or mallet to tap the second post firmly so the rails engage half-way into this post. You can now secure the rails in the previous post (by nailing if you are using timber posts). Check the second post is vertical and wedge it into place. Fit subsequent posts and rails in the same manner.

Fitting arris rail fence and concrete posts:
1 Tap second post onto rails **2a & 2b**
Alternative gravel board fixings **3a** *Nail through thicker edge of board into arris rail*
3b *Check vertical* **3c** *Use filler piece as final board* **3d** *Alternatively reverse board to finish*

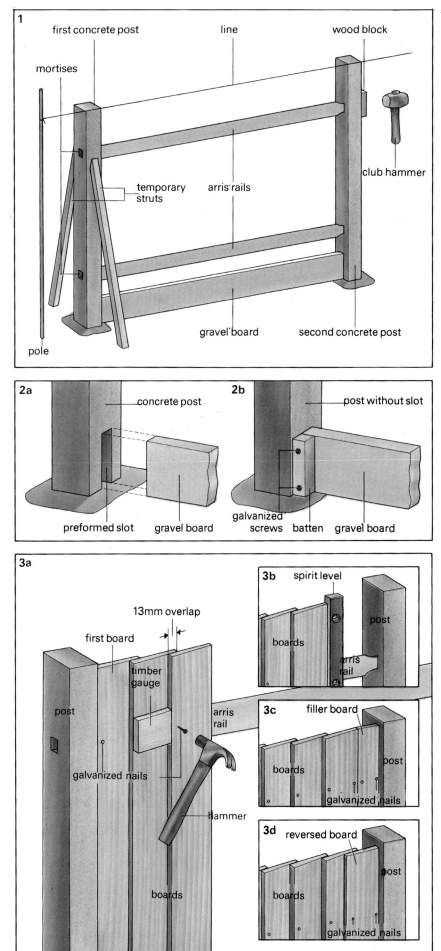

37

Fitting gravel boards

If you require them, gravel boards may be located in the preformed slots in the posts, if available; in this case they should be fitted at the same time as the arris rails. If you use timber posts without slots, fit battens alongside or nail them to the posts.

Fitting vertical boards

Finally fit the vertical boards with the thicker edge nearest to the first post; make sure you check they are vertical. Drive a nail through the thicker edge and into the centre of each rail; insert the nails at a slight angle so they will not pull straight out if the fence is subjected to pressure. Ensure the thicker edge of the board overlaps the thin edge of the first one by about 13mm ($\frac{1}{2}$ in).

Use a piece of timber cut to the size of this overlap to provide a uniform gap all the way down the board. Hold it in position at the top before nailing its overlapping neighbour through its thick edge, through the thin edge of the board below and finally into the rail; insert these nails at an angle. Use the gauge at the bottom before nailing through and finally nail the board to the centre rail – if you are using one. After you have fitted every fourth or fifth board, check the overlap of the board you have just nailed to make sure all the boards remain in line. If you wish to fit a gravel board afterwards, remember to leave a 150mm (6 in) gap below each board.

Final boards The overlap of the last two or three boards will have to be increased or decreased slightly to ensure the final board meets the end post. Alternatively you could continue with uniform overlaps and cut a filler board to finish off or reverse the last board so its thicker edge is against the post. Fit a capping piece to all boards since the end grain is subject to early rotting and splitting; skew-nail the capping piece to the posts.

CHAIN LINK FENCE

You can fix chain link fencing to timber, concrete or angle iron posts. It is very important to fix the posts solidly and brace the end posts because of the force exerted as you strain the fence during building.

Putting up timber posts

If you use timber posts, bolt timber struts to them within the top third of the post and concrete the struts into the ground to a depth of 450mm (18 in). Space intermediate posts about 2.8m (or 9 ft) apart and bury them to a depth of 450mm (18 in); for long runs you will need an intermediate straining post at 69m (226 ft) intervals.

Straining posts are also required at corners, changes in direction and where there is a substantial difference in the level of the ground. Line wires are strained between the

posts to support the fence. The number of wires depends upon the height of the fence; use two if it is under 1.2m (4 ft) and three if under 2.25m (7 ft 6 in). On long runs you can join up to three lengths of 25 m (82 ft) rolls and strain them quite safely.

Fitting chain link

Allow the concrete to set in the post holes. Use a brace and bit to drill a 10mm ($\frac{3}{8}$ in) diameter hole through the posts at the required wire height. Insert an eye bolt through each post so there is at least 50mm (2 in) of thread projecting. Fix the washer and nut to the bolt, thread the end of the wire through the loop and twist it several times with pliers.

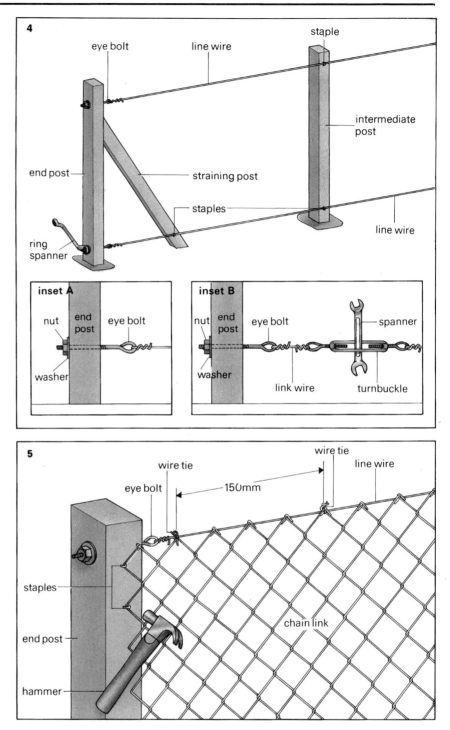

4 Fitting chain link fencing to timber posts; line wire fitted to end post using eye bolt (inset A) and turnbuckle fitted to stretch long runs of wire (inset B)

5 Stapling chain link fencing to timber end post; use wire ties to secure chain link to line wire

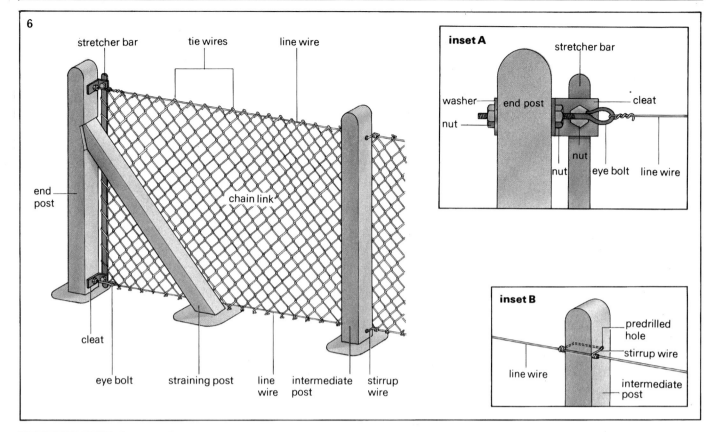

6 Fitting chain link fencing to concrete posts; stretcher bar fitted to end post using cleat and eye bolt (inset A) and stirrup wire used to fix line wire to intermediate post (inset B)

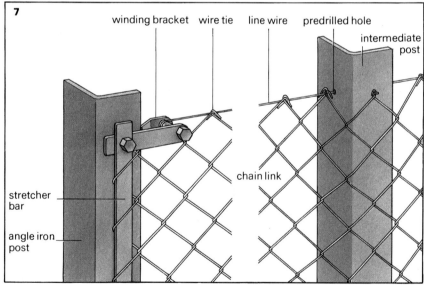

7 Fitting chain link fencing to angle iron posts; winding bracket secures stretcher bar

Unroll the wire and pass it through staples driven into the intermediate posts.

Fix the wire to the other end post with an eye bolt as before; use a spanner on the nut of the eye bolt to turn it to draw the wire tight – the eye bolt will stretch the wire by about 75mm (3 in). On long runs you will need to stretch the wire with a turnbuckle; cut the wire and twist its ends through the loops of the turnbuckle. Insert a spanner through its centre and turn it enough to tighten the wire: repeat this process for each wire.

Loosen the first end of the fencing and stand it alongside the post to fit it. Staple every loop of the mesh to the first post to prevent it sagging. You could use a stretcher bar instead of staples, as described below.

Unroll the fence, pull it taut by hand and fix it at 150mm (6 in) intervals to the line wires at the top; fix it every 450mm (18 in) to the other wires. To fix the fence, use tightly twisted fine galvanized wire; at corners or changes of direction, unravel a spiral and staple through each loop. Finally staple the free end to the last post.

Putting up concrete posts

You can use concrete posts in a similar way, with eye bolts to strain the wire and angled cleats to secure the stretcher bars, which are passed through the last rows of meshes on the chain link; the posts are predrilled to accept the eye bolts. Tension the wire with the eyebolts before tightening the securing nuts. Secure the line wire at intermediate posts by threading a stirrup wire through the predrilled holes and twisting its ends over the line wire. Concrete posts are supplied specially notched to accept the supporting struts.

Putting up angle iron posts

The difference here is merely the type of fixings used for the straining posts; special winding brackets are required to secure the stretcher bars and wires to the iron posts. The line wire passes through predrilled holes in the intermediate posts.

Joining rolls

To join rolls of chain link fencing, release the knuckles at the top and bottom of the first spiral on the roll to be joined, then detach the spiral from the roll by unscrewing it anti-clockwise. Join the ends of the rolls by twisting the loose spiral clockwise through the links of the next roll. When you have threaded it to the top, bend over the knuckles at the top and bottom.

DECORATIVE WIRE FENCE

You can build this type using timber posts or angle iron stakes set at 1.5m (5 ft) intervals. Fences 600 and 900mm (24 and 36 in) high require posts fixed between 450 and 600mm (18 and 24 in) below ground according to whether you have firm or weak soil. Use supporting struts for the end posts, which should be set into concrete.

Fixing wire fencing
Unravel the end of the fencing and fit it centrally to timber posts with 20mm ($\frac{3}{4}$ in) 20 gauge staples at roughly 75mm (3 in) intervals. It is always best to hammer home staples at a slight angle rather than straight to the grain where they might pull out. With angle iron posts, use plastic-coated wire as a fastener, twisted round to secure the fencing.

Fences 250 and 400mm (10 and 16 in) high will be self-supporting; but you should drive in small stakes at 1.8m (6 ft) intervals to ensure the fencing remains in place. Unravel the fence to the first post, pull it taut and fix it again; repeat along the roll.

On undulating sites it is worth providing additional support centrally between the posts by driving a 25mm (1 in) square stake into the ground and stapling the bottom of the fence to it. Any gaps in the bottom of fence, through which children or animals could crawl, will need to be filled in; you can do this by making up the ground, building a low wall or burying the bottom portion.

WIRE NETTING

Use timber, angle iron or special wire netting stakes at 1.8–2.4m (6–8 ft) intervals; each post should be buried for about one third of its height. The wire netting must not be over-tensioned since the mesh will distort and cause the fence to balloon out. To retain small animals such as rabbits, it is best to bury the bottom 150mm (6 in) in the ground.
Line wires The fence will be stronger if you use line wires. Use 3mm ($\frac{1}{8}$ in) galvanized wire; two lines for a fence under 1.2m (4 ft) high and three for higher fences. Space the line wires evenly down the posts and secure with netting fasteners or tie wires.
Posts Manufacturers advise holes for posts up to about 1400mm (56 in) should be 450 mm (18 in) square and 750mm (30 in) deep; set the posts in concrete. If you are using line wire, unroll it and strain it between the posts. fix the edge of the netting to the first post using 15mm, ($\frac{5}{8}$ in) 16 gauge staples (timber

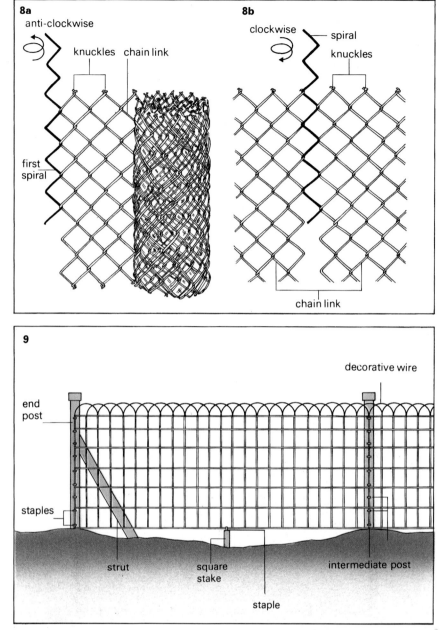

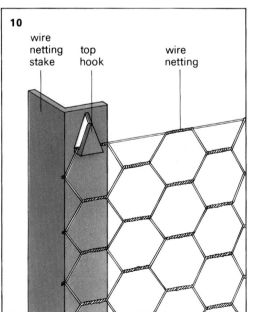

8a When joining rolls of chain link fencing, unscrew first spiral anti-clockwise
8b Thread spiral down by twisting it clockwise
9 Fitting decorative wire fence using timber posts; where ground undulates, staple bottom of fencing to timber stake
10 Fitting wire netting to special stake

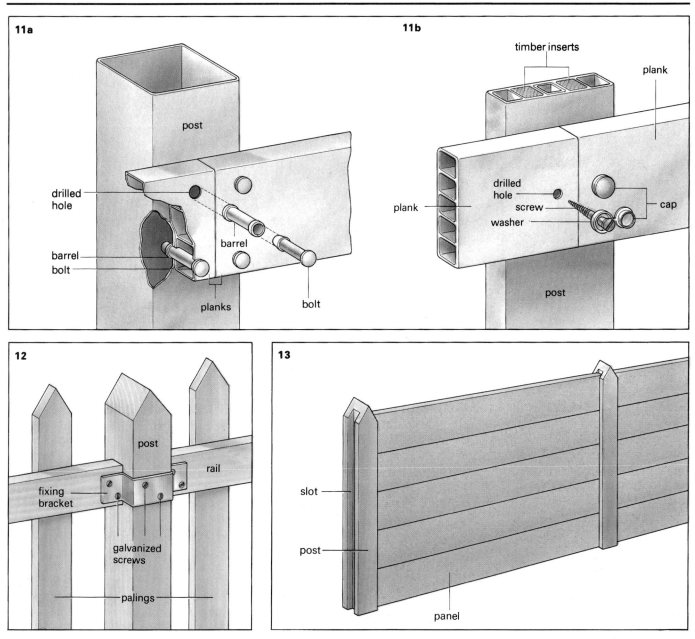

11a *When building snap-in plastic fence, bolt planks to post through drilled holes*
11b *When building screw-in plastic fence, screw planks to timber inserts in post*
12 *Building paling fence using brackets to fit rails to post*
13 *When building concrete fence, drop panels into slots in posts*

posts) or tie wire (angle iron).
Netting stakes To fix these, hook the top edge over the top hook and the lower edge over the bottom one; gradually unroll the fence, pulling it taut and securing it to the line wires and posts with tie wire.

PLASTIC FENCE

There are various types of proprietary plastic fence: manufacturers supply detailed fitting instructions which differ slightly with type.

One system uses posts slotted to accept 100mm (4 in) planks; you can buy posts capable of accepting two or three planks at heights of 1000 and 1300mm (40 and 52 in) respectively. You must carefully align the posts at 1.5m (5 ft) intervals so they will accept the planks. With 1000mm (40 in) posts, 300mm (12 in) should be below ground; with 1300mm (52 in) posts, 400mm (16 in) should be below ground.

Putting up plastic fencing
The fence is built in a similar manner to a timber fence; fit the post, check it is vertical, insert the planks and fit a second post to accept the ends of the planks. As with arris rails, insert planks half-way into a post where they butt the next plank. Planks are 1.5 and 3m (5 and 10 ft) long; use long and short planks alternately. Planks are retained in the posts by plastic nibs which project at the ends from the upper edge.

If you have to cut planks to suit your layout, for example if you need a short length to finish off, form new nibs by cutting a shallow groove across the top of a plank and prising up a nib with pincers. Support the posts as work proceeds and finally infill their holes with concrete; fit plank end caps and post top caps with the recommended adhesive.
Alternative methods You could set all the posts into the ground and fit the bottom plank to ensure the correct spacings. After

14
15
16
17
18

Building snap-in plastic fence system:
14 *Saw posts to length*
15 *Use jig to drill holes through planks and post*
16 *With fence laid on flat surface insert barrels and bolts*
17 *Check each section is vertical using spirit level*
18 *Fix subsequent sections in same way*
19 *Completed fence*

19

the infill concrete has set, insert further planks by springing in their ends.

Another common plastic fencing system has special plastic barrels and bolts which are snapped into place to hold the planks onto the faces of the posts. Drill the holes on site, through both posts and planks; it is best if you build the fence in small sections – three posts with planks fixed – by laying the components flat on the ground. The whole assembly is then joined up as the sections are positioned in the post holes. It is important to carry out this assembly on a flat surface so the planks are fitted square to the posts.

One manufacturer supplies a special jig which ensures the holes are accurately drilled. Lay the planks in their correct positions and spacings on the posts; place the jig on the face of the planks and drill the holes. Plastic barrels and bolts are snapped into place to lock the planks into position.

A further plastic fence system uses screws inserted through planks and posts and driven into timber inserts inside the posts. Again, the planks butt on the faces of the posts.

CLEFT CHESTNUT PALING FENCE
Use end posts 100mm (4 in) square with 75mm (3 in) square struts: set intermediate posts the same size as the struts at 2.7m (9 ft) intervals. Staple the top and bottom wire to the posts, retain the tension while stapling and pull the fence taut as work proceeds.

POST AND RAIL FENCE
Sawn posts should be 75mm (3 in) square and fixed at 1.8m (6 ft) intervals; rails should be 37×87mm ($1\frac{1}{2} \times 3\frac{1}{2}$ in) minimum, nailed to your side of the fence and butted up at the post centres. Stagger the joints in the rails so where the rails butt at a post, those above and below butt at the posts on each side. Allow 300mm (12 in) spaces between the rails and allow 260mm ($10\frac{1}{2}$ in) between the bottom rail and the ground.

Fitting palings
Post and rail fences with palings should have 75mm (3 in) square end posts set at 1.8m (6 ft) intervals. For fences up to 1050mm (42 in) you will need two rails; fences over this height should have three. Space palings with 50mm (2 in) gaps and nail them to all the rails. Proprietary fences supplied with ready made panels (cross rails with pales already fitted) are joined to the posts with special brackets.

CONCRETE FENCE
Set the posts in concrete at exact intervals to receive the particular width of panel you have ordered. The slots in the sides of the posts accept the panels which are simply dropped into place.

REPAIRING TIMBER FENCES

All timber exposed to the elements has to be protected to prevent it rotting. Hot sun dries out timber, making it shrink and develop cracks; in winter moisture penetrates these cracks and causes decay. A regular buffeting from the wind also causes minor defects to develop into major damage. Regular maintenance of your timber fence will keep it in good condition.

Most fences are treated with preservative by the manufacturer, but you should apply a fresh coat at least once every year. There are various brands of preservatives, available in 5lit (1 gal) cans from your local builders' merchant. The best time to apply the preservative is in late summer, after a dry spell when the timber is dry; preservative will not soak into damp timber. Apply it with a large paint brush, which you should keep solely for this purpose. You can also stand dry posts overnight in a container filled with preservative so the part of the post which will be below ground is immersed. If you intend to paint the posts, leave the bottom 150mm (6 in) bare so you can treat this portion (which is most liable to rot) each year with preservative.

1a Removing rotten gravel board 1b Gravel board fixed to batten on timber post 1c Gravel board fixed to batten driven into ground against concrete post

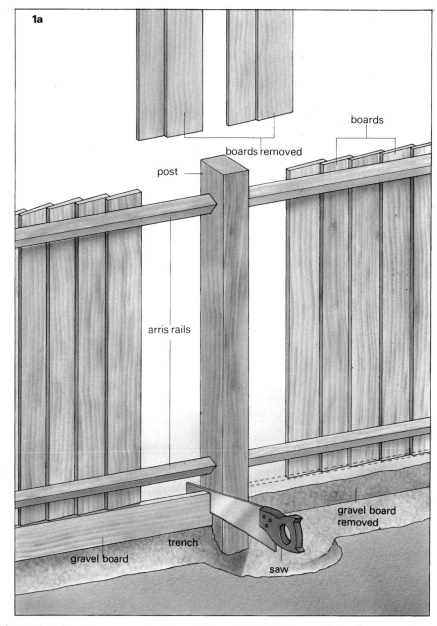

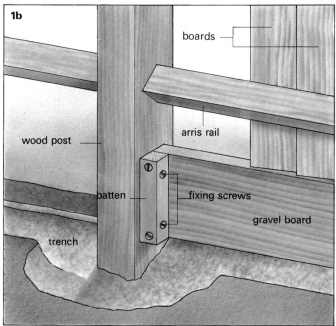

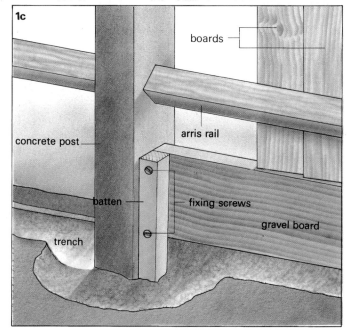

Protecting post tops

Timber posts are just as susceptible to rot at the top as at the bottom. Square-cut post tops allow rainwater to collect, which later sinks into the end grain and causes rot; the only way to remedy this is to remove the affected part with a saw.

A common way of protecting square-cut tops is to fix a protective capping of wood or metal onto the top of the post. Each wood capping should be about 19mm ($\frac{3}{4}$ in) thick and about 13mm ($\frac{1}{2}$ in) wider than the post all round. Soak the wood in preservative for 24 hours before nailing or screwing it in place.

Metal – zinc or aluminium – is a sounder capping material. Place the metal on top of the post and fold down the edges over the side of the post to form a lip of about 13mm ($\frac{1}{2}$ in) which you can then fix with aluminium or galvanized nails.

The simplest method of guarding against rot is to saw off the top of the post to an angle, making a slope for the water to run down. Alternatively you can cut both sides of the post to form a ridge; this does not give complete protection, however, and a capping of timber or metal should be fixed.

Replacing gravel boards

Gravel boards protect the bottom of a fence by preventing it touching the ground. A gravel board fixed between posts bears the brunt of the deterioration and can be replaced fairly easily when affected by rot.

To replace a rotting board, dig a trench round it to facilitate removal and to allow the new board to be manoeuvred into place between the fence and the posts. Saw off the end of the old board where it enters the posts. Check the base of the fence for rotting and replace any timber which shows signs of rot at the ends. Screw a 50 × 50mm (2 × 2 in) timber batten, which has been soaked in preservative, onto the base of each post to act as a fixing point for the new gravel boards; keep the top of the battens in line with the bottom of the fence panels or boards. Position the new gravel board and screw it to the battens flush with the front of the posts. Finally fill the trench; don't pack the soil against the new board since this will cause further deterioration.

Replacing panels

First remove the nails holding the panel to the posts. Panels usually come in standard widths and it should be easy to find a replacement of the same dimensions. If you cannot find a replacement of the exact size, buy one slightly undersize; the difference can be made up by screwing infill pieces to the posts and nailing the new panel to these. Make sure the infill pieces are well coated with preservative on both sides and fix them with 63mm ($2\frac{1}{2}$ in) long galvanized nails.

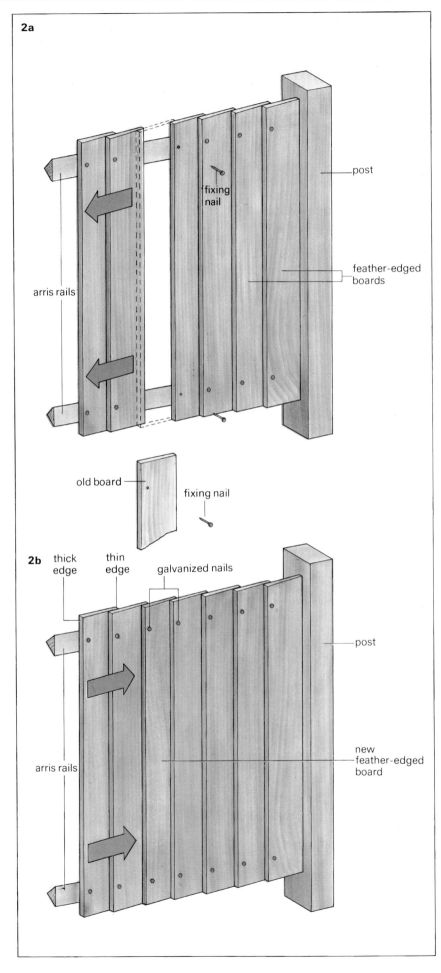

44

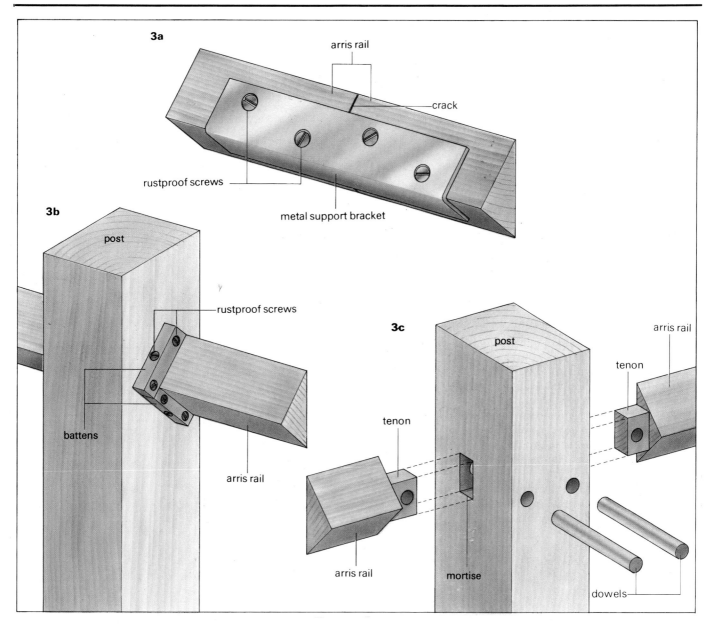

3a arris rail

crack

rustproof screws

metal support bracket

3b post

rustproof screws

battens

arris rail

3c post

arris rail

tenon

tenon

arris rail

mortise

dowels

2a *To remove rotten feather-edged board, take out nails and slide out rotten board*
2b *To replace feather-edged board, slide in new board thin edge first then fix with nails*
3a *To repair cracked arris rail, place metal support bracket over crack and fix with rustproof screws*
3b *To fit arris rail flush with post, use battens secured to post and rail with rustproof screws*
3c *To secure loosely fitting arris rail, drill holes in post and through tenon of arris rail; insert hardwood dowels to hold rail firmly in position*

Replacing feather-edged boards

Old, unprotected boards become brittle and eventually pull over the nails holding them to the arris rail. If the boards are worth saving, apply preservative and refix them with galvanized nails. Where a board has to be replaced, take out the fixing nails securing it to the boards on each side; if the nails will not move, drive them into the arris rail using a hammer and nail punch. Buy your replacement board and coat it with preservative; slip it into place. Fix it through both edges into the arris rail. Always fix through the thick edge of the board into the thin edge of the board it overlaps and then into the arris rail behind.

You can shape and protect the tops of feather-edged boards in the same way as you protect posts by fitting capping pieces.

Repairing arris rails

Arris rails take a lot of strain so slight defects are quickly magnified.

For cracks in the middle of the rail, simply fix a special arris rail support bracket and secure it with rustproof screws. Cracks in the ends of the rails where they enter the posts can also be secured with a rail-to-post bracket. You can make your own bracket from 25mm (1 in) thick pieces of wood. Soak the wood in preservative before fixing, then secure the rail to the 25mm (1 in) battens. If the end of the rail fits loosely into the post, drill a hole through the post into the rail and knock in a hardwood dowel to hold the rail securely in position. Before tapping the dowel home, cut a shallow groove along its length and coat it with a waterproof adhesive.

If you need a new rail, buy one 75mm (3 in) longer than the space between the posts. Shape the ends with a tenon saw.

Fitting a new rail is easier if one of the posts is sufficiently loose to be pushed sideways. If both posts are solidly fixed, cut a tenon in one end of the new rail and place this in a post mortise. Cut the other end square and secure it with a rail-to-post bracket.

FITTING GATES AND POSTS

Whatever type of gate you choose, it is essential the posts are substantial and well-fixed. These can be of timber, steel or reinforced concrete and piers of brick, stone or concrete blocks can also be used.

Timber posts Oak is the best timber for gate posts. It should be at least 100mm (4 in) square and 125mm (5 in) square if your gate is more than 1.8m (6 ft) high and 1m (or 3 ft) wide. Larch is suitable if you cannot obtain oak. For all five-bar gates, strong oak posts are very important. For gates of 1.2–2.1m (4–7 ft) wide, use 150mm (6 in) square posts 2.1m (7 ft) long. This allows 0.9m (3 ft) to be buried; for gates 2.4–3.6m (8–12 ft) wide 1.2m (4 ft) should be buried and the posts should be 2.4m (8 ft) long and 175mm (7 in) square. The post on the catch side can be 2.1m (7 ft) long and 150mm (6 in) square.

Metal posts Metal posts are available for metal gates. They are tubular, square or rectangular welded box section; hinge pins, catch and slam bars are usually welded in place. Paint ready-made posts with rust-resistant primer; dip the bottom in black bitumen paint to give extra protection.

Concrete posts You may be able to buy purpose-made concrete posts but it is usual to adapt standard concrete fence posts to hang a gate. The main problem is to fix the hinges and the catch. The posts may be predrilled so these fittings can be bolted through the holes, although more usually the hinges and catch have to be screwed to lengths of timber which are bolted through the post holes.

Masonry piers Piers must be substantial; the minimum size for a brick pier is a brick-and-a-half square – or 337mm (13 in) square. Use strong bricks or stones and strong mortar – one part Portland cement to three or four parts clean sand. Hinge and catch fittings are usually designed for building into the mortar joints as you construct the piers.

Obviously the gate must be purchased before you begin so you can position the fittings accurately. It is easier to use fittings which you plug and screw to the completed pier, although these fittings are not as strong.

Fitting gate posts

To measure, lay the gate on the ground and position the hinges, hinge post, gate catch and catch post. Measure the distance between the posts and allow a slight clearance to ensure the gate will swing freely when hung; check the distance is the same top and bottom. Cut a timber batten to this length and use it as a gauge to set the posts the correct distance apart. If you are fitting a pair of gates place a 6mm ($\frac{1}{4}$ in) thick batten as a spacer between the joining stiles of the gates

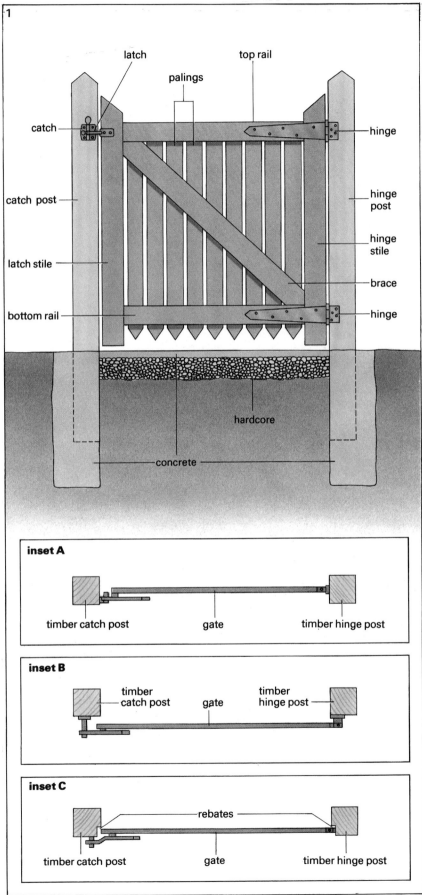

inset A

timber catch post   gate   timber hinge post

inset B

timber catch post / gate / timber hinge post

inset C

rebates

timber catch post   gate   timber hinge post

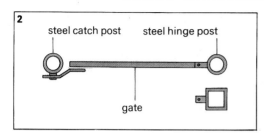

to ensure they will open and close freely.

Post holes If posts were supplied with the gate, make the depth of the holes sufficient to give a clearance of at least 50mm (2 in) under the gate. If the ground rises behind the gate, you may have to set the posts higher so the gate can be opened fully without scraping on the ground. If you are buying posts separately, make sure they are sufficiently long to allow 450mm (18 in) to be set in the ground if the gate is up to 1m (or 3 ft) high and 1m (or 3 ft) wide; if the gate is wider than this, 600mm (or 24 in) should be set into the ground. You will need a post hole borer for farm-style gates.

In soft ground you should dig a 150mm (6 in) deep trench between the post holes to form a concrete bridge between the posts in the gateway opening; this is to counter the considerable strain exerted on the hinge post. Place about 100mm (4 in) of concrete in the bottom of each post hole and position the posts; check they are lined up with the other posts in a fence run and are vertical on all faces. Use temporary struts of scrap timber to hold the posts steady and check the tops of the posts are level. Check your posts are the correct distance apart top and bottom and pack round the posts with concrete – or concrete and hardcore.

Metal gate posts often have welded-on metal projections near their bases; these must be set into concrete for a secure fixing. Allow about seven days for the concrete to harden before hanging any gates.

Post fittings Metal posts often have hinges and catches already fitted and hanging becomes a simple matter of placing the gate on the hinge pins and checking it swings freely and the catch operates. To prevent vandals removing a metal gate you can drill the hinge pins to take split pins; slip a washer over the hinge pin before fitting the split pin. If the gate fittings (hinges and catch) have to be screwed to the posts, place the gate in position and hold it clear of the ground on suitably sized blocks; check the gate is upright. In the case of a metal gate, hold the hinge pin in position on the gate and mark the fixing holes onto the post.

Fixing gate hinges
In the majority of cases, timber garden gates are hung using T-hinges. These are available in various sizes in either painted steel or a galvanized finish, the latter being preferable.

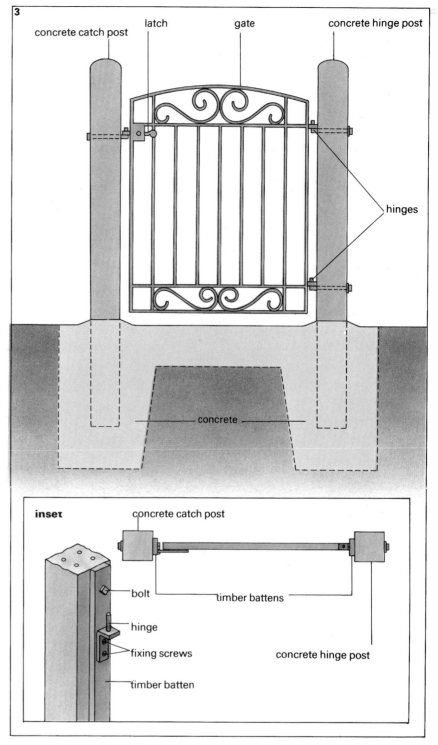

For an 'old world' look of wrought iron, rust-resistant malleable iron hinges are available. This type of hinge looks most effective with a sturdy ring latch set.

Garden gates Heavy garden gates need substantial hinges and it is best to use a cranked single strap and plate hinge (also called a hook and band hinge); alternatively you could use a heavy reversible cup hinge. With all the hinges, you screw the pin plate flap to the face of the post and the long strap portion to the gate itself; the latter should correspond with the horizontal rails on the gate. These heavy hinges have a square hole punched

1 Components of a typical timber gate and plans of hanging between posts (inset A), to the rear of posts (inset B) and on rebated posts (inset C)
2 Hanging a gate using either round or square steel posts
3 Hanging a metal gate between concrete posts; use predrilled concrete posts or screw a timber batten to the posts (inset)

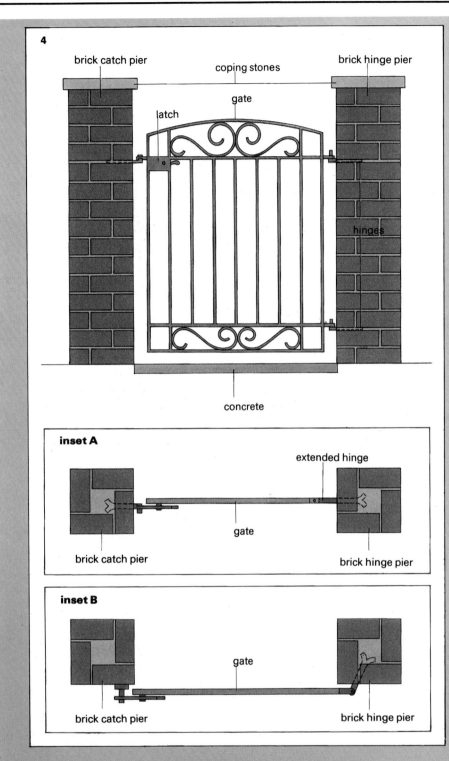

4

brick catch pier

coping stones

brick hinge pier

latch

gate

hinges

concrete

inset A

extended hinge

gate

brick catch pier

brick hinge pier

inset B

gate

brick catch pier

brick hinge pier

through them to take the collar of a coach bolt, which you pass through the hinge and bolt right through the gate.

Farm gates Use heavy-duty double strap and hook hinges. Most of the weight of the gate is taken by the top hinge, which should be larger than the bottom one. The top ride, as it is often called, extends some way along the top rail to which it is bolted. It hinges on the top hook, which is driven through the gate post and held in place with a nut and washer. The bottom hook is spiked so you can drive it securely into the post. The bottom ride is smaller than the top and it simply bolts through the hanging stile.

Fitting gate catches

A common type of catch for farm-style five-bar gates is the spring catch; sometimes an auto-catch is chosen because this type is drilled to take a padlock. Both catches will only work from one direction and the posts must be set so the gate closes onto them. If there is a clearance between the latch stile and the post, you could fit a Chelsea catch which allows the gate to open inwards or outwards.

Loop-over catch Where two farm-style gates meet, they are usually held closed with a simple loop-over catch. One gate is held closed with a heavy-duty drop bolt.

Conventional catch After hanging the gate align the fittings so the latch bar (the moving part) strikes the catch (which is fixed to the post) at around its mid-point. When a gate is slammed, the latch takes a good deal of strain; make sure it is securely fitted.

Thumb latch Also called a Suffolk, a thumb latch can be fitted to a gate by cutting a slot in the gate to allow the latch lifter to pass through. Fit the handle plate and lifter to the front side of the gate; position the latch bar on the reverse side so the lifter will raise the latch bar. Finally fit the catch plate.

Automatic catch This is a common latch for low gates; if used on a close-boarded side gate, you can drill the post and fit a release cord which you then fix to the release lever. On some types of catch, you can drill the lever so a small padlock can be fitted to hold the gate closed. For extra security, you may

5

7

6

4 *Hanging a gate between brick piers and plans of using extended hinges where the existing opening is too wide (inset A) and hanging the gate to the rear of the piers where the existing opening is too narrow (inset B)*

5 *Farm-style bottom ride and hook*

6 *Top ride and hook*

7 *Farm-style loop-over catch*

8 *Cranked single strap hinge*

9 *Chelsea catch set*

10 *Ring latch set*

11 *Automatic catch set*

12 *Drop bolt and socket*

13 *Fitting a split pin to prevent the gate being removed; drill through the hinge pin, insert the split pin and bend it round the hinge pin*

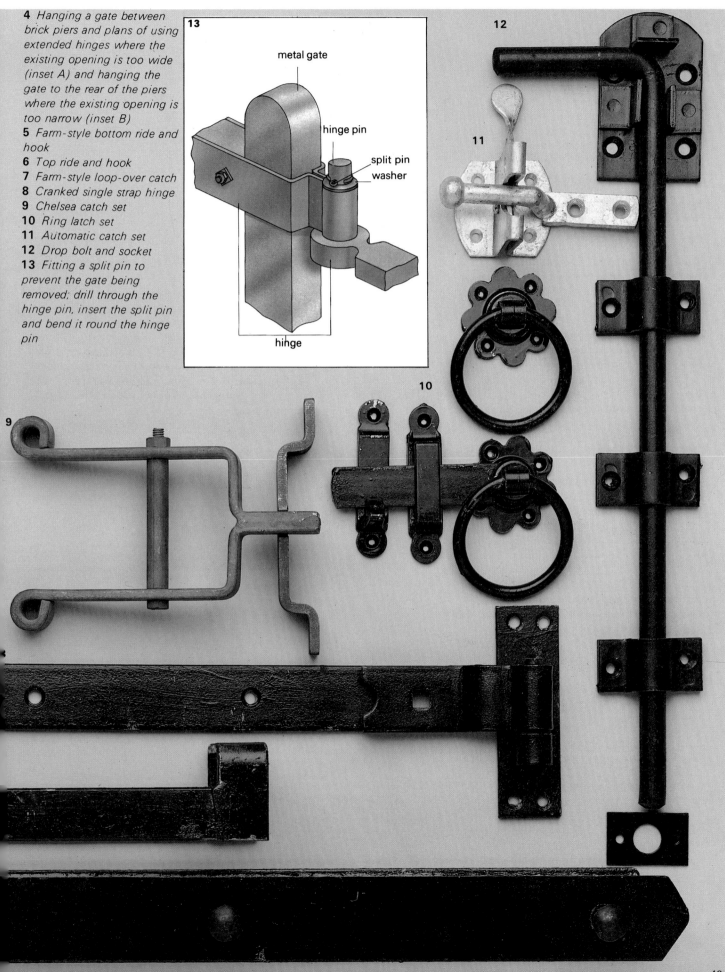

13
metal gate
hinge pin
split pin
washer
hinge

12

11

10

9

require a padlock hasp; fit the securing plates with large, long screws so when the hasp plate is in position it covers the screw heads.

Drop bolt If you are fitting double gates, you will require a drop bolt fitted to one gate to hold it closed; concrete a socket or flat plate into the ground to accept the drop bolt barrel. If you are fitting the gates over existing concrete, use a large masonry drill bit in a hammer drill to make the socket.

Gate closers You may also require a gate closer, of which there are several types. The most common is a gate spring, which consists of an adjustable tension coil spring; one end is screwed to the hinge post and the other to the hinge stile of the gate.

Fitting gate to piers

You should excavate the foundation for each pier to a depth of at least 450mm (18 in) and 150mm (6 in) wider all round than the pier; in clay soil the pier should be fitted into a 600mm (24 in) deep hole. Place a 150mm (6 in) depth of concrete into each foundation hole; if the ground is subject to movement, link the foundations between the piers.

Piers These must be built up carefully to ensure each is vertical without any twists; the courses of bricks must line up. Use a batten gauge which allows for the hinge and latch projection to ensure the piers are built the correct distance apart. Insert vertical battens on each side of the opening just clear of one outer corner of each pier; these will ensure the piers are built accurately. Make sure the battens are correctly aligned and check they are vertical with a spirit level. To ensure they do not move, join their tops with a crosspiece and secure the vertical battens with temporary struts. Mark each brick course on the battens, checking with a spirit level and straight-edge each course is level, and stretch a line between the marks as a guide to your bricklaying. Remember to build the hinge pins into the mortar joints as you work.

Fitting gates between existing piers

If you buy gates of the correct size, you can fit them between existing posts or piers. If the gates are too wide for your opening, you will have to reposition one of the posts or piers.

Gaps If the opening is too wide for your new gates, the biggest problem is to fill the gap. The best solution is to remount the hinges or the latch catch on a strip of timber, which is then bolted to one or both of the existing posts to fill the gap. The timber can be made up to 75mm (3 in) thick, so you could fill a gap of about 150mm (6 in) using this method. Fix the strip or strips of timber with coach bolts, which should pass right through the posts; in the case of a brick pier, fix them using projecting-type expansion bolts. Once the opening has been reduced to the correct width, you can hang the gate.

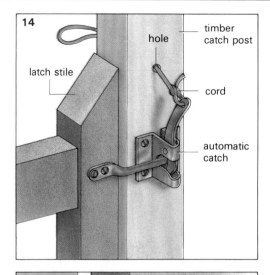

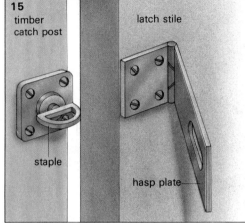

14 Fitting an automatic catch to a timber post; a release cord is fed through a hole drilled in the post
15 Fitting a padlock hasp for extra security; when the hasp plate is in position it conceals the fixing screws
16 Linking the foundations to form a strip between the piers if the ground is liable to movement; the hinge pins are set into the mortar joints as the hinge pier is built

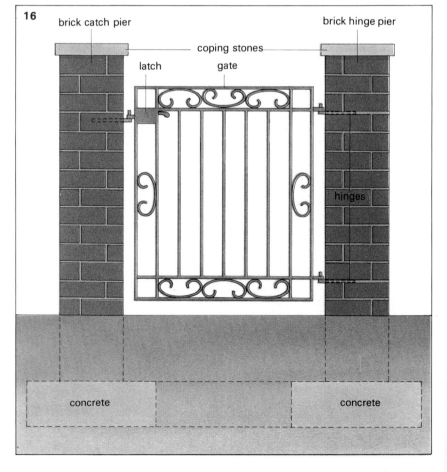

REPAIRING GATES AND POSTS

There are several repairs you can make to prolong the life of gates and posts.

TIMBER GATES

The most common problem you are likely to encounter with timber gates is when they bind on the ground or on their catch posts. Binding could be due to faulty hinges, loose joints, split or rotting timber or sagging.

First try this test. Partially open the gate, grasp the latch stile and attempt to lift it up and down; this will show up loose hinges and wear in the hinge pins. It will also show if the gate has loose joints or if the hinge post is loose or leaning to one side. Also test the latch for movement and make sure the stile is vertical with a spirit level.

All the above problems are discussed below; if they are not the cause or cannot be easily rectified, you should plane or saw the offending edge to give a clearance of about 6mm ($\frac{1}{4}$ in) between the stile and the catch post. You will need to remove the latch before planing – and it may be much easier if you remove the gate from its hinges.

Sagging gate
If the gate sags check it was properly hung; if a diagonal brace is fitted, it should run from the bottom corner on the hinge side to the top corner on the latch side. If this is not the case, remove the gate and rehang it.

Fitting diagonal brace If the gate does not have a diagonal brace, it is a good idea to fit one. Insert wedges under the bottom rail on the latch side to hold the gate in the required position. Cut the brace from 100 × 32mm (4 × 1$\frac{1}{2}$ in) timber – 100 × 50mm (4 × 2 in) timber for a large gate – and shape the ends so the brace fits tightly across the frame. Fix the brace into place with waterproof adhesive and zinc-plated screws.

Using wire brace If your gate has a brace which is not effective, you can correct the sag using a wire brace. Screw on metal plates at the corners on the opposite diagonal to the existing brace, fit a turnbuckle and straining wire between the plates and tighten the turnbuckle so the gate is pulled square.

Worn hinges
If the hinges seem to be loose, this means they are probably too small and should be replaced with larger versions. Alternatively the

Fitting hinge Hold the new hinge in place and drill new pilot holes if the old screw holes do not align. If the old holes are only very slightly out of alignment, plug them with short lengths of dowel coated with adhesive and drill new pilot holes.

Loose joints
If the gate joints are loose, you can be fairly certain parts of the gate are beginning to rot (see page 52, repairing rotted areas). The rot may not show up on the surface of the timber; but if you probe it with a pointed tool such as securing screws may be too small; replace them with longer zinc-plated screws or use galvanized nuts and bolts. A worn hinge pin is not worth repairing; if the hinges are corroded or fractured they should be replaced.

Garden gates over about 1.5m (5 ft) high and about 0.9m (3 ft) wide should be hung with three hinges, for extra support. If you have a large garden gate with only two hinges, add a third midway between them; this will give the gate extra strength and may avoid major repairs in the future. Replacement hinges should be of the same size and pattern, unless the old ones have worn and need to be replaced with hinges of a larger size. Ideally they should be galvanized or

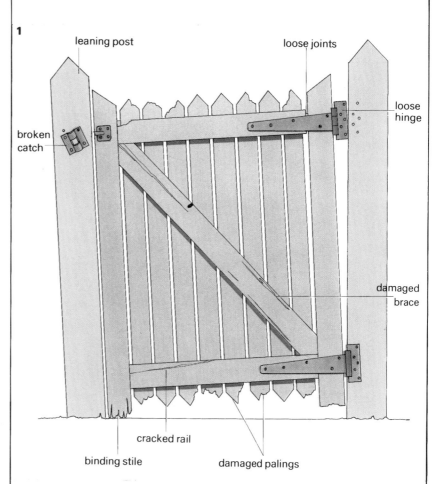

1 A gate can become damaged at various points through weathering, misuse or age; try to repair the damage as soon as it occurs to prevent further deterioration
2 (next page) Fit a diagonal brace to bring a sagging gate back into square; use wedges to hold the gate in the required position
3 (next page) Alternatively correct the sag by using a wire brace and turnbuckle mounted on metal plates; the wire brace should run in the opposite direction to the original timber brace

Figure labels: leaning post, loose joints, loose hinge, broken catch, damaged brace, cracked rail, binding stile, damaged palings

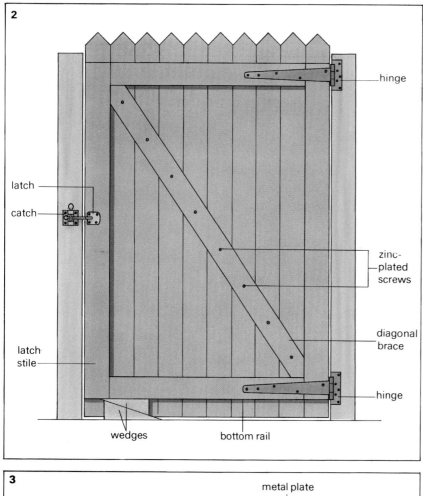

2

latch

catch

latch stile

hinge

zinc-plated screws

diagonal brace

hinge

wedges   bottom rail

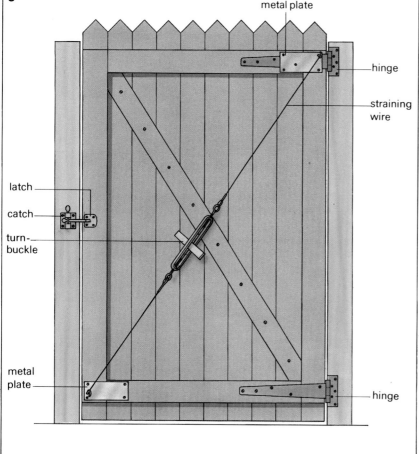

3

metal plate

hinge

straining wire

latch

catch

turn-buckle

metal plate

hinge

have a black japanned finish; if you use hinges which are bright steel, paint them on all faces before using them on the gate.
a penknife, you should find it. If it is extensive, the gate should be replaced.

Fitting timber brace If the timber is sound and the resulting sagging only slight, loose joints can be repaired with a corner-to-corner timber brace. Saw the brace roughly to shape and plane it until it is a tight fit; fix it securely to the gate with waterproof adhesive and screws. The timber brace should always run upwards from the bottom on the hinge side.

Rebuilding joints If many joints are loose, you will have to dismantle the gate and remake each joint; use waterproof adhesive and reinforce each joint with a hardwood dowel smeared with adhesive and inserted through the mortise and tenon.

If the end grain of the mortise and tenon shows on the surface of the stile, make a slot in the end grain with a chisel and apply waterproof adhesive before tapping a small hardwood wedge into the slot. This will force the sides of the joint apart and tighten it; once the adhesive has set hard you can cut the end of the wedge so it is flush with the joint. As the adhesive hardens, the gate should be held flat; use clamps to hold the joints together.

Fitting corner plates You can make a repair using corner plates or brackets. The plates are flat L or T-shaped or you can buy right-angled metal brackets. They are simply screwed into place over the loose joint or they can be recessed into the gate using a chisel; this leaves the plate flush with the surface.

To fit a corner plate, close the gate and place wedges under the bottom rail and between the catch post and latch stile to tighten the loose joints. Fit plates of the largest size and heaviest gauge possible to both sides of the damaged joint.

Split timber

Some types of timber may be prone to cracking and splitting: you can reinforce small cracks with a flat steel brace or plate screwed across the crack. More serious cracks need to be carefully prised open and injected with waterproof adhesive; hold the crack closed with slotted steel strip.

Rotted timber

Small areas of rot can be chiselled back to sound timber; treat the area with clear or horticultural wood preservative and fill the cavity when the preservative has dried. There are various waterproof fillers suitable for exterior grade timber.

Replacing timber Large areas of rot should be repaired by dismantling the gate and replacing the defective timber. You can use the old timber as a template and new timber can be fixed to sound old timber with screws, dowels or brackets and waterproof adhesive.

TIMBER POSTS

If your gate post has worked loose, dig out a collar of soil to a depth of about 150mm (6 in) round the post. Hold the post vertical and check with a spirit level before ramming large pieces of rubble or stones into the ground to secure the base of the post. Fill round the post with a concrete collar.

Sinking The post may sink straight down into the ground in some types of soil. This could prevent the latch working or make the bottom of the gate scrape on the ground. All you can do is reset the latch and/or hinges in the hope the post will not sink any further. If it does continue to sink, remove and reposition it on a paving slab set into the hole.

Leaning A leaning gate post will usually need to be reset into the ground. If the hinge post is leaning because of the weight of the gate, you may be able to place a packing piece of timber under the lower hinge plate; this may pull the gate upright. Alternatively, you could pull the hinge post upright with a turnbuckle and straining wire; a leaning catch post could be corrected in the same way. If the gate post is fixed to a wall with expansion or screw bolts, it may work loose as it is continually opened and closed. You may be able to secure it to the wall by turning the securing nut of the expansion bolt; if it again works loose, replace the bolts with ones of a larger size.

Damaged post

If you have to replace a gate post, the main problem is the same as for fence posts – it is often difficult to remove the old stump. The usual method, already described, is to lift out the post by breaking up the concrete and removing the rubble. To avoid damage, you can attempt to jack the post stump up and out of the ground.

Jacking Drill a substantial hole through the post at about 200mm (8 in) above ground. Secure metal blocks or offcuts of sturdy angle iron to each side of the post using a stout bolt through the drilled hole. With a car jack and a length of timber each side of the post you may be able to lift the post straight out of the ground.

Boring If your post has snapped off at ground level, you could bore it out of the ground piece by piece. Hire a timber auger or

4a *To secure a loose mortise and tenon joint, insert a hardwood dowel smeared with adhesive through the mortise and tenon*
4b *To secure a through mortise and tenon joint, tap a wedge into the tenon after applying waterproof adhesive*
4c *Hold the glued joints with a Spanish windlass until the adhesive has set*
5 *As a temporary measure you can repair split rails with metal plates secured with galvanized screws*

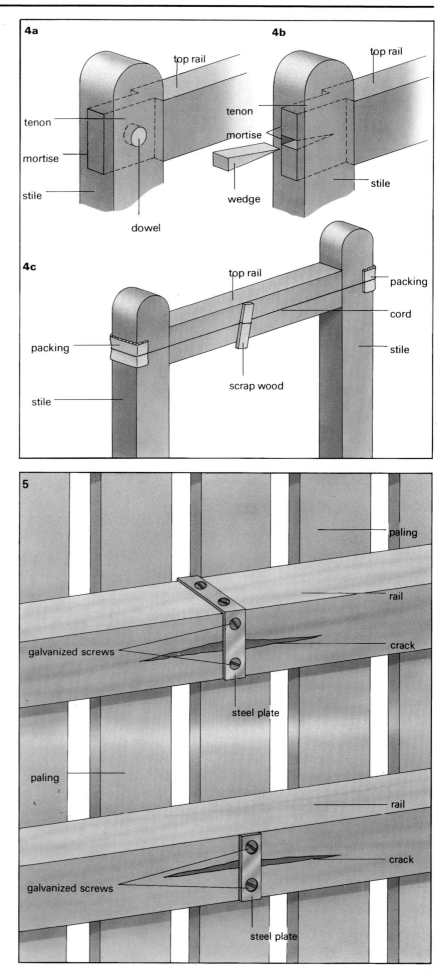

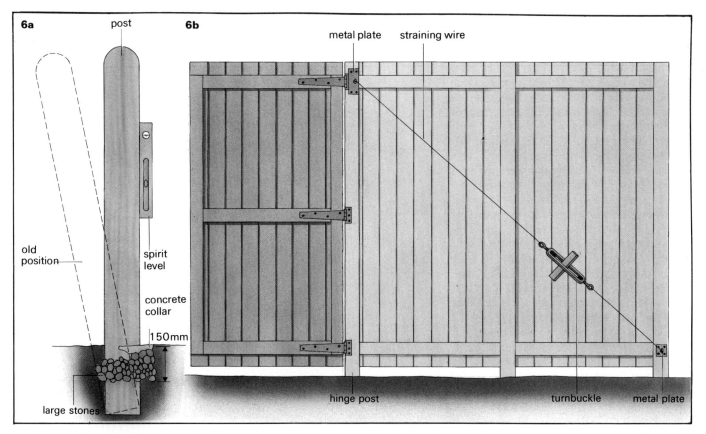

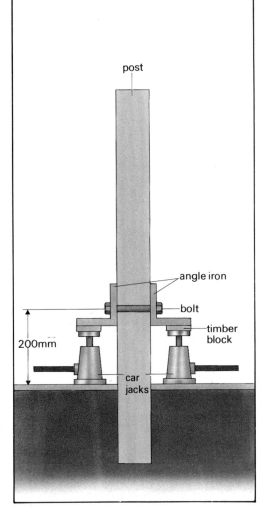

6a *To correct a leaning post, wedge the post in a vertical position with stones and cast a concrete collar to hold the post permanently in place*
6b *Alternatively you can fit a straining wire and turnbuckle between the top of the gate post and a rigid fixing*
7 *To remove a damaged post, use car jacks to lever it from the ground; raise each jack a little at a time*

post boring tool about 25mm (1 in) in diameter; place it on the stump and drill out the end grain of the timber. Repeat the process several times to remove as much timber as possible; sections which remain could be split off and removed with a long cold chisel. Use a long cold chisel or crow bar to remove lumps of concrete and rubble so the post hole is enlarged to allow at least 25mm (1 in) of packing concrete all round the replacement.

Rusted latch
Rusting is the most common problem on latch posts. If it is severe, you will have to replace the latch; otherwise use a wire brush to clean the latch and treat it with rust-resistant primer before repainting. All latches, bolts and closing devices should be regularly lubricated.

BRICK PIERS
Leaning or sinking brick piers must be rebuilt on deeper foundations, as described on page 51. If there is only slight leaning, you could pack the post with timber offcuts.

METAL GATES
The main problem here is corrosion. You can wire-brush metal gates and apply rust-resisting primer before repainting them. Wrought-iron or mild steel gates may break at the joints; repair them using welding or brazing techniques. Or make up a metal bracket from a strip of steel; secure it to the gate using self-tapping screws or rivets.

Walls, fences and hedges all create divisions within the garden and most people are content with these well-tried ideas.
However, there is one more useful device that merits close attention.

MAKE A FEDGE

A fedge is exactly what it sounds – a cross between a fence and a hedge. This is not as extraordinary as it seems, for a fedge is a useful device with a positive role to play in the garden.

Basically, a fedge consists of climbing plants covering a prefabricated framework; this might be an old wall, fence or purpose-built wire screen. Once the plants are established, the framework becomes incidental and completely obscured.

Such a feature opens up interesting design possibilities and combines an architectural form with the softer, sprawling nature of the climbers used, providing a useful link between house and garden.

By its nature a fedge is most effective up to a maximum height of 2m (6½ ft). Beyond this many climbers tend to get a little straggly and the bottom growth becomes sparse and untidy. For this reason fedges are not really suited for use on a boundary where screening is important but are better adapted to the garden's own internal divisions – perhaps between a lawn and a vegetable plot, or for marking off a play area.

Constructing a fedge

The traditional method of constructing a fedge is to use chestnut fencing, allowing the climber simply to ramble up and over it. Although cheap and flexible, it is likely to decay fairly quickly. A sturdier method, and one that can give rise to a wide range of architectural patterns, involves using a combination of 10mm (⅜ in) mild steel rods of the type used in reinforced concrete, in combination with plastic mesh such as Netlon.

First, decide on the height and length of the fedge, remembering that it need not be straight or a necessarily continuous run; if you are in doubt about the final result in relation to the rest of the garden, work out the pattern to scale on graph paper. Next, select the finished shape you want; this can be rectangular, hooped or wedge shaped. Each shape, being more or less formal, will have its own characteristic.

The reinforcing rods are then carefully bent in a vice to the shape of a simple template (a pattern used as a guide in cutting) made from plywood or hardboard, thus ensuring that each hoop matches the next.

The hoops in a fedge 1·5m (5 ft) high should be under a metre (or yard) apart.

An effective method of anchoring them is to slide each section into a length of scaffold pole set into the ground. The plastic mesh is then stretched over the finished line of hoops and neatly fixed by plastic-coated wire.

While this technique is suitable for fedges of considerable length and scale in the larger garden, another simple form of fedge can be made from railway sleepers set vertically into the ground 2m (6½ ft) apart. The netting in this case should be nailed to the outside of the sleepers, and climbers planted in the usual way.

Plants for fedges

Of all fedging plants, hedera (ivy) is undoubtedly the best – tough, evergreen, and relatively fast to cover a framework. The large-leaved varieties are the most suitable and *Hedera colchica*, with its bold, heart-shaped green leaves, is ideal. *H. c.* Variegata has the added bonus of really large leaves, the dark centres of which are in striking contrast to the soft, yellow, outer variegations. Hedera is also useful in that it tolerates shade – a point to

remember when screening some of those awkward features such as compost heaps and bonfire areas.

Of the other climbers, aristolochia (Dutchman's pipe), lonicera (honeysuckle), passiflora (passion flower) and *Polygonum baldschuanicum* (Russian vine) can all be used, but be sure the lonicera you choose is an evergreen and remember that some climbers, the Russian vine in particular, will need continual pruning to keep them in check.

Maintaining a fedge

Fedge maintenance is normally confined to keeping it neat and tidy, removing dead leaves before they get clogged in the structure and pruning the more prominent climbers to keep them in hand. Pruning need not be too severe; if there is room, the climber can be allowed to run along the ground too, sweeping up and over the fedge in a continuous run.

Once established, the fedge will be a permanent and attractive feature, part of the basic framework forming a background for softer elements in the design.

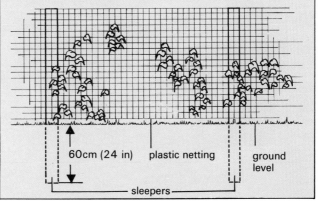

60cm (24 in)　plastic netting　ground level

sleepers

Left: fedge for the larger garden with climbers on plastic netting secured to the outside of railway sleepers
Below: climbers on wire frameworks bent to a variety of interesting shapes

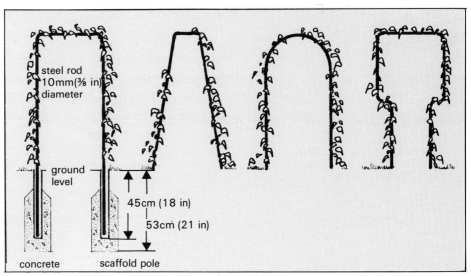

steel rod 10mm (⅜ in) diameter

ground level

concrete　scaffold pole

45cm (18 in)

53cm (21 in)

Surfaces

A variety of surfaces lends interest to your garden. Gravel, bricks, concrete or cobbles can alternate with grass for functional or visual effect; steps and ramps link different levels and, if you are enterprising, you can build your own patio garden.

GRAVEL SURFACING

When laying gravel, the various stages of preparation are very important, especially in driveways where heavy traffic can quickly cause havoc with a badly-executed job.

Preparation and laying

For the best results, really thorough consolidation is necessary at each juncture and, where space permits, you can hire a mechanical 'vibrating' roller and this will give ideal results in the minimum time. In cramped areas, or paths, a 500–750kg (10–15 cwt) hand roller may be all that is practical.

If you are thinking of using gravel for a drive, you will find that a 'sub base' is normally needed. This will have been carried out by a combination of the builders and traffic over the years on a developed site. When you are operating on virgin ground, it would be wise to call in a contractor to do at least the basic soil-shifting and levelling.

Lay a base of hardcore, crushed stone or clinker, and roll it to a finished thickness of 10cm (4 in). Then put down a

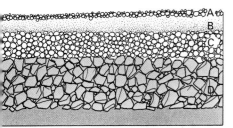

*Cross-section of gravel **A**, laid on 2·5cm (1 in) layer of hoggin **B**, and 5cm (2 in) layer of coarse gravel **C**, over hardcore **D***

layer of coarse gravel, small enough to pass through a 5cm (2 in) screen, and roll it to a finished thickness of 5cm (2 in). Roll on a 2·5cm (1 in) covering of fine gravel mixed with hoggin as a binder. 'Hoggin' is a technical term used by contractors and is simply a clay, usually from the same pit as the gravel, that seals and binds the surface together. Wet it just enough to achieve an even spread; if too wet, it will clog rollers and tools, sticking to everything except the surface of the drive itself.

On top, to finish with, spread and roll 13mm (½ in) washed 'pea' shingle. The surface should now be firm; there is nothing worse than a treadmill effect on your way to the front door.

Drainage

It is especially important to provide drainage with gravel and if, after digging a trial hole, you find the water-table to be within 60cm (2 ft) of the surface, lay a simple drain on one or both sides of the drive. (See bottom diagram).

Retaining edges

The gravel may well be retained by a building or some kind of paving but, where it meets a soft surface such as plantings or grass, you may need a definite edge. You can obtain a neat and

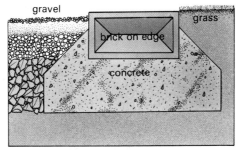

Above: cross-section showing edging brick set in concrete with gravel below on one side and grass above on the other

attractive finish by laying bricks on edge, but make sure that these are a hard, well-fired variety that will resist frost. Set the bricks in concrete and bring the gravel within 13mm (½ in) of the top. If the area abuts a lawn, the grass should, in turn, be 13mm (½ in) above the brick, allowing the mower to run easily along the top.

Plants for use with gravel

Architectural foliage blends well with gravel and enhances the composition by highlighting and ornamenting its edge. The large strongly-veined leaves of *Hosta sieboldiana*, a blue-leaved plantain lily, contrast effectively with the tall spiky uprights of *Yucca flaccida* (Adam's needle). Avoid 'spotty' effects of single specimens by planting in small groups.

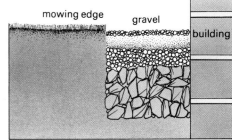

Above: cross-section of gravel abutting a lawn and laid against a building that acts as a retaining edge

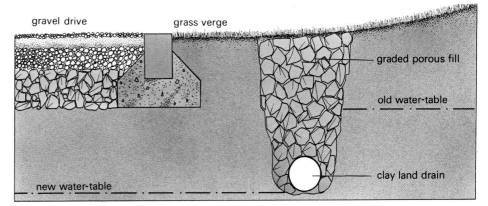

Above: cross-section of gravel set around the base of a tree beside paving; make sure there is no upstand between paving and gravel as it only collects rubbish

Below: cross-section of a 10cm (4 in) land drain installed on one side of the gravel area; graded porous fill allows seepage, making a new water-table

HOW TO LAY BRICK PATHS

Brick paving is like a good wine – it needs to be carefully laid down, is rich in flavour and improves with age.

As with all surfacing materials, brick has a character of its own, and because of its size, tends to be used where detail and intimacy are important. The incongruity of having vast areas of brick paving around some of the newer public buildings is immediately apparent because, besides being prohibitively expensive, it can be desperately monotonous.

It is, then, a surface to be used carefully, taking into consideration the immediate surroundings and any other relevant parts of the design.

Although bricks are available in a standard size of $225 \times 113 \times 75$mm ($9 \times 4\frac{1}{2} \times 3$ in), the range of textures and finishes is enormous. The density or hardness can also vary from a virtually indestructible 'engineering' brick to a much softer stock.

Taking these differences into account, it is quite obvious that while a perfectly uniform engineering brick could look superb in an austere modern composition, it would look out of place in a cottage garden.

The method of laying bricks also alters their character; open joints emphasize each module, while flush pointing provides a more uniform surface.

Remember, too, that bricks can be laid either flat or on edge and that this, as well as the type and direction of the bond, will affect the finished composition.

Assuming these factors have been taken into account during the design stage we can now start to look at the various methods of laying brick paving.

Laying a path

Ideally, the foundation for a path should consist of 8cm (3 in) of well-consolidated hardcore. If surface drainage is likely to

Above: Alchemilla mollis *spilling onto brick path laid in a stretcher bond*
Below: warm clay texture of this path leads eye and foot gently to conservatory

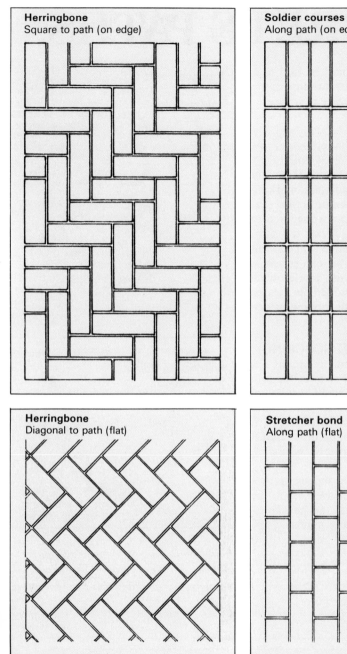

Herringbone
Square to path (on edge)

Herringbone
Diagonal to path (flat)

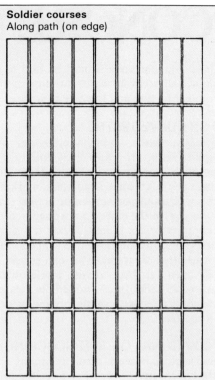

Soldier courses
Along path (on edge)

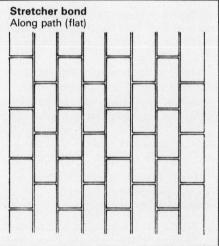

Stretcher bond
Along path (flat)

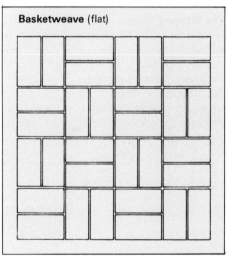

Basketweave (flat)

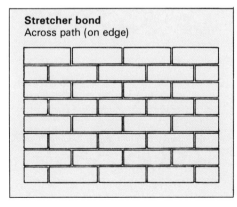

Stretcher bond
Across path (on edge)

weave – although there are modifications to these that will extend the range.

Stretcher bond This is exactly what it says, with the bricks laid end to end, as in a wall. The pattern can either be across or down the length of the path. This obviously has an effect on the overall design of the garden. If the line is down the path, the length and direction of the feature will be emphasized; bricks laid across a path give it a feeling of greater width. Stretcher bond also allows a camber to be easily incorporated and so will drain quickly after rain.

Herringbone You can see fine examples of this traditional paving pattern in its original form at many historic buildings. As with stretcher bond, the bricks can be laid flat or on edge, and either parallel or diagonally across the line of the path.

This is an intrinsically complicated design, and looks it. It is therefore better to use it in an intricate, detailed situation – too much of it could become fussy and oppressive to the eye. A camber is difficult to lay and the pattern should be worked to a straight cross fall.

be a problem, roughly shape the hardcore to a slight camber or cross fall.

The usual method of laying brick paving on the prepared hardcore foundation is as follows: bed the bricks on a 5cm (2 in) thick, dry layer of sand and cement (using – by volume – 1 part sand to 4 parts cement). When you have finished the path, or section of path, wet the surface with water from a can (keeping the rose on) and then brush the same mix into the open joints. When the joints have almost set you can rub them back to accentuate individual bricks and emphasize the pattern as a whole.

A choice of patterns
Bricks can be laid in three basic patterns – stretcher bond, herringbone and basket-

Above: illustrations of brick paving laid in three different patterns – herringbone, stretcher bond (soldier coursing is a variant of this, without the staggering) and basketweave

Basketweave Again, this pattern is a traditional one. Bricks can be laid flat in pairs, or on edge in threes. The effect is more static, as bolder squares give stability to the overall design.

If the path is on a slope and you don't need steps, it is possible to 'haunch', or lay the bricks at a slight angle, to obtain a better foothold. This is really only practical with a simple pattern, as in the stretcher bond, laid across the path.

Finally, it is essential to be neat in your work. Bricks are a small module and there are a lot of joints in relation to the total surface area. The beauty of a brick path lies in its precise pattern and texture; to spoil this with bad levelling or unsightly splashes of mortar is a sure sign of poor workmanship.

PRE-CAST CONCRETE PATHS

Paths are not only an essential part of any garden but also an important design element, leading the eye as well as the feet. Concrete slabs can be mixed with other materials for maximum effect.

Pre-cast concrete slabs are probably the most widely-used material for paving. They come in many different shapes, sizes and colours from a standard grey laid in conventional pattern to interesting hexagonal and interlocking designs. Their relatively low price makes them more competitive than natural stone. As well as being durable, various textures are available, the non-slip varieties being particularly useful in the garden.

For medium-to-heavy traffic Lay a base of rammed hardcore 15cm (6 in) thick. Bed slabs on a 5cm (2 in) layer of mortar, leaving 6mm ($\frac{1}{4}$ in) gaps for pointing.

For light traffic Lay each slab on five spots of mortar, in centre and at corners.

For stepping stones in a lawn Remove a section of turf and simply place slab in position, making sure that the hard surface is 13mm ($\frac{1}{2}$ in) below the lawn, to avoid damaging a mower.

For aggregate slabs With a surface of small stones or pebbles (exposed by brushing before concrete finally hardens)

these non-slip slabs should be laid to a slight 'fall' to avoid water standing in the rougher texture and freezing in winter.

FOR CURVED PATHS

Straight paths, using rectangular or square slabs, are relatively simple to lay but curves are more involved. Here you must peg out the line in advance, marking this with a sharpened stick or 'scribe' that is swung on the end of a cord secured to the appropriate radius. When the slabs are laid to this line a wedge-shaped joint ensues (see diagram). This can either be left open and planted with low-growing aromatic herbs or, if traffic is heavy, be carefully filled with small cobbles bedded in mortar.

HEXAGONAL OR INTERLOCKING

Six-sided slabs form attractive paths but the key to success here is to lay a random pattern that echoes the irregular shape of the module itself. This is particularly effective crossing a planted area, the hard and soft materials overlapping so that it is difficult to define a precise boundary between the two.

Interlocking concrete shapes, rather like pieces of jig-saw puzzle, should be treated in the same way as hexagonal paths, as a rigid edge looks clumsy.

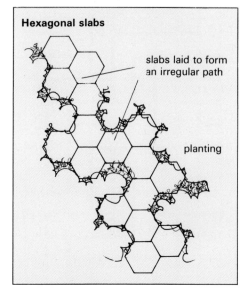

Hexagonal slabs

slabs laid to form an irregular path

planting

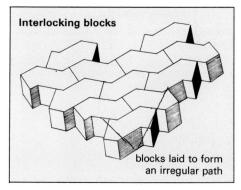

Interlocking blocks

blocks laid to form an irregular path

Hexagonal slabs or interlocking blocks both look better in irregular patterns, while with a curved path (left) you must work out your line in advance from radius points

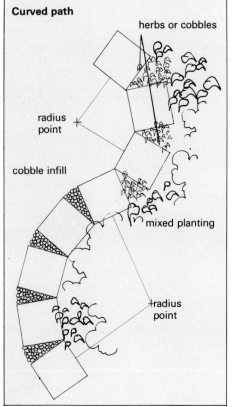

Curved path

herbs or cobbles

radius point

cobble infill

mixed planting

radius point

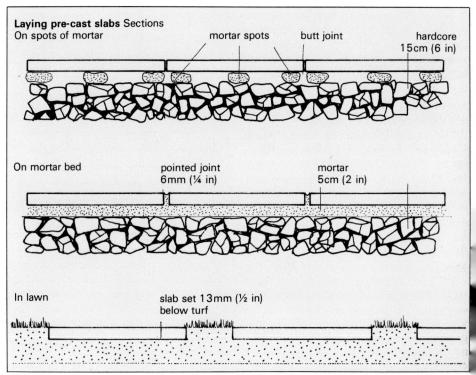

Laying pre-cast slabs Sections
On spots of mortar

mortar spots

butt joint

hardcore 15cm (6 in)

On mortar bed

pointed joint 6mm (¼ in)

mortar 5cm (2 in)

In lawn

slab set 13mm (½ in) below turf

COBBLES

Smooth surfaces, such as concrete, paving slabs and tarmac, invite pedestrian traffic. A surface area of small, uneven 'modules', such as a pebble path, has the opposite effect, while cobbles are a positive deterrent.

Cobbles are useful as they prevent people from cutting corners, protect beds by the front door from the delivery men, and generally direct the necessary tread of feet along the right paths.

They are round or oval stones, often flint, and similar to those found on the beach. Cobbles come in graded sizes up to 10cm (4 in) in diameter and can be laid in a variety of patterns, ranging from sophisticated formal designs, utilizing stones of different size, to loosely-arranged piles.

It is important to lay cobbles (or any small module) correctly, remembering that it's the material itself that counts, and not the background. The 'currant

*Cross section of cobbles **A**, laid on 5cm (2 in) layer of concrete **B**, and 5cm (2 in) layer of sand **C**, over a hardcore base **D***

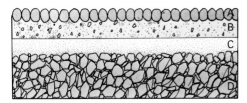

bun' effect, where a few cobbles are dotted at random in a sea of concrete, is to be avoided. The overall impression should be one of 'eggs in a crate', with little or no mortar showing between tightly-packed stones.

Where you intend cobbles to withstand cars (as an oil-drip), or pedestrians, a well-consolidated base of hardcore or crushed stone will be necessary. Put a layer of sand on top of this and roll it to a finished thickness of 5cm (2 in). Next, spread concrete (2 parts cement to 6 parts sand and gravel mixture) 5cm (2 in) thick and press the cobbles into this by hand. Use a straight-edge to ensure that the finished surface is flat and tamp any high stones down to the level of the rest.

An alternative, often used in Europe, is to lay the cobbles on a dry mortar or a concrete mix and then wet the mix from a watering can (with the rose on), thus preventing any of the cobbles becoming marked with cement which would be virtually impossible to remove.

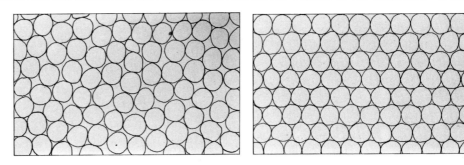

Above: plans of how to lay cobbles in a random pattern (left), and in courses (right)
Below: a more ambitious design, showing how to lay cobbles in a radius pattern

Below: cross-section showing combination of paving with informal planting, cobbles and larger boulders that will serve to deter people from cutting corners and so keep them on the path you would like them to use

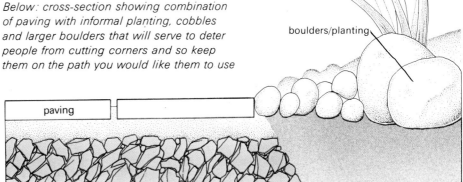

Below: use of paving, loose cobbles and brick edging as part of overall design scheme

CONCRETE BLOCK PAVING

If you use concrete blocks you will find laying an area of paving a fairly easy task. More traditional types of paving involve mixing a considerable amount of mortar and handling numerous paving slabs, some of which can be extremely heavy. Concrete blocks are comparatively easy to handle, both when stacking and using them, and do not require the use of a cement mix when you are bedding them into position.

Suitable for patios, paths and driveways, these blocks are strong enough to carry very weighty objects, such as a heavy fuel-delivery lorry, immediately after they have been put down. Area for area they are similar in price to any top quality coloured slab paving and are available in a variety of colours and shapes in sizes similar to house bricks – about 65mm (or 2½ in) thick. The range of colours and interlocking shapes means you can choose from a wide selection of patterns for use in contrasting areas for herringbone, zigzag and chequered effects, as well as for plain infills and borders.

Preparing the surface

The area to be paved must have a firm base, preferably consisting of well rammed hardcore. Make sure the overall surface of the base follows the required fall of the finished paving. It is important to remember the completed paving will be almost entirely impervious to water and you should consider this when setting out your levels. Puddles will form in any depressions remaining on the surface after laying has been completed.

Edge restraint You should provide an edge restraint around the outer perimeter of the area to be paved. Place 25mm (1 in) thick profile boards at the outer edges and fix them with 25mm (1 in) thick wood stakes driven well into the ground. Make sure the timber is well creosoted before fixing and set the top edge of the profile boards at the level the finished surface of the paving will reach. You do not need to place edge profiles against brick walls or the side of the house, but make sure the completed paving surface will be at a level at least one brick below the damp proof course and that there is a suitable fall-away from the house to carry off rain water.

Completing the base Spread a layer of washed, sharp sand over the entire area to be paved and level it by drawing a long timber straight-edge across the surface between the profile boards. The sand should be 65mm (or $2\frac{1}{2}$ in) thick and when the concrete blocks are placed on it their top surface should be about 13mm ($\frac{1}{2}$ in) above the edge of the profile board.

Laying the blocks

Once you have decided on the pattern you wish to follow, lay the concrete blocks as close to each other as possible across the width of the paving for about 1m (or 1yd). Cut to size any blocks which might be required at the ends to complete the section. To cut blocks you can use a sharp brick bolster with a club hammer; aim firm blows along a line marked on the top surface of the block with the block placed on a firm surface to make cutting as easy as possible. Alternatively, if you have a lot of cutting to carry out, hire a hydraulic guillotine.

Vibrate the first section down into the sand by passing a petrol-driven vibrating machine or plate vibrator over the surface. You can

Left: Concrete blocks laid to a pattern make an interesting driveway; they are available in a range of shapes and colours (inset)
1 *Levelling the sub-base with a timber straight-edge* **2** *Laying the blocks* **3** *Using a hydraulic guillotine to cut blocks to fit*

4

5

6

profile board

peg

blocks

sand

hardcore

earth

7

blocks

sand

hardcore

earth

concrete haunching

hire one of these from your supplier at not too much cost and, though it requires two people to lift it, it will fit easily into the boot of an average-sized family saloon car. The sand is compressed and forced up between the blocks so the paving level corresponds with the top edge of the profile boards.

When the first section is bedded into position, complete the second metre (or yard) using the same process of laying, cutting and vibrating and continue until the entire area is finished. Brush a thin layer of sand over the surface of the paving and follow up with the vibrating machine to drive fine grains of sand down between the blocks to complete the locking process.

Keep the profile boards around the outer edges of the paving in position after the job has been completed since the edge blocks will fall away if not supported. Alternatively, you can lift the boards and support the outer blocks with a concrete haunching, afterwards

putting turf down on top of the haunching to butt up close to the blocks.

Lifting blocks If it is necessary to lift blocks after they have been laid, you should start at a point on the outer edge. Break away the concrete haunching or lift the board. Once the outer blocks have been taken up, you will find it comparatively easy to lift others. You can then carry out any service repairs below paving level and, when these are completed, replace the blocks following the same procedure as for laying. If you are lifting areas of block for planting purposes, remember it will be necessary to use profile boards or concrete haunching on the internal faces of the finished area to prevent blocks falling into the flower bed.

Cleaning and drainage To keep the surface of the blocks in good order you simply have to sweep them lightly fairly regularly. If the falls have been set accurately, rain will run from the surface to suitable drainage points.

4 *Use a vibrator several times over the blocks to level the surface*
5 *Sweep fine sand over the surface and go over it with the vibrator to force the sand into the joints*
6 *Leave the supporting profile boards in place to prevent the edge blocks falling away*
7 *Alternatively remove the boards, laying in their place a concrete haunching covered with turf*

LAYING A CONCRETE PATH OR DRIVE

The method of laying a concrete path or drive is fairly straightforward and the surface will last indefinitely.

Laying concrete over a long narrow area, such as a drive or a path, involves the same basic techniques as laying a concrete slab, but there are certain extra things to be taken into account. The level along the length must be accurately plotted to avoid puddles collecting in the middle, a fall should be provided to allow for drainage and joints must be made along the length to prevent cracking.

Paths Use a mix of one part cement, two parts sand and three parts coarse aggregate; lay the concrete 75mm (3 in) thick and on a good base – firm soil is usually sufficient, but use fine, clean hardcore or hoggin where there is clay or the soil is poor.

Drives Use cement, sand and coarse aggregate in the proportions of 1:1½:3. For a drive to be used by cars and light vans, lay concrete 100mm (4 in) thick on firm subsoil, 125mm (5 in) thick on soft clay or poor subsoil. Increase the thickness by 50mm (2 in) if the drive is to be used for heavy vehicles.

Preparing the site

Establish the line the path or drive is to take and clear away topsoil, plants and roots from the site. Dig to the proposed level of the base of the concrete, allowing up to 75mm (3 in) extra depth for drives or where there is clay or poor subsoil. If the drive or path will be next to the house, the surface should be at least 150mm (6 in) below the damp proof course.

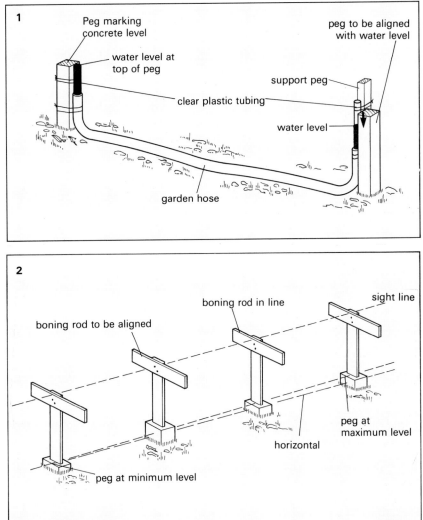

1
Peg marking concrete level
water level at top of peg
peg to be aligned with water level
support peg
clear plastic tubing
water level
garden hose

2
boning rod to be aligned
boning rod in line
sight line
peg at maximum level
horizontal
peg at minimum level

Obtaining a level

Use the water method to set levels at each end of the site. Drive a peg into the ground to the level of the finished concrete. Insert a short length of clear plastic tubing in each end of a hose and fill the hose with water until all air bubbles are forced out. Attach one end of the hose to the peg and the other end to a temporary support at the other side of the site; adjust the water level so it aligns with the top of the peg and hammer in a second peg to the level of the temporary support.

To establish a fall along the length of the site, lower the appropriate end peg to the required level and ensure a constant fall with boning rods. These consist of two pieces of timber fixed squarely together to form a right-angled 'T' piece at the top. You will need three or four boning rods of the same height to set the fall accurately.

Using boning rods Place pegs in the ground at equal distances along the site and place a boning rod on each. Look along the rods from one end and tap the intermediate pegs down until all the rods are in line.

Crossfall Allow for a fall of about 1 in 60 across the width of the site by lowering the pegs on one side. If the path or drive is next to the house, make sure the fall is away from it.

The formwork

Using the pegs as guides, stretch a string line on each side of the site along its length and fix it at both ends. Make the formwork to the dimensions of the site, using the string lines as guides, and check it is level with the pegs.

Curves You can produce curves in the formwork by making sawcuts part of the way through the timber, at about 250mm (or 10 in) intervals, to enable it to be bent.

Making joints

Depending on the width of the site, joints should be made at 2–2.5m (or 6–8 ft) intervals in paths and at 3m (10 ft) intervals in drives. For joint boards use softwood battens the full depth of the concrete and about 12mm ($\frac{1}{2}$ in) thick. Set the battens at the required intervals so they are at right-angles to the formwork and support them on one side with a strip of formwork timber pegged to the sub-base.

Lay the concrete right up to the exposed side of the batten and to within 50mm (2 in) of the back of the supporting board. Remove the support board, leaving the batten in place; fill the resulting gap and compact the concrete well on both sides of the joint with a tamping beam.

Alternate section method If the site is next to a wall, so you cannot use a tamping beam in the normal way to compact the concrete, use the alternate section method to lay the path or drive. Lay a thicker batten at right-angles to the formwork where each joint is to be made and concrete every other section. Use

the tamping beam across the battens over the section to compact the concrete.

When each section has set (after one or two days), remove the battens and concrete the remaining sections, making butt joints between each.

Curing the concrete

Cover the concrete with polythene sheeting and leave it to cure for about seven days (ten in cold weather). Keep the formwork in place during this time to protect the edges of the concrete against damage. Once the curing period is over you can use the path or drive, but don't allow heavy vehicles onto it for at least two weeks after laying.

1 *Establish the level at each end of the site by the water method*
2 *Set the fall by lining up boning rods along the length of the site*
3 *To make a curved path, cut the formwork at intervals so it can be bent as needed*
4 *Form joints using battens and support boards: lay the concrete, remove the support boards and fill in the gaps*
5 *Where a path is right next to a wall, lay it in alternate sections*

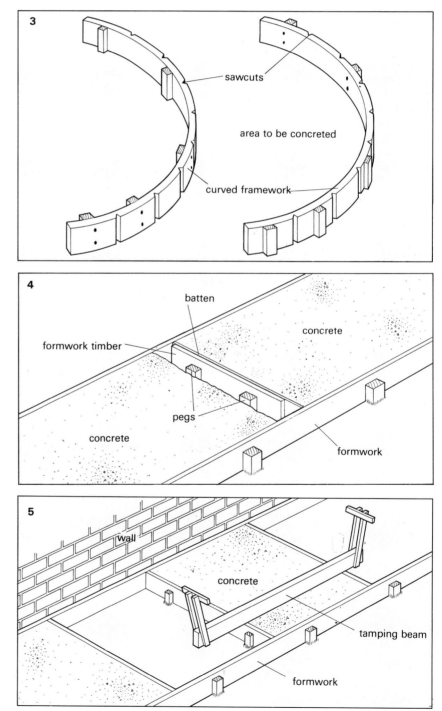

REPAIRING CONCRETE

When concrete deteriorates, the cause can nearly always be traced to an error when it was laid. You can repair concrete but, if you do not want the result to look patchy, make sure you use the same finishing technique and colour as for the original work.

PATHS AND DRIVES

Garden paths and drives are the most likely concrete areas to deteriorate, with faults ranging from minor cracking to subsidence.

Repairing dusty concrete

A common problem – and the simplest to correct – is a surface which is constantly dusty. Various proprietary sealing liquids are available which can be applied to the surface after you have brushed away the dirt.

Repairing cracks

If a concrete path was laid correctly, it will have been completed in sections, with contraction joints between. Hairline cracks following the run of the joints can be ignored, but cracks elsewhere forming random patterns need attention. They can be the result of omitting contraction joints or subsidence due to inadequate foundations. Usually it is best

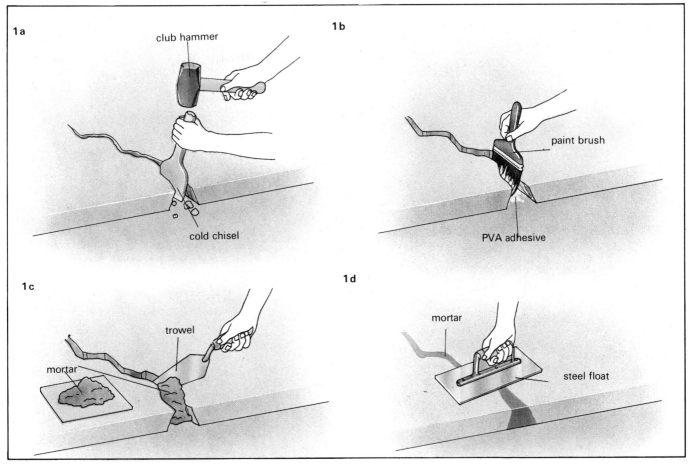

to live with such cracks for a year or so until you can see they have stopped growing. If you fill them before, the filling will crack.

Use a cold chisel and club hammer to undercut the edges of the crack. This is important if the filling is to be properly anchored. Clean out all dust and thoroughly brush on a PVA adhesive as a bonding agent to ensure a firm grip between the old and new concrete. PVA adhesive should be used whenever concrete repairs are made – but always dilute it in accordance with the manufacturer's instructions.

Filler Mix one part cement to three parts soft sand:add PVA adhesive and keep the mix on the dry side, adding water sparingly. Pack it well down into the edges of the crack and smooth off the surface with a steel float.

For small repairs it is often more convenient to use a bag of dry ready-mixed mortar than to buy separate ingredients.

Holes You will often find holes in the vicinity of cracks; these holes are probably attributable to poor foundations or a weak concrete and should be filled as for cracks.

Repairing crumbling edges

There are a number of reasons why the edges of paths or drives start to crumble. Poor foundation work could be one explanation; or it may be that the timber edge supports (positioned along the path to retain the concrete when it was laid) were removed

before the concrete was fully cured.

Another cause is failure to pack the concrete down into the sides of the timber framework. This leaves air pockets below what appears to be a solid surface: when weight is placed on the concrete the surface material is forced down to fill the cavities.

Use a cold chisel and a club hammer to break up the crumbling edge, remove all loose material and tamp the exposed foundations – using extra hardcore if necessary.

Place a length of timber alongside the edge and support it with pegs driven into the ground. Brush PVA adhesive onto the exposed edges. Mix a batch of one part cement to five parts sharp, washed sand and add PVA adhesive to the mix. Press the concrete well down into the edges of the timber, gradually building up to a level surface. Remove the timber after about four weeks.

Repairing depressions

Depressions, which allow puddles to form, are caused by subsidence, poor levelling off at the laying stage or failure to allow for a crossfall. They can be filled provided the new layer of concrete is more than 13mm ($\frac{1}{2}$ in) thick. Otherwise the area will have to be broken up to deepen the cavity.

Fill with a mix of one part cement and three parts sand, with added PVA adhesive, and fill as described earlier when repairing cracks.

1a *To repair a crack, undercut the edges with a club hammer and cold chisel*
1b *Brush on a PVA adhesive to ensure a firm bond*
1c *Trowel a fairly dry concrete mix into the crack and pack it down well*
1d *Smooth over the edges of the crack with a steel float*
2a *To repair crumbling edges, chip back the concrete with a club hammer and cold chisel*
2b *Lay a piece of timber, supported with pegs, along the edge to give you a guide for laying the new concrete*
2c *Fill in the gap with concrete, pressing hard into the side of the timber*
2d *Smooth the surface with a steel float*

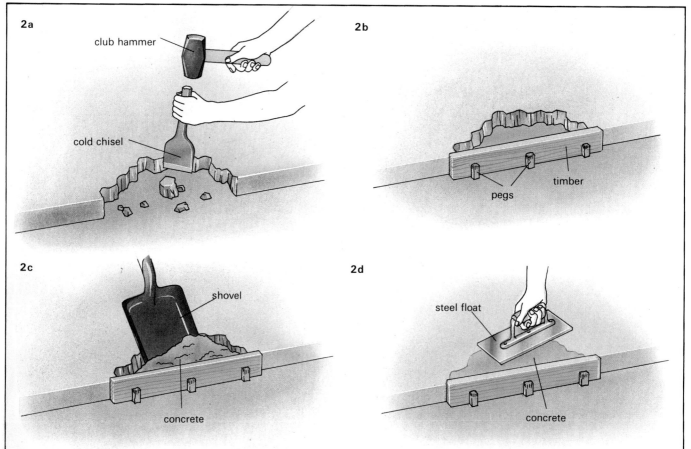

2a club hammer cold chisel
2b pegs timber
2c shovel concrete
2d steel float concrete

Extensive cracking, steps created when a path breaks or serious subsidence can only be remedied by breaking up the affected area and using hardcore to form new foundations.

STEPS, SILLS AND SLABS

Cracked and chipped concrete is not only unsightly but it can also be dangerous in the case of steps and paving stones. If repairs are done promptly you can prevent accidents and avoid more extensive repairs later.

Concrete steps

Damage and wear to steps may show as a generally poor, undulating surface or cracks and chips to the front and side edges.

Uneven surface To form a key for a new layer of concrete, score the surface with a cold chisel and club hammer and brush all debris from the step. Fit a timber framework round the step so it projects above the existing surface by at least 13mm ($\frac{1}{2}$ in), the minimum depth of the new mortar. Fix the timbers to a slight fall to allow for drainage. If possible, secure the timbers with stakes driven well into the ground. If the step is surrounded by concrete, use heavy weights to hold the framework.

Brush the step with a priming coat of PVA adhesive, following the manufacturer's instructions, and allow it to dry. Add a little adhesive to a mix of one part cement to three parts sharp, washed sand. Just before laying the mortar, apply another coat of adhesive to the step. Trowel on the mortar mix to a depth of at least 13mm ($\frac{1}{2}$ in) and level off the surface with a straight-edge.

Allow the mortar to set partially, then brush it crosswise with a stiff brush or broom to give a rippled surface; this will provide a firmer foothold than a smooth surface. When the mortar has hardened, cover with polythene or dampened hessian and leave it to cure for about ten days. If possible, leave for about one month before removing the timbers and using the step. If you must use the step, avoid treading on the edges.

Cracked front edge Chips and cracks can be quickly and economically filled with a hard-setting exterior-grade filler.

If the edge has completely broken away, cut it back with a chisel and club hammer and undercut the surface of the step to support the filling. Clean away all debris from the edge and fit supporting timbers round the step. Secure the timbers with stakes or heavy weights. If the step is high off the ground, secure the side pieces of the framework with masonry nails or plugs and screws and nail or screw the front piece to these. Apply PVA adhesive as described above, then fill with a mortar mix of one part cement to three parts sand plus a little PVA adhesive. Finish off as previously described.

3a *To level the surface of a step, first score with a club hammer and cold chisel*
3b *Fix a supporting framework round the step*
3c *Trowel on the mortar and smooth it level with the top of the framework*
3d *When partially dry, go over the surface with a brush*
4 *Repair the front edge of a step by undercutting the surface and fixing support battens round the step. Fill with mortar and smooth off*
5a *To resurface a sill, score the top with a club hammer and cold chisel*
5b *Fix a timber framework with a fall towards the front, fill with mortar mix and smooth level with the top of the timbers*
6a *Remove a concrete slab by inserting iron rods under it and using these to roll the slab to one side*
6b *To replace a slab, put mortar at the corners and in the centre of the bedding area and position the slab*
6c *Use a straight-edge to check the slab lies flush*

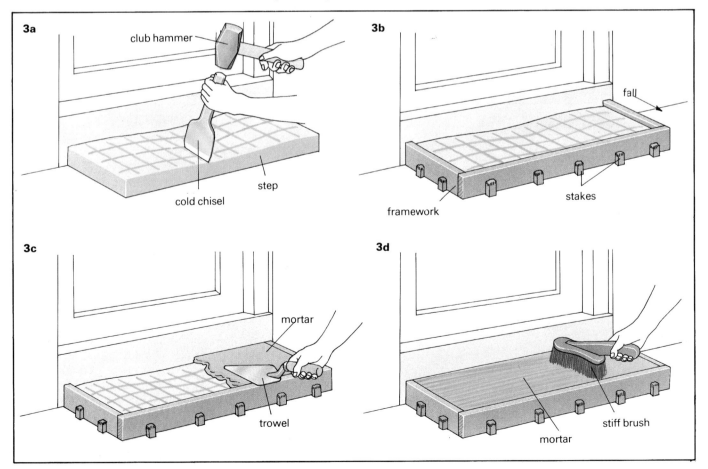

3a club hammer step cold chisel

3b fall framework stakes

3c mortar trowel

3d stiff brush mortar

Concrete window sill

An old, unpainted concrete window sill may weather badly and need to be resurfaced. To provide a key for the new material, score the surface with a cold chisel and club hammer. Clean away all debris, apply PVA adhesive and allow it to dry.

Fix a timber framework round the sill so it projects at least 13mm ($\frac{1}{2}$ in) above the sill level. Angle the top of each side frame to make a fall towards the front to allow water to drain off. Suspend the framework on a timber batten fixed to the wall immediately below the sill; screw the side pieces into the batten and the front into the sides. Make up a mortar mix of one part cement to three parts sand, including a little PVA adhesive and a waterproofing agent.

Before spreading the mix, add a second layer of PVA adhesive to the sill. Fill the supporting timbers with the mix making sure it is well packed into the edges. Level off against the top edges of the timbers. Use a wood float to flatten the mix, then polish with a steel float.

Concrete paving slabs

Concrete slabs are bedded down on either sand or blobs of mortar and should be relaid on the type of base originally used.

Removing slab Lever up the side of an

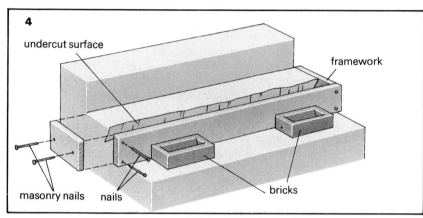

4

undercut surface

framework

masonry nails   nails

bricks

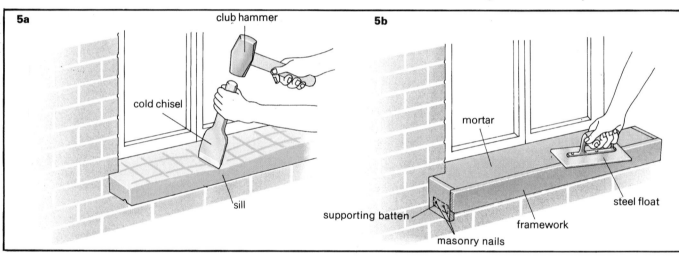

5a   club hammer

cold chisel

sill

5b

mortar

steel float

supporting batten

framework

masonry nails

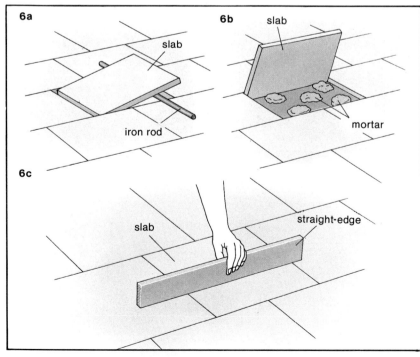

6a

slab

iron rod

6c

slab

6b   slab

mortar

straight-edge

slab

undamaged slab with a strong spade or other suitable tool and remove it intact. Alternatively insert a couple of iron rods or broom handles under the slab to act as rollers and push the slab to one side.

Break up a cracked slab with a club hammer and cold chisel and remove it in small, manageable pieces.

Relaying slab If the slab was laid on sand, add more sand, level out the base and replace the slab. Where mortar was used, mix up a small amount of new mortar, using one part cement to five parts sand; keep it on the dry side.

Lay a pat of mortar at each corner of the bedding area and one in the middle. Place the slab in position and tap it down gently with a club hammer and a block of wood, checking with a straight-edge until the replaced slab lies flush with those surrounding it.

Allow two days for the mortar to set before filling in the joints by sweeping a dry mix of sand and cement into the cavities surrounding the slab.

STEPS FOR SLOPES

Most people think of steps situated in the garden as being regularly spaced, rectangular and straight. As a result, the majority of flights are built to a standard pattern, when often a different approach could provide interest and create an attractive feature.

You can construct steps from a wide variety of materials. Cobbles and stone, timber and gravel, concrete and brick are all available to form numerous permutations. The shape of the individual steps can be round or hexagonal and the flights can be staggered or straight. Whatever the composition, it can be softened by planting.

Steps for steep slopes

A steep slope normally requires a sensible, neat flight with a number of closely-spaced treads. You should vary your material to suit the situation: timber is less formal than brick which is not as formal as stone, pre-cast slabs and concrete. With stone or pre-cast slabs, make the tread overhang the riser by about 5cm (2 in). This will then cast an aesthetically pleasing shadow on the tread below.

Steps for gentle slopes

Gentle slopes give a wider range of choice, but remember that simplicity is the key to all design and in building steps, you are forming a pattern that should not become 'fussy'. If, for example, you are using a combination of brick and pre-cast slabs, be sure to arrange them in sensible proportions. Brick is dominant visually and is therefore particularly suitable at the top and bottom of the flight. Use a well-fired variety, and avoid soft bricks that may shatter in frosty weather. 'Bull-nosed' bricks, with a specially-rounded leading edge, are available for the front of the step.

Irregular steps

Steps that have free or irregular outlines present problems of their own. Slabs, stone and even brick are unsuitable as they have to be cut at the edges. This is a lengthy, laborious and expensive proposition, especially if you have to hire a contractor to carry it out. In this instance, materials such as concrete, tarmac and very small paving modules like cobbles, come into their own as they can all be adapted to a specific shape.

Big steps

Do not be put off by the idea of big steps; they give an impression of space and tranquillity. The infill is of brushed concrete and takes advantage of a technique used all too little in this country. It simply involves laying a normal concrete mix of 1:2:3 – one part cement, two parts sand, three parts aggregate – ensuring that the aggregate is made up from an attractive selection of small rounded pebbles. Once the job starts to harden, or 'go off', brush the surface carefully with a stiff broom. This will expose the aggregate and produce a striking marbled effect when dry. In very hot weather cover the surface with damp sacking to prevent damage. In frosty weather dry sacking will suffice.

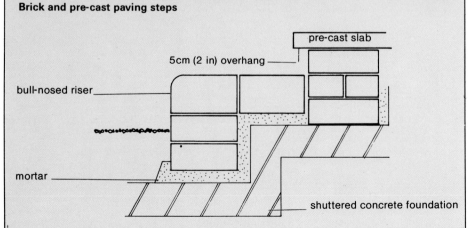

Above left: the charm of irregular steps of natural stone, seen at Wisley
Left: construction of overhanging treads, and bull-nosed riser for a bottom step

Brick and pre-cast paving steps

pre-cast slab

5cm (2 in) overhang

bull-nosed riser

mortar

shuttered concrete foundation

STEPS FOR SLOPES
Cantilever and hexagonal

A change of level in your garden gives you an excuse to build an imaginative flight of steps. Opposite we give ideas for steep and gentle slopes, and tell you how to make steps from brick and pre-cast paving. Here we suggest more ambitious designs to form focal points in your garden.

Cantilever steps

These are unusual steps and can be built to negotiate the face of a retaining wall. Concrete is best for this operation as you can bed reinforcing rods into the basic structure. You can easily adapt some types of lintel and these can be bought ready-made from a builder's merchant. Natural stone can be used in a similar way. Be sure that at least half the step is bedded into the wall and, as a general rule, try to match the materials so that the flight is compatible with its background.

Above right: set a graceful flight of cantilevered steps into a retaining wall Below: ground plan, showing how steps are set 50 per cent into the wall. Allow 5 cm (2 in) overlap between each step

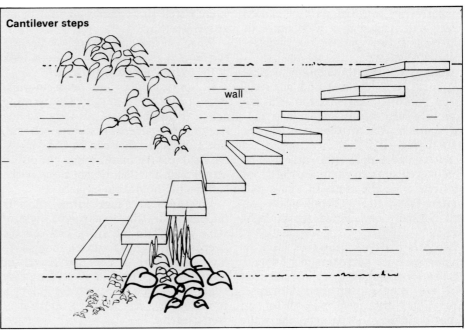

Cantilever steps

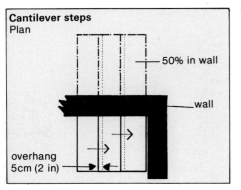

Cantilever steps
Plan
— 50% in wall
— wall
overhang 5cm (2 in)

Hexagonal steps

In the ground plan drawing we show a series of interlocking hexagonal steps that would be ideal for linking two levels close to a building; the obvious geometry provides a strong visual link with the house. Each hexagon could be anything from up to 3m (10 ft) across with one step overlapping another to give a feeling of gentle progression. The low retaining walls forming the risers are approximately 15cm (6 in) high and built of brick. With big steps, 23cm (9 in) brickwork looks far better than 11cm (4½ in) and the extra effort is amply repaid by the end result.

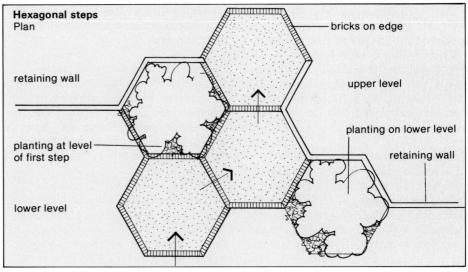

Hexagonal steps
Plan
— bricks on edge
retaining wall
upper level
planting at level of first step
planting on lower level
retaining wall
lower level

Above: ground plan showing successful use of hexagonal steps to link a relatively large area. Below: section showing foundation details of hexagonal steps

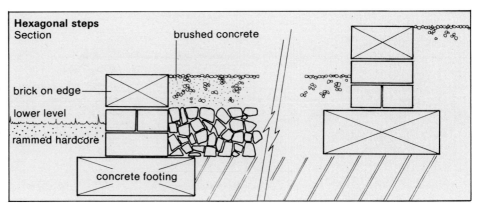

Hexagonal steps
Section
brushed concrete
brick on edge
lower level
rammed hardcore
concrete footing

Railway sleepers constitute a versatile material that will blend well into a natural setting. You can give a new lease of life to these solid timbers by using them as steps, paving or a retaining wall.

RAILWAY SLEEPERS for steps and slopes

Timber is an essential part of garden design and is used in a wide range of applications from fencing to summer-houses and steps.

Railway sleepers, though often neglected, form an interesting and relatively cheap constructional material and are now becoming readily available as railways switch over to using concrete for track-laying.

Sources of supply vary; they can be obtained either from your local rail depot or from a middle man. In any event, enquire first at the rail depot, where you will normally be referred to the right person.

Sleepers are dark brown or black in colour, measure approximately 2·45m × 20cm × 13cm (8 ft × 8 in × 5 in), and need only two people to lift them with ease. This makes them ideal material for the rapid building of steps, retaining walls and raised beds.

As they have been weather-proofed with tar, you can expect sleepers to last indefinitely, and they can be maintained by a biennial treatment with a non-toxic wood preservative. Although creosote is in common use, remember that it is toxic and needs at least twelve months to become neutral and safe for any plants you want to put in.

Preparation and laying
In aesthetic terms, sleepers blend equally well with an architectural feature or a softly-planted bank, as their long, solid outline provides a feeling of stability and sympathy with the immediate surroundings. This is due largely to the fact that they are man-made from a natural material and so can adapt themselves

equally well to fit into a natural or an artificial setting.

When you are considering how sleepers can be used in a particular situation, look at the overall design of the area.

If, for example, you need informal steps, use them in a staggered pattern and soften the outline with planting, adding one or two boulders for sculptural detail. In this instance, they can be laid 'dry' as the bank can be quite simply cut out to accept them and their weight alone will be sufficient to hold them in place.

You can create a more formal effect by building a straight or staggered flight of steps and filling the space between the sleepers with rolled gravel, hoggin (a binding mixture of clay and gravel) or crushed stone. This will give a long easy climb that would be perfect for linking a terrace with a less formal woodland or wild garden.

If the tops of sleepers are going to be exposed, as in the case of steps or paving, they should be laid upside down, to hide the bolt holes.

Paving slabs and retaining walls
You can achieve a really crisp architectural design by using sleepers in conjunction with pre-cast paving. The slab can either overhang the sleeper, possibly bedded in concrete, or sit flush behind it; the latter method allows the edge of the

Below: a natural effect; front view of railway sleepers for steps and slopes, using a staggered pattern and softening the outline with plants and boulders
Below right: a side section of the same
Right: a formal effect; retaining wall, with sleepers and paving slabs in mortar

step to be clearly seen.

When you are building retaining walls and raised beds, work out the design in advance. Cutting sleepers can be hard work with a manual bow saw so try to borrow or hire a chain saw. The sleepers are stretcher-bonded in the same way as brickwork and either laid dry, or bedded on the soil, allowing plants to grow in between the joints.

You do not need complicated foundations for simple structures. Merely sink the first course into the ground so that the tops are flush with the surface. If the ground is heavy or unstable and high retaining walls of over a metre (or yard) are necessary, it may be advisable to bolt the sleepers onto steel angles in the ground before work starts. The wall can also be built to a slight angle, with several joints left open along its length to provide drainage.

A light or open-textured fill behind the wall will help drainage and lengthen the life of the timber.

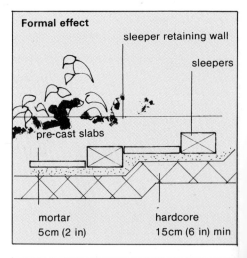

Formal effect

sleeper retaining wall

sleepers

pre-cast slabs

mortar 5cm (2 in)

hardcore 15cm (6 in) min

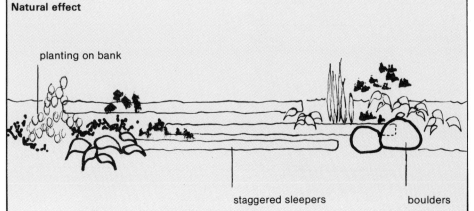

Natural effect

planting on bank

staggered sleepers

boulders

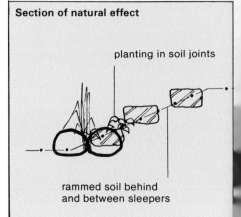

Section of natural effect

planting in soil joints

rammed soil behind and between sleepers

LOGS FOR STEPS

If you are lucky enough to live in an area where timber is readily available in the form of logs, you will find that you have the basic material for a number of interesting garden projects.

Logs have an informal character and are ideal in a softly-planted woodland or in the farthest reaches of a garden where different features need to blend with one another. They can also be used in more architectural patterns as a link between the obvious, regular geometry around a building and the natural setting of the open areas beyond.

You can use virtually any type of timber; the hardwoods include beech, oak and elm, and last the longest. If you are thinking of using elm, remember that it may have been affected by Dutch Elm disease and still be capable of harbouring infection. It is wise to strip the bark off any elm logs and burn it immediately.

Making steps

Steps can be formed in a number of ways, using long or short lengths. Don't worry if the longer logs are slightly bent or twisted, as this will add to the character of the flight of steps.

You can make wide steps using single tree trunks quite simply by bedding them into the slope and driving wedges into the ground in front of each log to prevent movement. The treads can then be filled with crushed stone, hoggin or rammed soil. The length between each step need not be constant as some variety adds interest to the flight. It's also a good idea to 'stagger' the logs and encourage plant growth at the sides to soften and hide the ends of the timber.

If you can only obtain short logs, say 50cm (20 in) long, you can still make steps out of them. In this instance, drive them vertically into the ground, close together, so that the complete row forms a riser of the desired length.

Retaining walls

You can extend this technique by using longer logs to hold back sections of a slope and create retaining walls. Once again, the pattern can be varied, allowing the height of each platform to be slightly different. If the bank is in an informal part of the garden, the spaces between the log walls can be filled with softly-spreading foliage. If, on the other hand, the area is more formal, it might be better to use loose cobbles in conjunction with boulders and architectural planting.

Paving and stepping stones

Offcuts can be particularly useful in a number of ways, either as paving or as stepping stones. As paving, sections can be bedded into mortar in the usual way, or laid dry, allowing the occasional low plant to grow in soil that has been brushed into the joints.

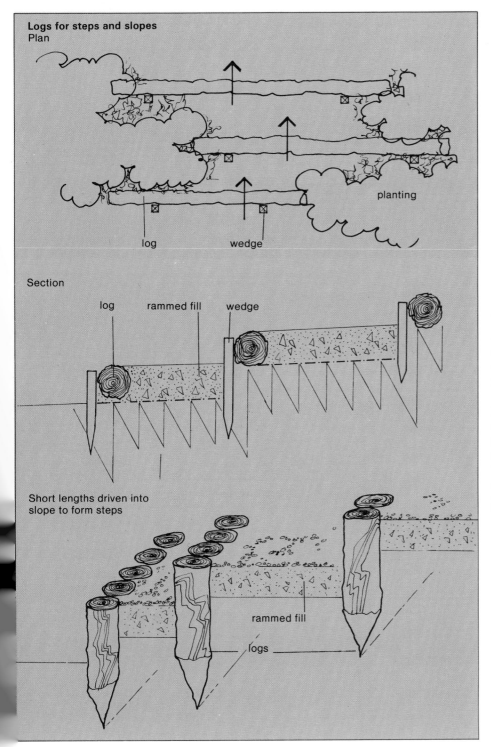

Logs for steps and slopes
Plan

planting

log   wedge

Section

log   rammed fill   wedge

Short lengths driven into slope to form steps

rammed fill

logs

Above left: ground plan (top) and section of single logs laid lengthwise to form shallow steps. The filling can be dispensed with if the ground is firm and the traffic light
Left: short logs, sharpened at one end and driven into the ground, also blend well into a country setting

Stepping stones can be laid dry, but if they are to cross a lawn, make sure that the logs are set just below the surface of the turf so that a mower can run smoothly over the top.

The 'stones' made of wood achieve just the right visual balance through planting and woodland, where real stone or precast slabs might seem out of place.

Right: offcuts used as stepping stones make an effective pathway
Below: plan (top) and sections showing how to arrange logs as a retaining wall

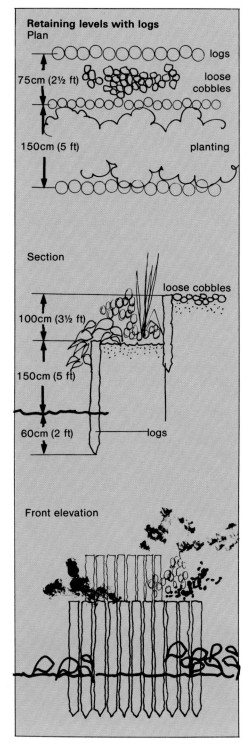

Retaining levels with logs
Plan

logs

75cm (2½ ft)

loose cobbles

150cm (5 ft)

planting

Section

loose cobbles

100cm (3½ ft)

150cm (5 ft)

60cm (2 ft)

logs

Front elevation

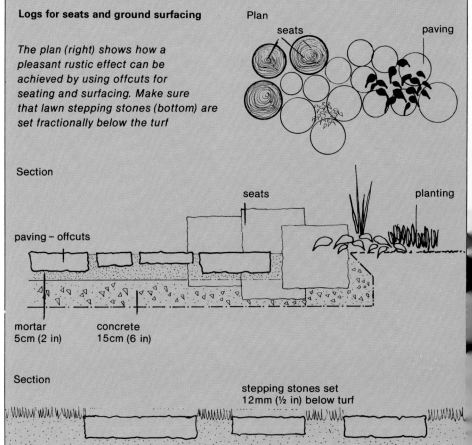

Logs for seats and ground surfacing

Plan

seats

paving

The plan (right) shows how a pleasant rustic effect can be achieved by using offcuts for seating and surfacing. Make sure that lawn stepping stones (bottom) are set fractionally below the turf

Section

seats

planting

paving – offcuts

mortar
5cm (2 in)

concrete
15cm (6 in)

Section

stepping stones set
12mm (½ in) below turf

RAMPS FOR SLOPES

In previous pages we have described the many uses of steps in a garden. Here we look at an alternative – ramps – and give practical advice on how to build them

Steps, circular or otherwise, are not always practical on a slope requiring wheeled access. Here a different solution is needed to cater for bicycles, wheelbarrows, prams or wheelchairs. A ramp is the obvious answer and the ways in which this can be constructed are as numerous as steps.

As a general rule the gradient should remain constant, both from a visual and a practical point of view. Steep ramps are tiring and if the slope is too great to tackle in one run, you should incorporate a 'hairpin' so that you go up in two evenly-graded sections.

Concrete for ramps

Concrete is the obvious material for this purpose. Laid on a suitably-compacted layer of hardcore, a final level is achieved by using wooden shutters, held in place by pegs. The finish with concrete can be varied, the easiest way being simply to tamp the top, between the shutters, with a long straight-edge. This will produce a ribbed effect, giving better traction for wheels and feet alike.

Brushed concrete (see page 18) can look effective and there is a wheeled tool available with an embossed face that you run over the concrete when partially dry to achieve the dimpled effect often seen in driveways and pavement edges laid by the local authorities. An important point to remember is to keep the concrete mix fairly 'dry'. As work progresses you will find that the tamping and trowelling will bring ample moisture to the surface. Too much moisture weakens the mix.

Brick, stone, cobbles or setts

Ramps can be made from brick, stone, or cobbles. Granite setts are also suitable and you can sometimes obtain old ones from city streets being demolished.

Setts are either full-sized (about the size of a thick brick), or half-sized (virtually square). The advantage this type of module has over concrete or tarmac is that it can be 'haunched' up at an angle,

each course being tilted to obtain a better foothold on the slope.

When laying any small-scale material make sure you keep the surface clear from mortar; there is nothing worse than seeing the finished job spoilt in this way – it is also the trademark of a poor workman.

A ramp, with steps alongside to provide extra safety for pedestrians

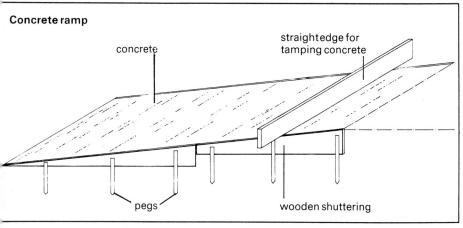

Concrete ramp

concrete

straight edge for
tamping concrete

pegs

wooden shuttering

*Left: tamp concrete for a non-slip surface
Below: angled granite setts make a good alternative to a ramp-type driveway*

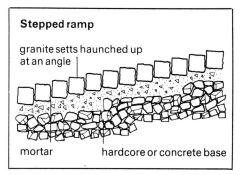

Stepped ramp

granite setts haunched up
at an angle

mortar

hardcore or concrete base

MAKING CIRCULAR STEPS

As a general rule rectangular shapes link naturally with the house while circular patterns are more suitable for informal situations, woodland and the further reaches of the garden. Such basic rules also apply to individual features and circular steps can be particularly interesting in this context.

Circular steps

These may be of any size and can be built in a number of attractive ways. Where space is unlimited large circular brick retaining walls, up to 3m (10 ft) in diameter can overlap one another to form the risers of a slow, lazy flight. You can vary the sizes of the circle and fill them with a wide range of materials, including grass, concrete, cobbles and even tarmac, the choice depending on the underlying design of the area. The point to remember when dealing with 'free' shapes is that the infill material must be flexible, thus cobbles are fine, while pre-cast concrete slabs or stone would involve a great deal of cutting to conform to the pattern.

A 23cm (9 in) wall is structurally correct for the surround and this will need to stand on a concrete footing 45cm (18 in) wide, the depth being dependent on the conditions of the ground.

Concrete pipes for steps

Another simple and relatively cheap step is formed by using large-diameter concrete pipes. Sewer pipes are ideal, as they are available in a wide range of sizes from 1–3m (3–10 ft). Here you sink most of the pipe in the ground, leaving just enough of one end above the surface to form the riser of the step. Again you can vary sizes within the flight and a staggered pattern looks most attractive, with planting to soften the outline.

This technique need not be confined to dry land, stepping stones across a large pool being made in a similar way. In this case paint the outside of the pipe with a bituminous sealer (such as Synthaprufe) thus effectively disguising the depth of concrete below the surface. Fill the pipes with any of the materials already mentioned. It is, of course, essential to drain the pool while work is in progress.

Above: a dramatic effect achieved with the use of granite setts for risers, with half-setts for treads and cobbles as a top surface
Below: plan of another set of steps shows how circle sizes and surface materials can vary
Right: cross-section, with brick surround set below lawn level to facilitate mowing

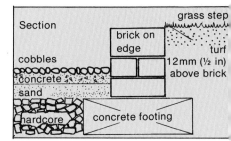

Section
cobbles
concrete
sand
hardcore
brick on edge
concrete footing
grass step
turf
12mm (½ in) above brick

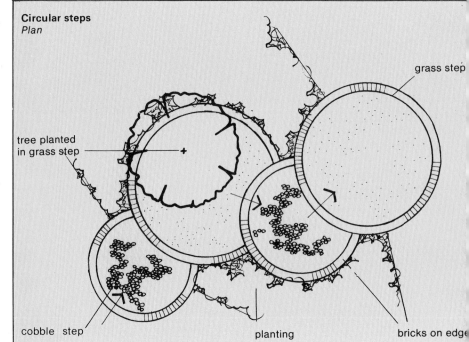

Circular steps
Plan

tree planted in grass step

grass step

cobble step

planting

bricks on edge

LAYING A PATIO FOUNDATION

A patio is an exciting feature in any garden, providing a semi-formal area for eating or sunbathing. The patio design suggested here may not suit your purposes entirely, but it may give you some ideas. It forms an enclosed garden area 7 metres (23 feet) square. We start with laying the foundation and continue right through to erecting a trellis and other features.

When carrying out work of this type it is essential to undertake the various jobs involved in an organized way so as to avoid unnecessary shifting of materials and to allow the work to proceed smoothly.

SCHEDULE OF WORK Stage 1

After you have completed any necessary repointing of the brickwork and painting of the exterior walls, you must clear the site of all unwanted vegetation and roughly level it. Remove the topsoil from the areas to be excavated and deposit it in the pergola area, for re-use in the plantings there. This not only saves having to import topsoil at a later date and carry it through the house, but also uses up the unwanted soil from the other areas.

Before any excavation work is started you must establish a 'datum' to which all other levels can be quickly related. Normally for this type of work the datum should be located at the highest level and in the case of our Patio Garden this would be at the finished level of the paved area adjacent to the house. Any paved or planted areas must be kept at least 15cm (6 in) below the house damp proof course (DPC) level.

To establish the datum, first excavate a small area adjacent to the house wall and with a base about 40cm (15 in) below the house DPC level. Now hammer a wooden peg into the ground so that the top is 15cm (6 in) lower than the DPC (see raised area diagram, page 80).

Main retaining wall

Using timber pegs and the brick line of the house wall, mark the boundary of the raised, paved area. A brick retaining wall must be built at this line in order

to support the paving slabs and to retain safely the trapped earth (see the section plan diagram, page 80). A wall of this type is normally reckoned to retain a height of three times its thickness. So for the wall specified, a 22·5cm (9 in) thickness, i.e. two bricks, is necessary. To be stable the wall must sit on a firm concrete foundation as illustrated in the section plan and raised area diagrams.

Retaining wall foundation

To establish the depth of the foundation trench, dig away some earth immediately below the marked border line. Using the original datum peg as a reference for the level, hammer a second peg about 60cm

Ground plan, drawn to scale, is an essential reference while you work on the patio site

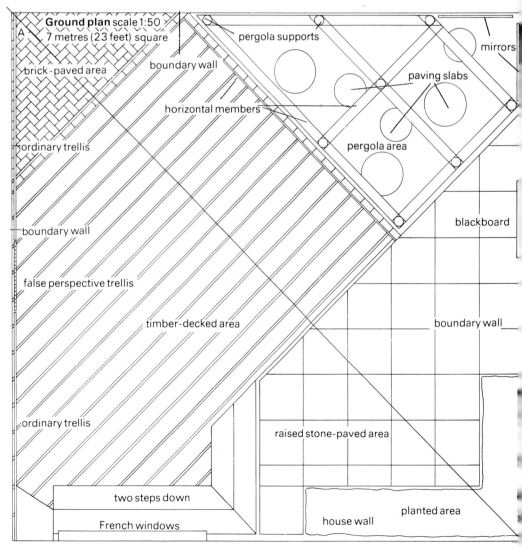

Ground plan scale 1:50
7 metres (23 feet) square

brick-paved area

ordinary trellis

boundary wall

false perspective trellis

ordinary trellis

boundary wall

horizontal members

pergola supports

mirrors

paving slabs

pergola area

blackboard

timber-decked area

boundary wall

raised stone-paved area

two steps down

French windows

house wall

planted area

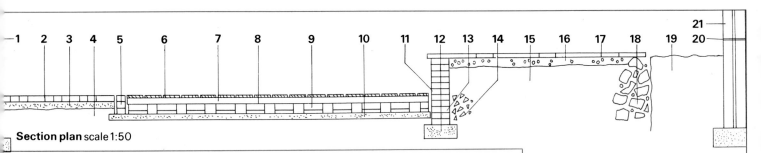

Section plan scale 1:50

(24 in) inside the paved area confine and level off, using the timber straight-edge and spirit level (as shown in the raised area diagram).

With the straight-edge laid on top of the two pegs, some measure can be gained of the excavation necessary to complete the wall foundation trench.

Next dig the trench and hammer in pegs to the finished concrete level (raised area diagram). Pile up the subsoil as you remove it ready for back-filling after the wall has been completed. With the trench neatly finished pour in concrete and level it to the tops of the wooden pegs.

Concrete mix

A suitable mix for this purpose is 1 part cement to 4·5 parts 20mm ($\frac{3}{4}$ in) all-in ballast. Mix dry ingredients first on a clean surface and then add sufficient water to produce a stiff mix. This must be poured into the foundation trench and carefully tamped level with the peg tops. Take care at this stage to produce a neat, flat surface as this will do much to simplify subsequent bricklaying.

SCHEDULE OF WORK Stage 2

For a wall that is subject to virtually constant dampness from the retained earth, a hard type of brick will prove more durable than a soft or 'common' type. Similarly, hard bricks will also be required for the brick-paved corner in the patio. It is worth spending some time finding the best type of brick available.

Mortar for bricklaying

Bricks are laid using a mortar mix of 3 parts soft sand to 1 part cement. Adding a plasticizer will make the mix more workable as well as minimizing subsequent shrinkage or cracking.

Mix the dry ingredients first on a clean surface and then add the water and plasticizer to produce a fairly stiff, but workable, mix. Transfer 2–3 shovels of mortar to your spot board which should be positioned near the work.

Building the main retaining wall

The art of bricklaying is something that can only be acquired with practice, but a relatively low wall of this type should be within the scope of most people provided the work is tackled in the order shown. Be sure to use the spirit level constantly to check that you are building the wall absolutely vertical.

Using the timber straight-edge as a guide, lay a line of bricks along the complete length of the wall. Next build up the ends and then the angled corner. Use a length of timber, marked with the brick courses and mortar joints, as a gauge to ensure that the building of the three columns proceeds accurately.

Key
1 boundary wall **2** brick paving
3 sand/cement base **4** subsoil/hardcore
5 retaining wall **6** timber decking
7 75mm x 50mm (3in x 2in) joist
8 DPC between bricks and timber
9 brick sleeper wall **10** concrete raft
11 main retaining wall
12 concrete foundation
13 drainage weep-holes **14** hardcore infill
15 subsoil/hardcore **16** ballast infill
17 paving stones **18** loose-laid rubble wall
19 topsoil (planted area) **20** DPC **21** house wall

Once this part of the work has been completed, 'filling in' is simply a matter of stretching the brick line to the courses of bricks and progressively building upward, one course at a time. The mortar joints, or pointing, should be finished as described on page 11.

Drainage weep-holes

To prevent a possible build-up of water behind the retaining wall, leave weep-holes in the course of bricks immediately above the concrete raft level for the timber decking (see section plan). To do this, simply omit the vertical mortar joint at about 70cm (27 in) intervals as the bricks are laid.

Raised area diagram reference for Stage 1

HARDCORE AND BALLAST

Hardcore consists of broken-up pieces of brick and other building materials. Quality and size of particles varies, but it is essential to get hardcore that is composed mainly of solid material, otherwise it will gradually break down and be detrimental to the foundations.

Ideally you should obtain brick hardcore that is free from foreign matter. You can buy it from builders or break up bricks yourself.

Ballast (or aggregate) adds bulk and strength to concrete. It consists of fine and coarse sand and small pebbles in different sizes, according to the job requirement.

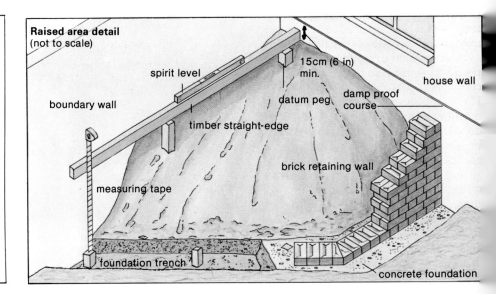

Raised area detail (not to scale)

spirit level

boundary wall

timber straight-edge

measuring tape

datum peg

15cm (6 in) min.

house wall

damp proof course

brick retaining wall

foundation trench

concrete foundation

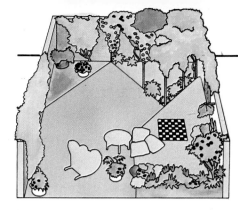

PREPARING THE PATIO
for decking and paving

You are now in the thick of making your own patio and for Stages 3 and 4 of the Schedule of Work you must check with the ground plan illustrated to scale on page 79.

SCHEDULE OF WORK Stage 3

With the main wall completed, you can proceed with further levelling and re-shaping of the site by piling the surplus subsoil from the lower level into the higher level. Take care to see that no pressure is applied to this main retaining wall until the mortar has set solidly. Now prepare the timber-decked area.

The ground plan and general detail diagram illustrate the layout of the timber decking. For this you must make a concrete raft foundation to which the timber structure will be laid.

Preparing for the raft foundation

The first stage of the work involves removing the topsoil to the pergola area. Once this has been accomplished, and fairly firm subsoil exposed, you can begin work adjusting the whole area to the necessary level. Lay straight-edge across the two previously positioned high-level datum pegs so that it overhangs the retaining wall. Now measure vertically down to the lower level, using the spirit level as a guide, as shown in the raised area diagram opposite. Hammer in a supplementary datum peg to the finished top level of the concrete raft. You can then carry out further levelling using the straight-edge and spirit level for a regular surface over all the raft site.

Where the excavation work has exposed reasonably firm subsoil, then concrete may be laid directly onto this. However, where topsoil removal has reduced the level below that required, the difference must be made up with clean, broken brick, stones or similar 'hard-core' material.

The concrete raft must be approximately 30cm (12 in) oversize to the timber decking along the pergola and brick-paved edges. This is to provide a foundation for the retaining walls that are necessary to cope with the difference in levels at these junctions (see general detail diagram, page 82).

Laying the shuttering

Concrete shuttering, or formwork, consists of planks of timber laid to the edges of the area to be concreted. This forms an edge to which the top of the concrete can easily be levelled and also contains, and provides, a clean edge to the work.

Timber for shuttering must be solid: scaffolding boards are ideal. With the aid of the spirit level and straight-edge, lay the top edge of the boards flush to the top of the supplementary datum peg. Hammer supporting timber pegs into the outside edge of the shuttering so that it does not move under the pressure of the poured concrete.

Drainage holes

The raft foundation will be surrounded by walls when the work is completed and for this reason drainage holes must be left through the concrete at about 1m (3 ft 3 in) centres. To do this, lay blocks of wood in the area prior to pouring the concrete, and then remove them before the concrete finally sets.

Where the subsoil consists of heavy clay and is not self-draining, it may be necessary to excavate a soakaway pit to ensure adequate drainage.

This would normally mean digging a 60cm (24 in) cube-shaped hole and filling it with hardcore under one main drainage hole. It would also be necessary to slope the concrete surface slightly towards the drainage point.

Use a scaffolding board, first across, then along the raft concrete, on the top surface of the shuttering timbers

Pouring the raft concrete

A suitable mix for the raft concrete is 1 part cement to 4·5 parts 20mm (¾ in) all-in ballast. Mix the dry ingredients first on a clean surface and then add sufficient water to produce a stiff mix. After pouring, tamp and level the concrete ready for the next stage of the work. Tamping and levelling can be carried out with a scaffolding board used on edge along the top surface of the shuttering (see below).

Decked area retaining walls

Next build brick retaining walls to the edge of the concrete raft (see the section plan and general detail diagram). As the height of this wall is only 22·5cm (9 in), a single skin wall will prove adequate.

Do the bricklaying by the same method described for the main retaining wall for the raised area opposite, the only difference being in the bond used, which you can see illustrated in the general detail diagram.

SCHEDULE OF WORK Stage 4

With all the retaining walls built and dry, you can proceed with the final back-filling and levelling work. Some broken brick or other hardcore must be laid at the inside base of the main retaining wall (see section plan), to allow free drainage through the weep-holes. Then use well-compacted hardcore and excavated subsoil to fill the main raised area. The division between paved and planted area is built up as necessary, using loosely-laid brick or stone as back-filling proceeds. The planted area should also be back-filled with topsoil.

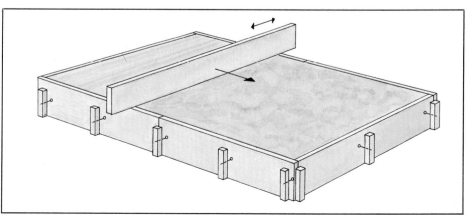

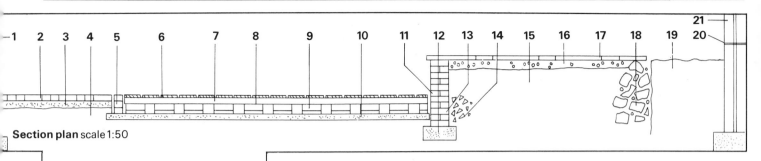

Section plan scale 1:50

Key
1 boundary wall **2** brick paving
3 sand/cement base **4** subsoil/hardcore
5 retaining wall **6** timber decking
7 75mm x 50mm (3in x 2in) joist
8 DPC between bricks and timber
9 brick sleeper wall **10** concrete raft
11 main retaining wall
12 concrete foundation
13 drainage weep-holes **14** hardcore infill
15 subsoil/hardcore **16** ballast infill
17 paving stones **18** loose-laid rubble wall
19 topsoil (planted area) **20** DPC **21** house wall

Levelling the brick-paved area

This area must be levelled in a similar way, with hardcore and subsoil being well compacted as a foundation for paving. Be sure to include pockets of subsoil as work proceeds, ready for subsequent planting of trees and shrubs. We have allowed for a *Magnolia grandiflora* to grow out of such a pocket against the trellised wall. Otherwise you must confine your plantings to tubs.

Preparing for the pergola

The first task here is to provide sockets for the rustic timber uprights. For this you should use 600mm (24 in) lengths of 100mm (4 in) diameter salt-glazed soil pipe. Position these in the ground (as shown in the general detail diagram); set them upright, using a post and the spirit level as a guide.

The main pergola area consists of topsoil that will support the woodland and other shade-loving plants to be planted here. Circular paving slabs give easy access, and to make a foundation for these, lay subsoil and ballast in the appropriate spots as you carry out the back-filling with topsoil.

Laying the raised area paving

As with bricklaying, the skill of laying paving stones can only be finally achieved through practice. However, by taking extra care and frequently using the spirit level and string guide, the beginner can produce a neat job.

Prepare the ground (see next page),

noting that the finished level of the ballast must be flush with the top of the main retaining wall (see general detail diagram).

Before starting to lay the paving stones, carefully set out the pattern to which the stones will be laid so as to avoid the use of small pieces of cut stone. The ground plan illustrates this point, where the cut stones along the retaining wall edge are all kept to a reasonable size.

Using the brick line and pegs, establish a line at right-angles to the planted area edge and as parallel as possible to the adjoining boundary wall. The line must be one paving stone width plus 2·5cm (1 in) maximum from the wall and positioned to represent the finished paving level, which should of course be flush with the top of the original datum peg.

Lay the first line of stones to the string line and then work backwards over the whole area until all the whole stones have been laid checking levels as you go.

Refer to the general detail diagram (below) and section plan (above) at all stages

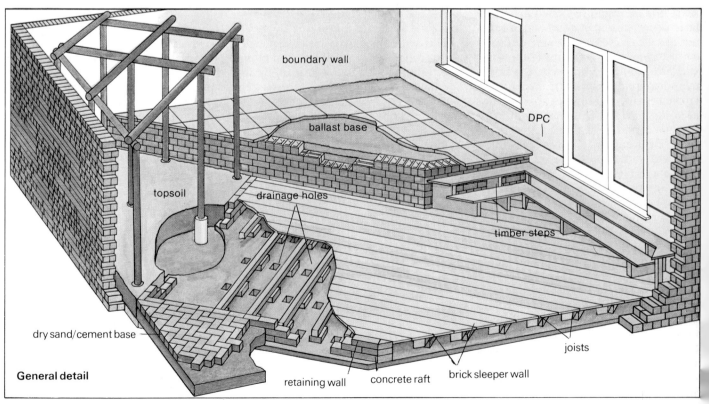

General detail

LAYING PAVING STONES

Having chosen your type of paving, estimated the quantity of stones needed and arranged for them to be delivered, it is time to prepare the ground.

If necessary, remove soil to a depth of 7–10cm (3–4 in) below the final required level. Then roll or tamp in a 5cm (2 in) layer of ballast. On springy or spongy soil use a 5cm layer of hardcore topped with sand. Check with a spirit level to ensure that the finished surface of your foundation is flat and accurate in all directions. Extra care taken at this stage will do much to simplify subsequent paving work.

You will need to mark out the area for paving with string, and then set out the pattern of your stones in such a way as to avoid having to use small, cut pieces. The stone supplier may be able to supply stones according to your specifications. Sizes and shapes for the cut stones should be taken direct from the plan of your paved area. To cut the stones yourself, follow the instructions below and practise on a spare bit of paving.

1 Mark out the edge of the first row with a string line. Each paving stone is then set on five blobs of a stiff 3 to 1 sand/cement mortar mix (that is, four blobs set just in from each corner and one in the centre).

2 To allow 9mm ($\frac{3}{8}$ in) gap between

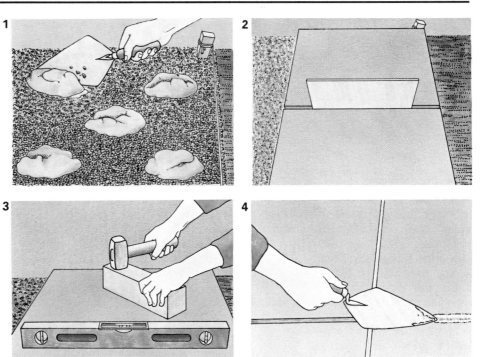

stones for final pointing, you need to use pieces of chipboard or plywood as temporary spacers.

3 Then tap each stone level, using a club hammer over a block of wood, until it lies level with its neighbours and no longer rocks on the foundation. With a trowel, cut away any surplus cement that may be squeezed out.

Always work backwards from your first row of paving, and refer frequently to your spirit level and string guide during laying so as to maintain a flat and even surface.

4 About a week after laying the paving you will need to point the spaces between the stones. For this, use the same 3 to 1 part sand/cement mortar mix and pack it into the joints, smoothing it with a trowel to slightly below level of stones.

CUTTING PAVING STONES

While it is possible to cut the stones by using a club hammer and bolster (or brick chisel), a far more satisfactory method is to hire a purpose-made power cutter from a tool hire firm. However, if you decide to do-it-yourself, it is worth taking your time to achieve a neat job.

1 Mark your cutting line, with a chalk or even a soft pencil, across both faces and edges of the stone.

Place the stone to be cut on a bed of soft soil and press it firmly down so that it will remain steady while you are chiselling.

2 Using a club hammer and bolster, cut a shallow scratch, about 2mm ($\frac{1}{16}$ in) deep, as evenly and straight as possible. At the end of your cutting line, chisel across the thickness of the stone. Then turn the stone over carefully and chisel across the second face.

3 Place a block of wood at one end of the scratch and strike it firmly with the club hammer. Repeat the process along the length of the scratch. You should hear the ringing tone turn to a dull thud.

4 Clean off any uneven edges with the bolster to obtain a neat join.

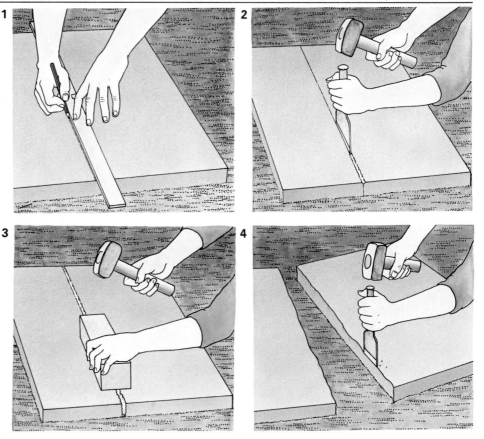

COMPLETING THE FINAL STAGES
in the patio

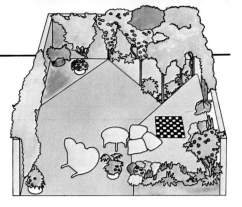

Following our Patio Garden design and work schedule, you are now in the final stages of building. The schedule guides you – from preparing foundations, laying a damp proof course and building brick walls, to the surface work of laying stone or brick paving and timber decking, as well as repointing and painting old brickwork.

Next come the decorative features, such as a trellis and pergola, then all that is left is the pleasure of choosing what plants to grow where, the right containers for them, and how to plant the deep bed in the raised, paved area.

SCHEDULE OF WORK Stage 5

When you have successfully completed the first four stages of work you will be ready to lay the decorative brick paving in the far left corner, opposite the French windows.

Laying the brick-paved area

For this brick paving a slightly different laying technique is employed from that for the stone-paved area described on page 83.

Here you should lay a 5cm (2 in) thick bed of a very stiff 5 to 1 sand/cement mix and carefully level it so that when the bricks are laid in position and gently tapped, the surface will become flush to the adjacent 11–12cm (4½ in) thick retaining wall.

You can obtain the right stiff mix by adding just sufficient water to produce a crumbly texture. Use a string line in conjunction with the spirit level to help you make a neat job of it. The dry sand/cement bed should be lightly dampened as work proceeds, using a watering can with a sprinkler rose.

Leave a 9mm (⅜ in) pointing gap between all the bricks and fill this with a 3 to 1 mortar mix after you have completed all the paving. Lay all the full-sized bricks first, before you insert any necessary cut pieces. You can cut the bricks to the required size with a club hammer and brick chisel. (You can follow the same laying technique if you wish to use a broken stone paving.)

Timber for decking and joists

An ideal timber for this purpose is Western red cedar, but if this type is too costly or not readily available, you should consult your local timber merchant as to the best alternative available. With some types of timber the supplier may suggest pre-impregnation with a preservative.

The 250 × 25mm (10 × 1 in) decking is fitted to 75 × 50mm (3 × 2 in) joists, which

Fix trellis either side of your false perspective arched pathway, and paint to choice, or protect with preservative

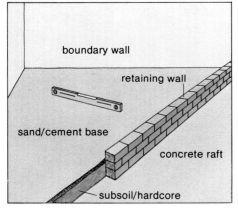

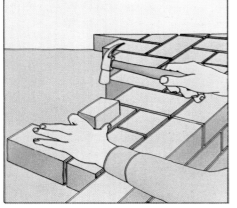

For brick paving: (top) level the sand/ cement base; (top right) keep the bed lightly dampened as you lay the bricks;

(above left) if gently tapped, the laid bricks become flush to retaining wall; (above) point the gaps between bricks

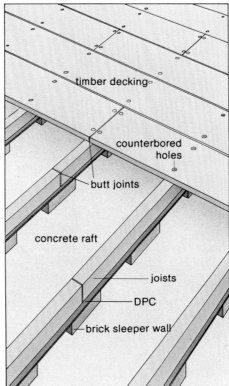

For timber decking: fit timber to joists supported on brick sleeper wall, with DPC between timber and bricks. Fill counter-sunk screw-holes with plugs

in turn are supported on a brick sleeper wall with a damp proof course between brick and timber. The joists must be set at 40cm (16 in) centres and the planks of the decking laid with 9mm ($\frac{3}{8}$ in) gaps between each to allow surface water to run through (see ground and section plans and general detail diagram). Take care with all the timber work to ensure that the timber never comes into direct contact with any concrete or masonry.

Building the sleeper wall
Set one brick in a corner accurately to the sleeper wall height and then use this as a datum to transfer the levels, through the straight-edge and spirit level, to a second brick positioned at the far end of this first sleeper wall. You can then stretch a string line to the bricks to lay the remainder of the wall accurately. The space between bricks should be about 15cm (6 in); see section plan. Build the balance of sleeper walls the same way.
Note For Patio ground plan, see page 79 for section plan, pages 80 and 82, and general detail diagram, pages 82.

SCHEDULE OF WORK Stage 6
Having fitted the decking to the joists, now follow the correct sequence of work.

Laying the decking
After the mortar has set, lay a strip of DPC material on top of the wall before laying the joists in position. Then fix the decking to the joists, using rust-proofed screws (ideally brass ones), counter-sunk below the surface. Fill the holes with a matching timber plug.

Timber for steps
To give access from the house down to the timber decking and also up to the raised paved area, you will need steps. Build these up from timber left over from decking (see general detail diagram).

Erecting the pergola
Cut the vertical rustic poles, all about 100mm (4 in) in diameter, to a 2·8m length (9 ft) and then drop them into the previously prepared sockets (see Stage 4 page 82). Cut the three horizontal under members to length and fit them to the tops of the vertical members by nailing through. Then fix the second horizontal layer (see general detail diagram).

SCHEDULE OF WORK Stage 7
No matter how small a patio, a trellis like this one, designed to give the illusion of depth, looks effective. We fitted ours to the left-hand boundary wall.

False perspective trellis work

This is quite simple to carry out if you follow our grid pattern. First of all, lightly pencil 10cm (4 in) squares onto a sheet of 12mm (½ in) thick marine plywood. You can then 'transfer' the design to the plywood panel by reference to the grid pattern. Cutting is best carried out using either a self-powered or drill jig saw attachment. After cutting, smooth all edges by sanding before painting with one coat of primer, two undercoats and one top coat of oil paint.

This false perspective trellis is flanked on both sides by the more conventional rectangular trellis which you buy ready-made. You can paint this any colour to suit your scheme, or leave it natural and protect it with wood preservative.

To fix all the trellis work to the brick walls, use conventional plastic wall plugs and screws. In order to prevent contact between the trellis timber and wall brickwork (as this provides a point where early rotting and staining may occur) use 100mm (4 in) long fixing screws with 35mm (1½ in) long plastic tube spacers fitted over the screw shank between the trellis and wall.

Fixing the mirrors and blackboard

Reflections from the two square mirrors fitted to the boundary walls under the pergola (see ground plan) add an air of mystery to the patio. Be sure to get the waterproof-backed type and fit them to the walls with standard-type plastic wall fixing plugs and brass screws through holes pre-drilled in the mirrors. The holes for the screws must be loosely-sized and a thick rubber washer fitted to the screw shank between mirror and wall to allow for expansion and contraction of the glass during extremes of temperature.

For the children's benefit it is well worth making an outdoor blackboard. Cut this yourself from a sheet of waterproof plywood and treat it with a special blackboard paint (and renew this as necessary). Fix it to the wall near to the main paved area (see ground plan) in the same way as the mirrors.

Painting the chequerboard

You can paint any pattern you like on the raised paving, but we thought a simple chequerboard was useful for the games enthusiasts and decorative in its own right. The area must be completely dust-free and lightly dampened before you start applying an emulsion paint.

Use grid to transfer your perspective pattern to marine plywood. You can add mirror glass panels here to good effect

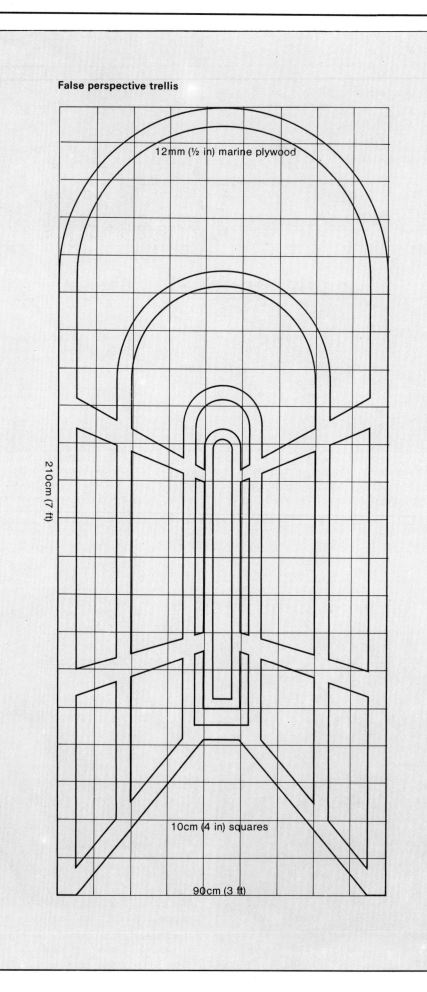

False perspective trellis

12mm (½ in) marine plywood

210cm (7 ft)

10cm (4 in) squares

90cm (3 ft)

Buildings

A professionally built greenhouse or coldframe may be prohibitively expensive, so follow our advice and erect them yourself; there are untold rewards for the keen gardener. We give directions, too, for a small tool shed for convenient storage.

ERECTING AND SITING A GREENHOUSE

In most cases it is wise to choose an open position for the greenhouse where it will get as much sunshine as possible. This generally means that you should try to position the unit with one of the longest sides facing south. It is a simple matter to shade the glass when you want to reduce light entry, but it is difficult to increase light without the trouble and expense of artificial lighting.

Remember that, in winter, nearly all plants will enjoy plenty of sunlight – even summer shade-lovers. Winter sunlight also means plenty of free warmth and your heating costs will be reduced.

Shady and windy sites
Avoid, where possible, a site that is near large trees (especially evergreens). Falling branches may break the glass, and spreading roots may upset the foundations. Falling leaves and exuded gums from some species dirty the glass, and you may also find that the roof is covered with bird droppings. Evergreens cast shade all year round, and many trees harbour numerous pests and diseases that can attack greenhouse plants and crops.

Small shrubs and trees are not usually a menace; these can even be planted (far enough away so that they do not cast shade) to act as windbreaks in windy areas. Strong, cold winds, usually from the north and east, can add greatly to the fuel bill. Other suitable windbreaks are fences, walls and hedges – as long as they are not too high.

Low ground and hollows
When choosing a site for your greenhouse, look carefully at the ground contours of your garden. In all cases where the site is at the foot of a hill there is a danger of frost pockets forming. Cold, frosty air can run off a slope almost like water, and surround a greenhouse that is set in a hollow. Where no other site is available, a low brick wall can help to deflect icy air currents.

In hollows and on low ground, water may collect or the ground may become very damp. These conditions are particularly unhealthy in winter when the greenhouse should be as dry as possible.

Sites near the house
Many people put their greenhouse at the far end of the garden – some distance from the house. There is often no good reason why it should be tucked away out of sight. Modern structures are rarely 'eyesores' and some designs are very attractive, especially when filled with decorative plants. There are many advantages in having the greenhouse within close reach of the house. Both water and electricity can be run to the greenhouse easily. Electricity, even if you don't want it for heating, may be needed for automatic aids or lighting; you may also wish to run natural gas from the house.

When the greenhouse is to be heated by solid fuel or paraffin, remember that the fuel will have to be carried to the greenhouse and, in the case of solid fuel, the ash carried away – yet another reason for avoiding remote sites. If you don't want to see a greenhouse from the windows of your home, you can always screen it with low shrubs or small ornamental trees.

In some cases greenhouses can be heated economically by an extension of the same central heating system used in your home. In this case the greenhouse should, preferably, come into contact with the house wall, and a lean-to is usually the best design. Where high temperatures are required it is always an advantage if the greenhouse can be set against a house wall, or a south-facing garden wall. Such a wall usually absorbs warmth from the sun during the day and radiates it at night, thus saving fuel and acting as a kind of free storage heater.

Laying the foundations
Most modern, prefabricated, amateur greenhouses are easy to erect single-handed, though with the larger sizes you may need assistance. The ground must always be firm and level, so laying a shallow foundation (by digging a trench and filling it with a fluid concrete mix that finds its own level) is often a wise move. However, some greenhouse manufacturers recommend their own base plinths and the small additional cost of these is well worth while. Some designs do not need elaborate foundations but are secured by 'ground anchors'. A separate

hole is dug for each anchor and the framework is then bolted onto these before the glazing is put in.

Brick or concrete base walls, if required, are best constructed by a professional builder – unless you are reasonably expert in this sort of work. Greenhouse manufacturers always provide a detailed groundplan of the structure, so follow this closely when putting in foundations or base walls.

When erecting your greenhouse, use a spirit level and plumb line to make frequent checks on levels and verticals. A period of calm weather when rain is not expected is the best time for the job.

Fitting the glazing
Stand glass panes in a dry, covered place until you are ready to use them. If they get wet they are very difficult to separate and you risk breaking them. Glazing is best done when the weather is not too cold or your fingers may be too numb for careful handling. Do any metal or timber painting before the glass is put in. If you are using putty, only put it below the glass as a bed for the panes – not over the top as well, as in ordinary domestic glazing. Top putty wastes material, adds unnecessary weight to the glazing bars and increases costs. Always be sure that surfaces to be puttied are clean and dry.

Plastic greenhouses
Be especially careful, when erecting and siting plastic greenhouses, to avoid possible wind damage. The suppliers usually issue special anchoring instructions and recommendations. When plastic is to be fastened to a timber framework, don't use creosote preservatives on the wood. Some plastics will become weakened by contact and all will be severely discoloured, making the greenhouse most unsightly. Moreover, creosote fumes are harmful to plants. For the same reason creosote should not be used on any timbers in close contact with plants in a confined area – such as in greenhouses or frames. Instead use one of the proprietary horticultural timber preservatives on the market.

Tending the site
The surroundings of your greenhouse should be kept tidy and weed-free. Weeds will harbour many troublesome pests; for example nearby stinging nettles may bring you an infestation of whitefly. A paved area or a path right round the greenhouse, however, can help to reduce the numbers of garden pests (such as slugs, woodlice or earwigs) that manage to find their way in.

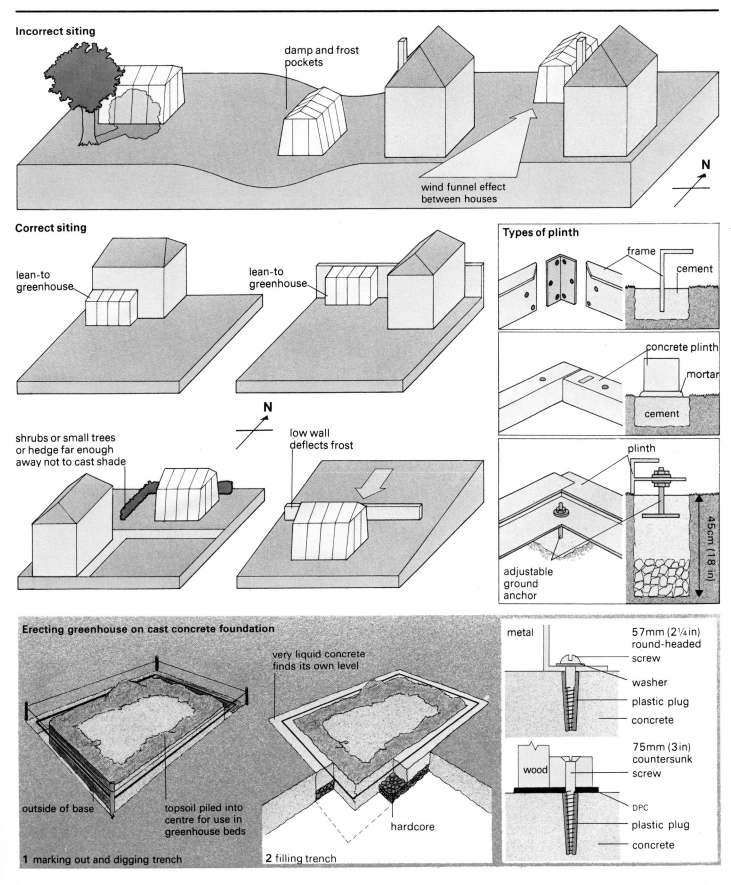

Incorrect siting

damp and frost pockets

wind funnel effect between houses

N

Correct siting

lean-to greenhouse

lean-to greenhouse

N

shrubs or small trees or hedge far enough away not to cast shade

low wall deflects frost

Types of plinth

frame
cement

concrete plinth
mortar
cement

plinth

adjustable ground anchor

45cm (18 in)

Erecting greenhouse on cast concrete foundation

very liquid concrete finds its own level

outside of base

topsoil piled into centre for use in greenhouse beds

1 marking out and digging trench

hardcore

2 filling trench

metal

57mm (2¼ in) round-headed screw

washer

plastic plug

concrete

wood

75mm (3 in) countersunk screw

DPC

plastic plug

concrete

Top: avoid shade, damp, frost and wind – enemies of the greenhouse
Centre left: use house or garden walls for economical lean-to greenhouses; make use of low-growing shrubs or low walls to help protect against wind and frost

Bottom left: dig trench on a firm, level spot, remembering to place soil in centre for future use. Concrete over hardcore provides a solid base for the greenhouse that can be anchored with the right type of plugs and screws (bottom right)

Centre right: ready-made base plinths in in metal or concrete need only very very simple foundations, and are easy for the amateur to put together. The adjustable ground anchor system requires a solid concrete base

COLD FRAME

A cold frame is an asset to any garden and makes a much easier job of growing seedlings. This frame is both practical and good-looking and can cope with a large number of plants at once.

TOOLS AND MATERIALS

timber (see cutting list)
measuring tape, pencil and try square
protractor, sliding bevel, marking gauge
fine-tooth panel saw, tenon saw, mitre box (or guide)
medium fine and fine glasspaper
12mm chisel, block plane
hand or electric drill, 2 and 5mm bits
screwdriver, bradawl, countersink bit
hammer and nail punch, four G-clamps
water-resistant woodworking adhesive and clean cloth

For assembly

No 8 black japanned round head screws 19, 32 and 50mm long, panel pins 25mm long
two 895 × 535 × 3mm glass panes (obtain cut to size)
6m of 16mm quadrant moulding
6m of 12mm square softwood batten (for fixing glass)
six 50mm long brass butt hinges and 25mm long brass screws to fit
600mm of brass chain (for door stays)

For finish

exterior grade cellulose filler or matching plastic wood
natural or coloured wood preservative (suitable for horticultural use)
old paint brush

Overall dimensions

1200mm long, 923mm wide, 610mm high (47 × 36 × 24in).
Project dimensions are in metric only and do not allow for cutting wastages.

Cutting list for softwood & plywood

Description	Key	Quantity	Dimensions
Front and back planks	A	6	1200 x 145 x 16mm
Side planks	B	6	864 x 145 x 16mm
Front corner posts	C	2	297 x 22 x 22mm
Back corner posts	D	2	574 x 22 x 22mm
Side edge battens	E	2	871 x 22 x 22mm
Door frame uprights	F	4	960 x 32 x 22mm
Door frame cross rails	G	4	600 x 32 x 22mm
Ventilator (plywood)	H	1	150 x 90 x 6mm

Stage 1

Measure and cut with a tenon saw all the pieces of timber according to the dimensions shown (see cutting list). Using a protractor and a sliding bevel, mark out the 72 degree angle on the top edge of the top back plank A1 and the top front plank A5 (see side elevation) and remove the waste from both planks with a block plane. Mark out the 72 degree angle at the top end of the front and back corner posts C and D (see assembly diagram). Cut off the waste from these battens with a tenon saw.
Place two of the side planks B together and mark on the shaping lines (see 1); cut the pair diagonally in half with a fine-tooth panel saw and plane down to the lines to form the top side planks (see assembly diagram). Smooth all cut and planed edges with medium fine, then fine glasspaper to remove any roughness.

Stage 2

Drill all the 5mm diameter clearance holes in the front and back planks A and side planks B according to the dimensions shown (see 2) and countersink them to a depth of 5mm on what will be the outside faces.
Hold the top front plank A5 squarely against the front face of the front corner posts C so there is a 16mm overhang at each end and the top edges form a continuous slope (see plan and side elevation) and mark with a bradawl through the clearance holes in A5 onto the posts. Drill 2mm pilot holes at these points, apply some water-resistant woodworking adhesive to the fixing area of both posts and fix A5 firmly in position with the 32mm long No 8 round head screws through the two lower holes. Wipe off excess adhesive with a clean dampened cloth. Glue and screw the bottom front plank in position in the same way. Fix the four bottom side planks B to the corner posts C and D as before, making certain all joints are square. Glue and screw the top four side planks to the back corner posts D1 and D2 (see assembly diagram).
Drill all the 5mm diameter clearance holes in the side edge battens E according to the dimensions shown (see 3) and countersink them to a depth of 5mm on what will be the inside faces. Mark out the 72 degree angle at both ends of E with a sliding bevel and cut off the waste with a tenon saw. Remember to make one left-hand and one right-hand batten.
Hold the battens E1 and E2 in the required position inside the cold frame carcase (see assembly diagram) and mark with a bradawl through the clearance holes onto the side planks. Turning the carcase onto one end at a time, drill 2mm pilot holes 10mm deep in the side planks where you have marked with the bradawl. Apply adhesive to the fixing face and both ends of the side edge battens and fix them firmly in position to the side planks with the 32mm long No 8 round head screws. Wipe off excess adhesive. Screw through the top holes in the front plank A5, through C1 and C2, into the ends of E1

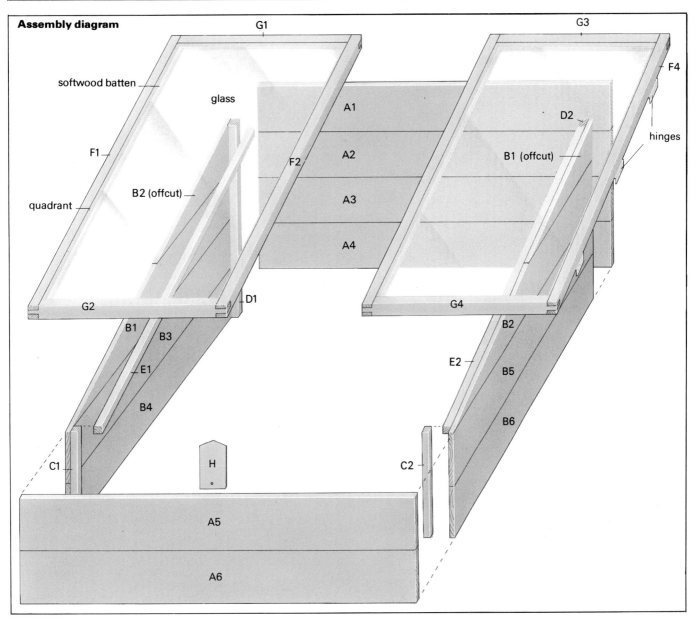

Assembly diagram

and E2 with the 50mm long round head screws.

Stage 3

Using a marking gauge, mark out the bridle joint slot at both ends of the door frame uprights F and the tenon at both ends of the door frame cross rails G according to the dimensions shown (**see 4**). Remove the waste from each slot in the uprights by making two cuts to the depth line with a tenon saw and chopping out the area from between the cut lines with a 12mm chisel. Cut off the waste from the cross rails with a tenon saw. Apply adhesive to the fixing surfaces of the bridle joints and assemble the door frames, tightening a G-clamp round

each joint until the adhesive has set. Check the frames are square and wipe off excess adhesive.
When all the adhesive has set hard, remove the clamps and cut the quadrant moulding into four 896mm lengths and four 536mm lengths, mitring both ends in each case (**see assembly diagram**). Glue and fix these mouldings to the insides of the door frames flush with the top face (**see 5**), using 25mm long panel pins. Punch the pin heads below the surface with a nail punch and wipe off excess adhesive.
Mark out and cut the hinge recesses in the door frame uprights F1 and F4 and the top side planks B according to the dimensions shown (**see side elevation**); the

hinge knuckles should lie just clear of the outside of the frames.
Cut the plywood ventilator H to shape and drill the 5mm diameter clearance hole in it at the dimensions shown (**see 6**).
Cut the 12mm square softwood batten into four 872mm lengths and four 536mm lengths.

Stage 4

Fill any holes, cracks and abrasions with exterior grade cellulose filler or matching plastic wood and rub all surfaces smooth with fine glasspaper. Apply three coats of wood preservative to all surfaces with an old paint brush; don't forget the ventilator and the softwood

battens.
Warning The preservative must be suitable for horticultural use or it may damage your plants.

When all the wood preservative has dried thoroughly, fix the ventilator H centrally to the top front plank A5 with the 19mm long round head screw, placing a washer between the plywood and the timber (**see 6 inset**). Lay the glass panes inside the door frame and glue and pin the softwood battens to the uprights F and cross rails G to secure the glass tightly.
Fix the doors in position with the brass butt hinges and the 25mm long brass screws, making pilot holes with a bradawl for the fixing screws. Cut the brass chain with a

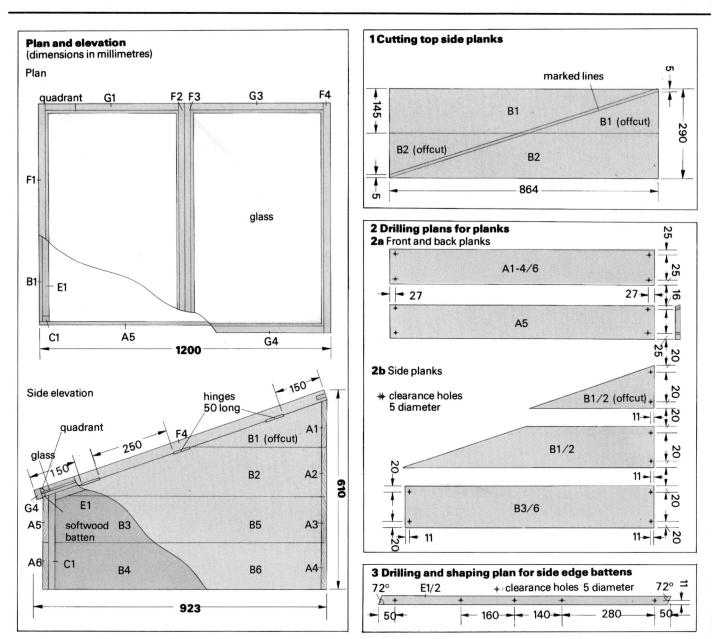

Plan and elevation
(dimensions in millimetres)

Plan

quadrant   G1   F2 F3   G3   F4

glass

F1

B1   E1

C1   A5   G4

1200

Side elevation

hinges
50 long   150

quadrant   F4   A1

glass   B1 (offcut)

150   250

B2   A2

G4   E1

A5   softwood   B3   B5   A3
batten

A6   C1   B4   B6   A4

610

923

1 Cutting top side planks

5

marked lines

145   B1

B1 (offcut)   290

B2 (offcut)   B2

5   864

2 Drilling plans for planks

2a Front and back planks

25

A1-4/6   25

27   27   16

A5

25

2b Side planks

20

clearance holes
5 diameter

B1/2 (offcut)   20

11   20

20   B1/2

11   20

B3/6   20

20   11   11   20

3 Drilling and shaping plan for side edge battens

72°   E1/2   clearance holes 5 diameter   72°   11

50   160   140   280   50

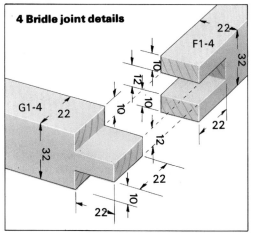

4 Bridle joint details

22

F1-4   32

12   10

10   10

G1-4   22   22

32   12

22

22   10

22

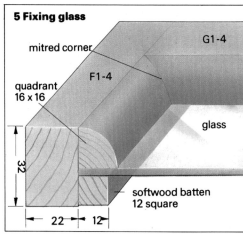

5 Fixing glass

G1-4

mitred corner

F1-4

quadrant
16 x 16

glass

32

softwood batten
12 square

22   12

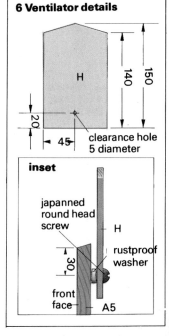

6 Ventilator details

H   150   140

20

45   clearance hole
5 diameter

inset

japanned
round head
screw   H

rustproof
washer

30

front
face   A5

hacksaw into two 300mm
lengths and screw one end of
each length to the side plank
B and the other end to the
inside of the door frame
upright F; make sure the
door can be opened to about

120 degrees before the chain
stops it going any further.
Leave the cold frame outside,
preferably with a cover over
it, for at least four days for
the preservative to dry out
before you start using it.

MAKE A TUCK-AWAY SHED

Materials

(approximate quantities)

52m (170 ft) of 40mm (1½ in) square sawn softwood

4 sheets Royal hardboard, 2·4×1·2m (8×4 ft) × 3mm (⅛ in) thick

piece of roofing felt 2×1m (6½×3¼ ft)

100 corrugated fasteners, 18mm (¾ in)

20 oval nails, 50mm (2 in)

25 galvanized felt nails

250g (½ lb) plated panel pins, 25mm (1 in)

3 coachbolts, nuts and washers, 90×6mm (3½×¼ in)

8 woodscrews, 50mm (2 in) × No 10

3 T-hinges, 3 fixing screws, 250mm (10 in)

hasp and padlock

500 ml (1 pt) aluminium primer

1 lit (1 qt) undercoat paint

500 ml (1 pt) top coat paint

Cascamite waterproof wood glue

4 paving slabs, 600mm (24 in) square

bolts or screws, *for anchoring*

Tools

measuring tape

panel saw

hammer

screwdriver

hand drill and wood bits

woodworking plane

pointed knife

50mm (2 in) paint brush

paint-roller and tray

The actual construction work involves simple carpentry only, and can be tackled using the basic woodworking tools listed. The shed is built from 40mm (1½ in) square softwood timber, assembled into frames, and then covered with Royal hardboard, ready for painting *before* the final assembly. This method has been well tried and tested, and provided you follow the instructions in respect of pre-conditioning and weatherproofing, the structure will provide you with many years of useful service.

Depending on your site and storage needs you may wish to modify the dimensions of the shed. Ours measures approximately 2m (7 ft) high, the short sides 1·2m (4 ft), and the front 1·65m (5½ ft), to take a standard 75×180cm (2½×6 ft) door. Where a lower shed would be more in keeping the height could be reduced and the shed made more in the form of a cupboard.

Garden tools such as a spade and fork only require a height of 1·2m (4 ft), and even a long-handled rake, hoe or broom can be stored in a height of 1·5m (5 ft). To reduce the height the only modifications necessary would be to shorten all vertical members by an equal amount, and to reposition the intermediate horizontal members to even spacings.

Many gardens are irregularly shaped, and as a result corners are rarely square. A minor deviation will be of little or no consequence, as long as you allow a small gap between shed and fence. But if you want a really snug fit you will have to check the proportions of the shed side frames against the angle of the corner you propose using.

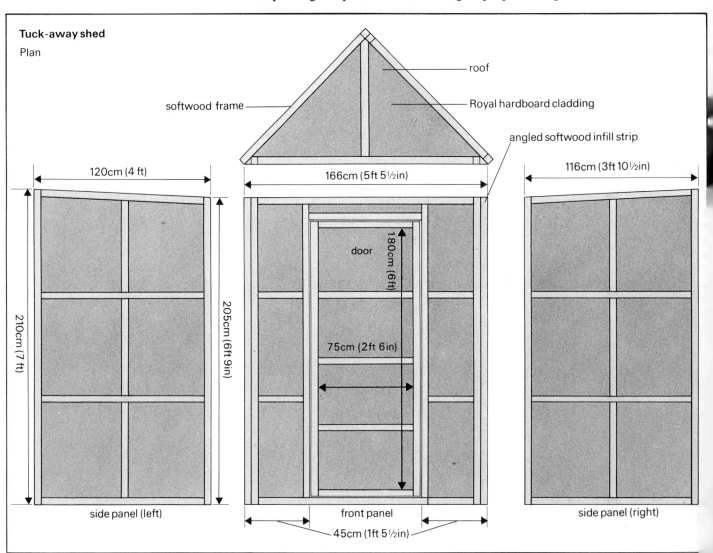

Tuck-away shed

Plan

Right: when assembling side panels make sure rear vertical member of right-hand frame is angled to give neat fit where it abuts left-hand frame;
for ease of working hang door while front frame is flat on ground;
raised base, formed from paving slabs, can be extended to provide firm area in front of and around shed

A simple way to do this is to take two lengths of 40mm (1½ in) square timber, and cut them to represent the side frames: make one piece 122cm (4 ft) long, and the other 118cm (3 ft 10½in). Lay them in the positions the side panels will occupy in the garden and the distance between the inner extremes will be the width to make your front frame (see measurement plan). Provided it is within 100mm (4 in) of the measurement given in our plan, your softwood infill strips can be cut at the angle shown; but if the difference is greater you will have to get the strips cut to suit the angle. Most timber suppliers will cut infill strips at the angle you require for a modest charge when you order the timber for the main frame. The rear vertical member of the right side panel must be angled to give a neat fit where it abuts the left frame. You can do this quite simply after assembly by planing the panel to shape.

It is important that you anchor the shed against possible damage by high winds. Generally, you will be able to put a bolt or screw through the main frame members and into an adjacent fence post. However, where the fence is the property of a neighbour prior approval must be obtained. If fixing to the fence is not suitable or desirable, you can hammer 90cm (3 ft) long pieces of 25mm (1 in) diameter pipe firmly into the ground and bolt the shed to these.

It is advisable to stand your shed on a raised base to protect the timber and hardboard from damage resulting from dampness. Four standard 60cm (24 in) square paving slabs would be ideal for this purpose and can be arranged as shown in the diagram, or even extended to provide a firm area in front and around the shed. (Instructions for laying paving stones or slabs are on page 60.) Before you position the shed on the base you will need to lay a damp-proof course consisting of a strip of roofing felt or heavy-gauge polythene placed between base and frames.

The roof is designed to throw surface water forward, both to avoid possible annoyance to your neighbour, and to prevent an unnecessary build-up of water between fence and shed.

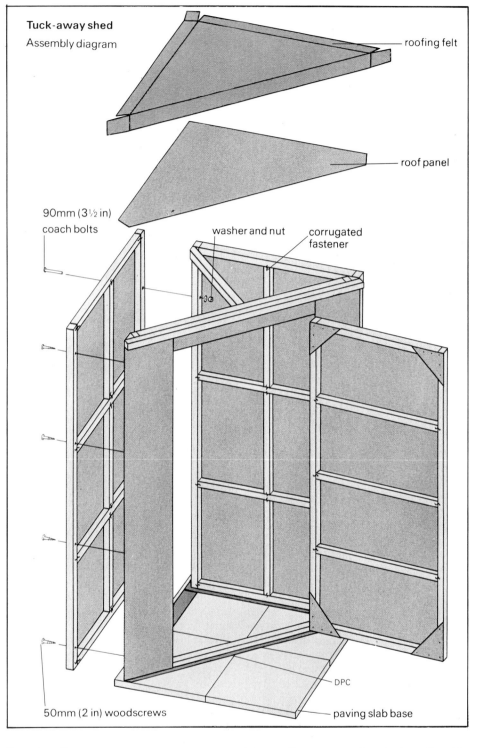

Tuck-away shed
Assembly diagram

roofing felt

roof panel

90mm (3½ in) coach bolts

washer and nut

corrugated fastener

50mm (2 in) woodscrews

DPC

paving slab base

Construction
First assemble the timber frames (follow step photographs on next page). Cut the main vertical and horizontal members to length and lay them out, ideally on a flat concrete floor, ready for fixing. Hammer corrugated fasteners across the join to fix the simple butt joints used in the structure (see **1**). At this stage the frame need not be exactly square, as you can use Royal hardboard cladding to pull it square later on in the operation.

Once you have fitted the main members, you can take sizes for the shorter intermediate spacers (vertical on the side frames and horizontal on the centre frame) direct from the structure.

With one side fixed, you must turn the frame over carefully – it will be quite flimsy at this stage – and hammer more fasteners into each joint from the reverse side. To ensure accuracy it is best to assemble the door frame in its opening in the main front frame (see **2**). The main frames are now ready for cladding.

With the front main frame, two angled infill strips are required at both vertical side edges (see **2**) to provide a flat mating

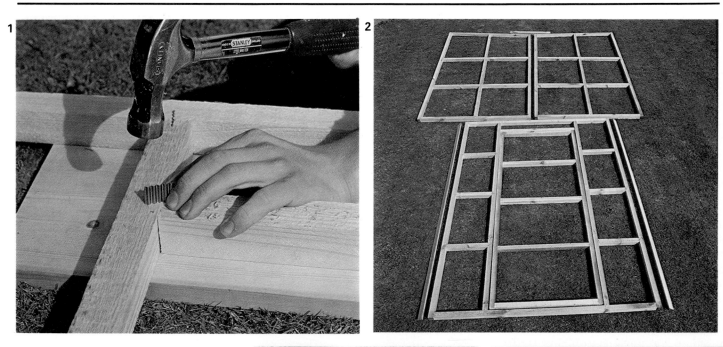

To construct front and side frames

1 *Fix main vertical and horizontal members with corrugated fasteners*
2 *For accuracy assemble door frame in its opening in front frame*
3 *Apply generous coat of waterproof glue to all frame members*
4 *Position hardboard, mesh side to frame lining up along one edge*
5 *Nail edge in position, pull frame square and nail other edges*
6 *Make trial assembly*
7 *Insert coach bolts through drilled holes inside frames*
8 *Tighten nuts inside frames with spanner to ensure firm fixing*

surface for the side frames. These two pieces can be cut from one length of the main frame material, sawn across at an angle of 45 degrees, if your structure is right-angled like ours. You will need a power saw if you intend doing this job yourself. The infill strips are located as in the front panel plan detail, and fixed with 50mm (2 in) oval nails.

Royal hardboard cladding

You will have to 'condition' the Royal hardboard thoroughly before using it, to minimize the possibility of buckling after exposure to weather. This merely means scrubbing about 1 litre (2 pints) of water into the mesh side of each sheet and this can be done with a broom. Then stack the dampened sheets flat and back to back, away from wind and sun, to allow the water to penetrate. The board will swell slightly after about 36 hours, and this is when it should be fixed. As it subsequently dries out, it will shrink, forming a taut covering to the frame, and this

built-in tension is normally quite sufficient to prevent the material distorting in a damp atmosphere. You must apply at least two undercoats and one top coat of a good quality oil paint to complete waterproofing, taking special care to give all exposed edges a good covering.

If you aim to make the shed in one go, you will have to condition the Royal hardboard before you build the frames, to avoid any delay.

Fixing the cladding

Once you have conditioned the Royal hardboard and have it ready for application, you should cut it to size, using the assembled frame as a marking template. Then apply a generous coat of Cascamite waterproof wood glue with a brush to all frame members (see **3**) and position the Royal hardboard mesh side to frame, and lined up along one edge (see **4**). You can then nail this edge in position (see **5**), using 25mm (1 in) plated panel pins. Pull

4

5

7

8

the frame square to a second Royal hardboard edge and complete the job with nails at about 100mm (4 in) centres.

With the cladding firmly nailed in position, you should lay the frames flat on a surface to allow the glue and dampened board to dry. When cladding the two side panels, be sure to apply the material to the 'correct' outer face of each frame. The tallest sides of the frames come together to form the right-angled rear corner, while the shorter sides mate with the outer sides of the main front frame, giving the roof a downward slope towards the front of the assembled shed.

After cladding the front frame, add a strip of frame timber along the front edge to provide a weather overhang for the roof panel. After cladding the door, turn it over and pin and glue four corner-reinforcing members (cut from offcuts of Royal board) into position, as shown in the assembly diagram: the dimensions of these pieces aren't critical. Once panels are really dry, plane the edges smooth.

Next, you should undertake a trial assembly. Stand the two side panels up and align them as in the assembly diagram. This is really a two-person job, but if there is nobody to help you, a temporary fixing can be achieved using a G-cramp applied to the top mating corners of the frames. You can then drill the assembly bolt-holes through both frames simultaneously, insert the bolts, and make a firm fixing.

Hold the front frame against the assembled side frames and check for fit and alignment. Then drill holes for the fixing screws through the side frames, allowing for the screwheads to be well recessed (see final assembly **6–10**). Take a measurement direct from the structure for the central roof beam (see measurement plan), and for the Royal hardboard roof panel. Also at this stage, you can position the shed to check whether any minor adjustments will be necessary for accurate siting, which will also enable you to test the base for level.

Painting

Ideally, you should do the painting under cover, but you would have to dismantle the shed first. Apply a coat of aluminium primer, taking particular care that all Royal hardboard edges are well covered. Next, apply one or two undercoats, followed by one top coat. The simplest method is to do the edges with a brush, and fill in main areas with a roller.

Final on-site assembly

When the paint is thoroughly hardened assemble and site the components. Fix the two side panels first (see **6–8**), using 90mm (3½ in) coach bolts, washers and nuts. Where access to the rear of the sited shed would not be possible, you should carry out the initial assembly as close as possible to the final location. The structure will be sufficiently light to allow final positioning after assembly.

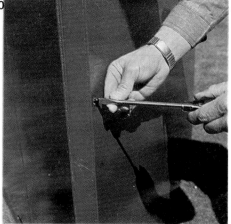

continuing shed construction.
9 *Stand up front frame and align it with assembled side frames*
10 *Screw frame in place with coach bolts before positioning on site*

11 *Cut roofing felt, using hardboard roof panel as template*
12 *The finished shed. The door can be hung left or right according to the way you want it to open*

For ease of working, the door is best hung with the front frame flat on the ground. Also at this stage, you can fit a padlock hasp or catch, together with a door stop (a piece of scrap timber fitted internally against which the door closes flush to the outside).

Line up the front frame next, fixing it in position (see **9** and **10**), and then lift the structure into position on the site. Slip strips of damp-proof material in place as the structure is finally sited. If ground anchorage is necessary, you should also arrange this in conjunction with the final location of the shed.

Nail the central beam of the roof in position. Before you fit the Royal hardboard roof panel, you can use it as a template for the roofing felt (see **11**), which should be cut approximately 75mm (3 in) oversize all round. Then fit the roofing panel, pinning it in position using 25mm (1 in) panel pins. Add the roofing felt next, and after trimming, secure it to the front and side frames with galvanized felt nails.

Recreation

Whether you want sturdy furniture for lounging in the garden, shades to keep off the sun or a barbecue for entertaining friends, instructions for making your own are all here. Don't forget playtime ideas for the children too.

'RECLINER'

Just right for the garden, this reclining seat is easily wheeled to wherever the sun is shining and, with a simple adjustment, you can sit up or stretch out. The backrest fits neatly underneath the assembly for storage when not in use.

Tools and materials

timber (see cutting list)
measuring tape, pencil and try square, mortise gauge
panel saw, tenon saw, coping saw
block or bench plane
electric or hand drill, 2 and 5mm bits
pair of compasses, protractor
screwdriver, bradawl, countersink bit
hammer and nail punch, mallet, vice, round file
6 and 18mm chisels
medium and fine glasspaper
web-clamp or length of strong rope
water-resistant woodworking adhesive

For assembly
panel pins 19 and 38mm long
two wheels and fixing bolts (with wing nuts and washers)
No 8 rustproof countersunk screws 38mm long
No 10 rustproof countersunk screws 50mm long

For finish
cellulose filler or plastic wood
clear matt polyurethane lacquer, 50mm paint brush

Overall dimensions (when stored)
2000mm long, 800mm wide, 322mm deep without wheels
(79 × 31 × 13in). Project dimensions are given in metric only
and do not allow for cutting wastages.

Stage 1

Measure and mark out, then cut with a panel saw, all the pieces of timber according to the dimensions shown (**see cutting list and plan**).
Mark out with a mortise gauge the tenon at each end of each backrest cross slat E according to the dimensions shown (**see 1b**) and cut to size with a tenon saw.
To make the wedged stub tenons, saw out two slits in each tenon and make wedges (**see 1b**) out of scrap pieces of wood. Mark out mortises (**see 1a**) on the inside edge of both backrest uprights F (there are four on each) at the dimensions shown then chop out the waste with a 6mm chisel. Cut a recess at one end of both rails according to the dimensions shown (**see 1**).
Mark out the shape of the halving joint at either end of

the backrest top G and both backrest uprights F at the dimensions shown (**see 1c**). Pour some water-resistant woodworking adhesive inside all the mortises in the two uprights F and insert the tenons on the backrest cross slats E (**see 1**), ramming them firmly home with a mallet. Apply adhesive to the halving joints on the backrest top G and on the two backrest uprights F, and pin them together with the 19mm panel pins. Punch the heads below the surface. Wipe off all excess adhesive with a clean dampened cloth and place a G-clamp over both halving joints and a web-clamp round the edges of the assembly; tighten the clamps making sure all joints are square.
When clamped more adhesive will be squeezed out — wipe off immediately.
If you do not have a web-

clamp you can improvise with a length of strong rope. Put newspaper or cloth padding between the rope and the frame to prevent bruising the wood, tie the rope round the backrest assembly and tighten it with a screwdriver.

Stage 2

For the handles, draw a circle at one end of one of the main side rails A at the dimensions shown (**see 2**) with your compass set to a radius of 30mm. Draw the

Cutting list for softwood

Description	Key	Quantity	Dimensions
Main side rails	A	2	2000 × 124 × 22mm
Main end rails	B	2	800 × 124 × 22mm
Cross slats	C	16	800 × 72 × 22mm
Shaped cross slat	D	1	800 × 44 × 22mm
Backrest cross slats	E	4	736 × 72 × 22mm
Backrest uprights	F	2	750 × 72 × 22mm
Backrest top	G	1	800 × 72 × 22mm
Legs	H	2	300 × 44 × 44mm

curved cutting lines approximately to the dimensions shown (**see 2**) and cut off the waste with a coping saw; smooth the cut edges with medium fine, then fine, glasspaper. Trace the shape of the handle onto one end of the other main side rail A and cut off the waste as before. This ensures both handles will be identical.

Assembly diagram

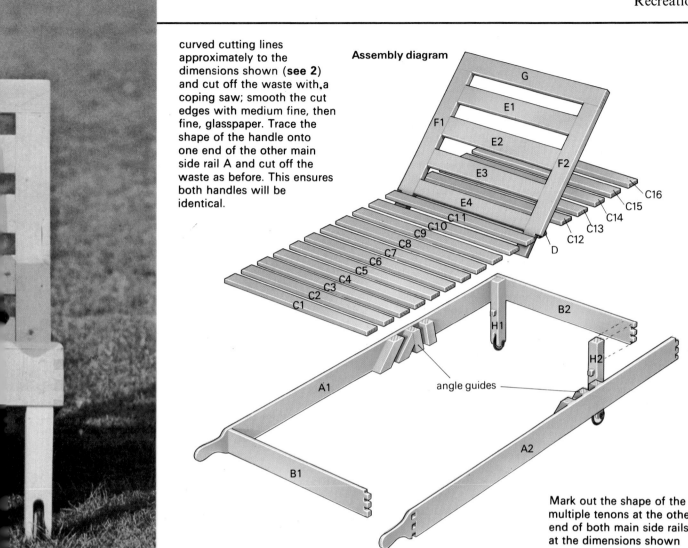

Mark out the shape of the multiple tenons at the other end of both main side rails A at the dimensions shown (**see 3a**) and cut them out with a tenon saw and an 18mm chisel.

Mark out and cut the tenons at either end of the main end rails B in the same way (**see 3c**). Mark out the required positions of the multiple mortises near the handles in both main side rails A at the dimensions shown (**see 3b**); chop out the waste with an 18mm chisel.

Cut with a tenon saw the backrest angle guides out of pieces of scrap wood to the dimensions shown (**see 4a**). To do this, use a protractor to mark the cutting lines on the timber; place each piece in a vice and cut very carefully along the cutting lines with a tenon saw. These angle guides must be cut very accurately or the backrest will not slide easily and squarely in position. Don't forget there are four angle guides to make for each main side rail A. Drill 5mm clearance holes in each backrest angle guide

Cutting plan for softwood

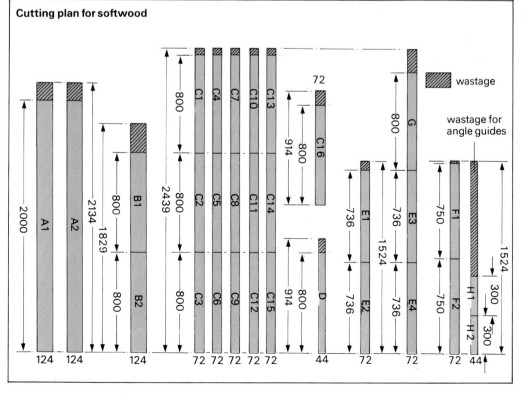

30mm centrally in from each end and countersink them to take No 8 screws. Hold each guide at the required position on the inside face of main side rail A1 (**see 4**) and mark through the clearance holes onto A with a long-bladed bradawl. Drill 2mm pilot holes at these points, apply adhesive to the fixing edge of each angle guide and screw the four guides firmly in position with the No 8 screws. Fix the other four angle guides to A2 in the same way.

Apply adhesive to the fixing edges of all the box joints and join main end rail B1 to the handle end of the two main side rails A (**see assembly diagram**). Wipe off excess adhesive. Slide the main end rail B2 into position at the leg end of the main side rails A and secure all joints with 38mm long panel pins (**see assembly diagram**), sinking the heads below the surface of the timber with a nail punch. The holes that remain can be filled later. Wipe off excess adhesive and make

absolutely sure all box joints are square and will remain so until the adhesive has set hard.

Cut a slot with a tenon saw in the bottom end of both legs H (**see 5**) by making two cuts with a tenon saw and chopping out the waste from between the cut lines with a chisel. Make the slot big enough to house the wheel with about 10mm clearance between the top of the wheel and the top of the slot. Make the arch shape at the top of the slot with a round file. Drill holes in each side of the slot of the same diameter as the fixing bolt for the wheel (**see 5**). Hold the wheel in position and slide the bolt through the holes and the wheel; tighten up with a wing nut, placing a washer between the nut and the wood.

Using a tenon saw, cut a 22mm square out of a piece of scrap wood, apply adhesive to one edge of it and fix it in position with 38mm long panel pins on the back face of the leg H so the top edge of the block is 150mm down

from top edge of H (**see 5**). Sink the pin heads below the surface of the timber with a nail punch. These small blocks stop the backrest falling out when it is strapped to the underside of the recliner while it is not being used.

Stage 3

Shape cross slat D by marking the cutting lines at each end and 100mm along the length of the slat (**see 6a**) using a protractor to mark the angles accurately. Remove the waste with a sharp chisel.

Drill two 5mm clearance holes 11mm in from each end and 20mm in from each edge (**see plan**) of all 16 cross slats C and one 5mm clearance hole 11mm in from each end of shaped cross slat D 12mm in from one edge. Lay these slats in the required position over the two main side rails A at the dimensions shown (**see side elevation**) and mark with a bradawl through the clearance holes in the slats onto the top edge of A1 and A2. When positioning the cross slats, don't forget to place the shaped cross slat D and mark through it with a bradawl in the same way. Remove the slats and drill 2mm pilot holes at these points, apply adhesive to the top edge of both main side rails A and screw all the cross slats C and the shaped cross slat D firmly down with the No 8 screws. Wipe off excess adhesive.

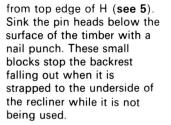

End elevation

G
E1
E2
E3

F2   C16   F1

clearance holes 5 diameter

44
74
H2   B1   H1

B2

25

25

800

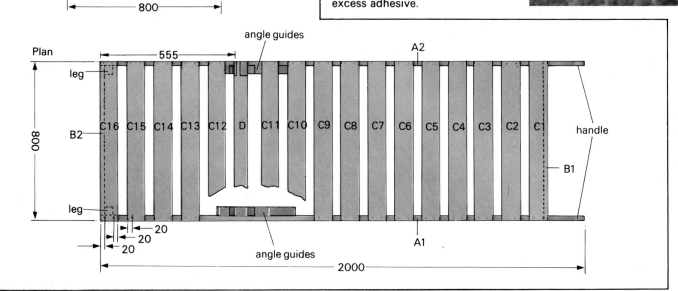

Plan

leg

angle guides

A2

555

B2   C16   C15   C14   C13   C12   D   C11   C10   C9   C8   C7   C6   C5   C4   C3   C2   C1

handle

B1

800

leg

20
20
20

angle guides

A1

2000

Stage 4

To fix the legs drill two 5mm clearance holes at each end of the main end rail B2 at the dimensions shown (**see end elevation**) and one 5mm clearance hole at the square end of each main side rail A at the dimensions shown (**see side elevation**) and countersink them to take No 10 screws.

Hold one of the legs in the required position and mark with a bradawl through these clearance holes onto the leg. Drill 2mm pilot holes at these points, apply adhesive to the fixing edges of H, spreading the adhesive no more than 124mm down from the top, then screw the leg firmly in position with the No 10 screws. Fix the second leg to the other main end rail

Elevations and plan
(dimensions in millimetres)

Side elevation

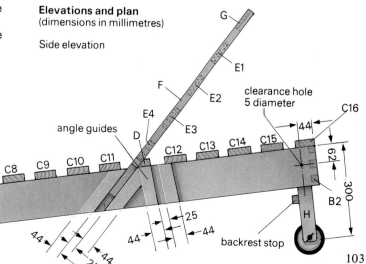

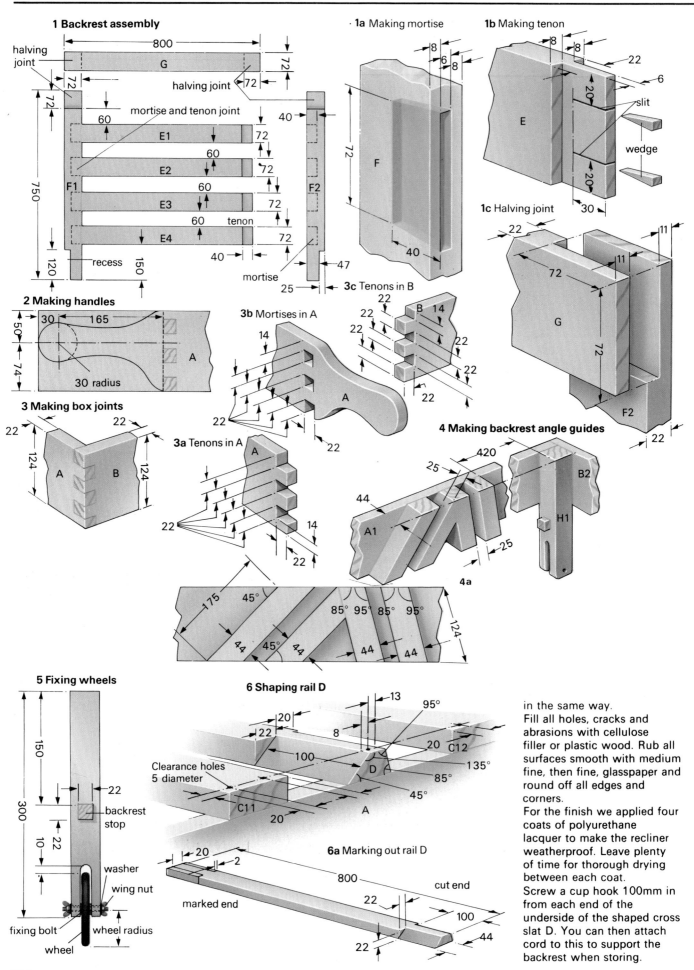

1 Backrest assembly

halving joint

800

72

halving joint 72

G

72

72

72

mortise and tenon joint

60

E1 72

750

60

E2 72

F1 60

E3 72

40

60 tenon

E4 72

120 recess 150 40

F2 47

mortise

25

1a Making mortise

8
6
8

72

F

40

1b Making tenon

8
8 22
6

20

E slit

wedge

20

30

1c Halving joint

22 11

72 11

G

72

F2

22

3c Tenons in B

22
22 B 14
22 22
22
22

3b Mortises in A

14

A

22

22

2 Making handles

30 165

50

74

A

30 radius

3 Making box joints

22 22

124 124

A B

3a Tenons in A

A

22

14

22

4 Making backrest angle guides

420

25

44 B2

A1 H1

25

4a

175 45°

85° 95° 85° 95°

124

44 45° 44 44 44

5 Fixing wheels

150

300

22

backrest stop

22

10

washer

wing nut

fixing bolt wheel radius

wheel

6 Shaping rail D

13

20 95°

22

8 20 C12

100 135°

Clearance holes 5 diameter 85°

C11 45°

20 A

6a Marking out rail D

20 2

800 cut end

marked end 22

100

22 44

in the same way.
Fill all holes, cracks and abrasions with cellulose filler or plastic wood. Rub all surfaces smooth with medium fine, then fine, glasspaper and round off all edges and corners.
For the finish we applied four coats of polyurethane lacquer to make the recliner weatherproof. Leave plenty of time for thorough drying between each coat.
Screw a cup hook 100mm in from each end of the underside of the shaped cross slat D. You can then attach cord to this to support the backrest when storing.

GARDEN BENCH

This slatted timber garden bench finished in teak-coloured preservative will look well in any setting and can seat three adults comfortably.

TOOLS AND MATERIALS

timber (see cutting list)
measuring tape, pencil and try square
protractor, sliding bevel and marking gauge
medium fine and fine glasspaper
tenon saw and coping saw, block plane, 16mm chisel
hand or electric drill, 2, 5, 9 and 12mm bits
three sash cramps and two G-clamps
screwdriver, countersink bit, mallet
850mm of 9mm diameter dowel
No 8 brass countersunk screws 38mm long, sockets to fit
water-resistant woodworking adhesive and clean cloth
wood preservative and 25mm paint brush (for finish)

Cutting list for softwood

Description	Key	Quantity	Dimensions
Slats	A	16	1500 x 45 x 22mm
Back legs	B	2	830 x 70 x 44mm
Front legs	C	2	334 x 70 x 44mm
Horizontals	D	2	490 x 70 x 44mm
Brace	E	1	1250 x 73 x 33mm
Feet	F	2	556 x 70 x 44mm

Stage 1

Measure and cut with a tenon saw all the pieces of timber according to the dimensions shown (**see cutting list**).
Cut off the waste with a tenon saw from the top end of both back legs B according to the dimensions shown (**see 1**), mark out the curve in the front edge of both back legs and cut out the waste with a coping saw. Using a protractor, sliding bevel and marking gauge, mark out the angled tenon at the bottom end of both the back legs according to the dimensions shown (**see 1**) and remove the waste from each one with a tenon saw; keep slightly to the waste side of the cutting line in every case.
Mark out the angled mortise in the front edge of both back legs according to the dimensions shown (**see 1**), drill out the bulk of the waste

from each one with a 12mm diameter bit and remove the rest of the waste with a sharp 16mm chisel.

Stage 2

Mark out and cut the angled tenon at both ends of both front legs C according to the dimensions shown (**see 2**). Mark out and cut the angled tenon at one end of both horizontals D to the dimensions shown (**see 3**). Mark out and cut off the waste from the other end of both horizontals, then mark and chop out the angled mortise in the bottom edge of each one according to the dimensions shown (**see 3**). Mark out the 77 degree angle at the front end of both feet F (**see 4**) and cut off the waste from each one with a tenon saw. Mark and chop out the two angled mortises in the top edges of both feet according to the dimensions shown (**see 4**).

Assembly diagram
(slats removed)

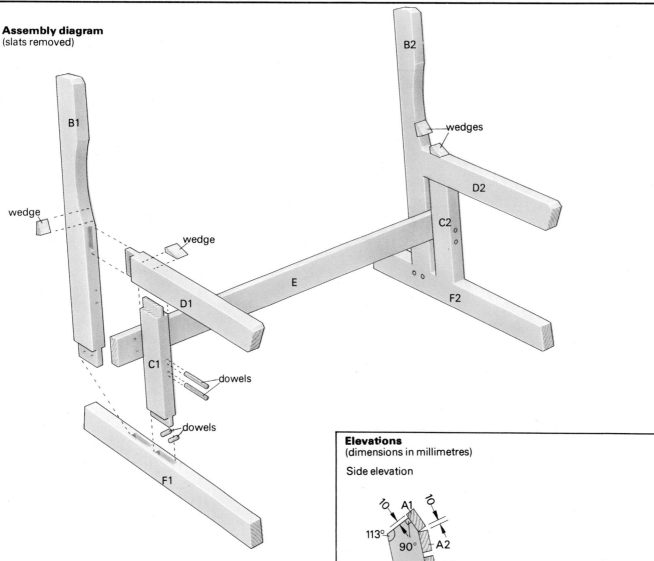

wedge

wedge

wedge

B2

B1

D2

C2

E

D1

F2

C1

dowels

dowels

F1

Stage 3

Fit the front legs C into the horizontals D, then fit the horizontals into the back legs B (**see assembly diagram**). Fit the feet F onto the front and back legs and check all joints fit neatly and tightly together. Trim with a sharp chisel joints that do not fit. Rub smooth all surfaces of all pieces in the end frames (B, C, D and F) with medium fine, then fine, glasspaper. Apply water-resistant woodworking adhesive to all joint surfaces and assemble the end frames in the same order as before, tightening sash cramps over the joints and placing wedge-shaped pieces of scrap wood between the cramps and the timber both for protection and to keep the cramps in the required position (**see 5**). Wipe off all excess adhesive with a clean dampened cloth and leave the cramps tightly

in position until the adhesive has set hard.
When the adhesive has set, remove the cramps and drill two 9mm diameter holes 35mm deep in each foot and back leg tenon and in each back leg and horizontal tenon at the dimensions shown (**see side elevation**). Cut eight 35mm lengths of the 9mm diameter dowel, apply adhesive to the cut lengths and ram them firmly into the holes with a mallet. Wipe off excess adhesive and trim the dowels flush with the surface using a block plane.

Stage 4

Using a block plane chamfer the top edges of all 16 slats A. Drill a 5mm diameter clearance hole 222mm in from both ends of each one (**see 6**), countersink them to take No 8 screws and hammer the brass sockets into the clearance holes.

Elevations
(dimensions in millimetres)

Side elevation

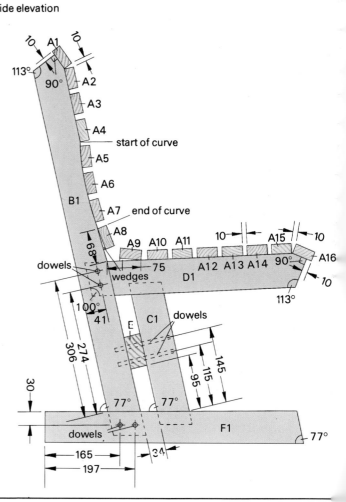

10   A1   10

113°   90°   A2

A3

A4

start of curve

A5

A6

B1   A7   end of curve

A8

68°   A9   A10   A11   10   A15   10

dowels   75   A12 A13 A14   90°   A16

wedges   D1   10

100°   113°

41   E   C1   dowels

306   274   145

115   95

30   77°   77°

dowels   F1   77°

165   34

197

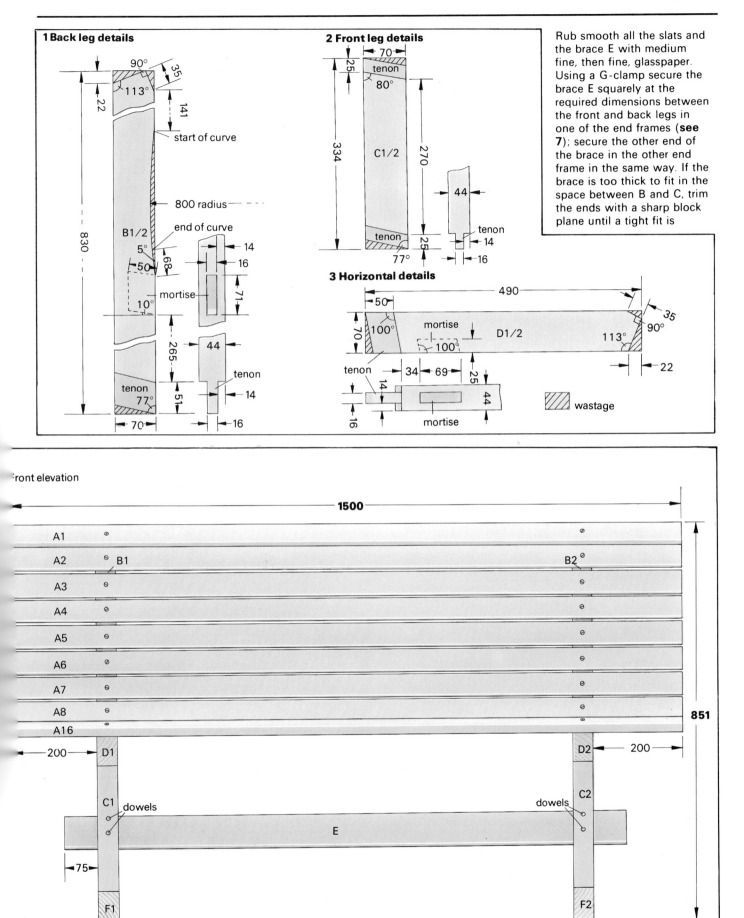

1 Back leg details

90°
35
113°
22
141
start of curve

830

800 radius

B1/2
end of curve
5°
50
68
mortise
10°
265
44
tenon
tenon
77°
14
70
16
14
16
71
51

2 Front leg details

70
25
tenon
80°
334
C1/2
270
44
tenon
tenon
77°
14
25
16

3 Horizontal details

50
490
mortise
35
70
100°
D1/2
90°
100°
113°
tenon
34
69
25
22
tenon
14
44
16
mortise

wastage

Rub smooth all the slats and the brace E with medium fine, then fine, glasspaper. Using a G-clamp secure the brace E squarely at the required dimensions between the front and back legs in one of the end frames (**see 7**); secure the other end of the brace in the other end frame in the same way. If the brace is too thick to fit in the space between B and C, trim the ends with a sharp block plane until a tight fit is

Front elevation

1500

A1
A2 B1   B2
A3
A4
A5
A6
A7
A8
A16

851

200 D1   D2 200
C1 dowels   dowels C2
75
E
F1   F2

1012

4 Foot details

mortises

44

6 14

72 · 34 · 72 · 225

50 · 77° · 77° · 25

70 · mortises · F1/2 · 77°

556

5 Cramping end frames

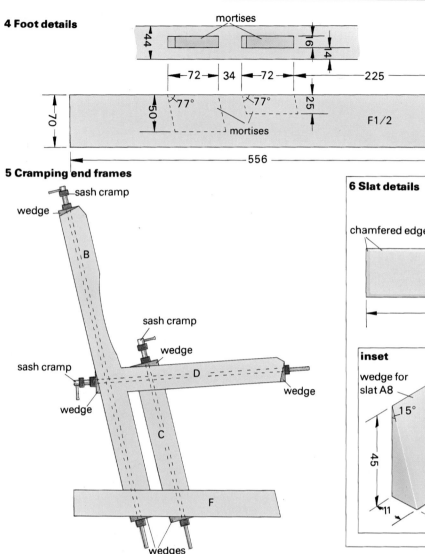

sash cramp

wedge

B

sash cramp

wedge

sash cramp

D

wedge

wedge

wedge

C

F

wedges

6 Slat details

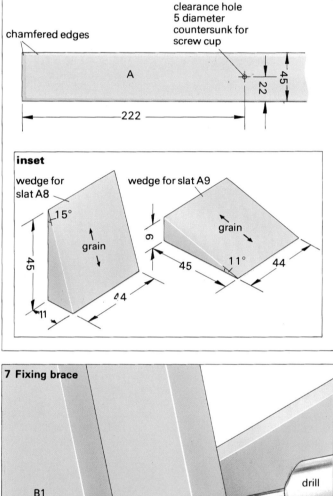

chamfered edges

clearance hole
5 diameter
countersunk for
screw cup

A

45

22

222

inset

wedge for
slat A8

wedge for slat A9

15°

grain

grain

45

6

45

11°

44

44

11

7 Fixing brace

B1

C1

E

drill

dowel hole
9 diameter
130 deep

scrap wood

scrap wood

G-clamp

achieved. Check the brace is square to both end frames and drill the two 9mm diameter dowel holes, 130mm deep, at the dimensions shown (**see side elevation**).

Cut four 140mm lengths of 9mm diameter dowel, remove the G-clamps, apply adhesive to the areas of the brace which will be in contact with the front and back legs and clamp the brace in position in the end frames as before. Pour some adhesive into the dowel holes and push the cut lengths of dowel into position, ramming them firmly home with a mallet.

Cut the four softwood wedges out of a piece of scrap wood according to the dimensions shown (**see 6 inset**); these are used when fixing the slats A8 and A9 to create a smooth curve (**see side elevation**). Apply adhesive to the fixing area of the slats A1–8 and fix the

slats firmly and squarely in position, with the 38mm long brass screws, at the required dimensions (**see elevations**), remembering to drill a 2mm pilot hole for each screw and to place the larger wedges under the slat A8. Wipe off excess adhesive and fix the slats A9–16 to the top face of the horizontals D in the same way, placing the wedges under the slat A9.

When the adhesive has set hard, remove the protruding dowels in the front legs C with a sharp chisel and block plane.

For the finish, apply three coats of wood preservative; we chose a natural wood colour although there are many bright colours available if you prefer.

SWING SEAT

Our swing seat is a simple design using gas pipe tubing for economy. The whole structure can be taken apart for winter storage, the seat cushions are removable and the canopy is adjustable.

Cutting list for gas pipe

Description	Key	Quantity	Dimensions
Uprights	A	4	1700 x 12mm*
Top	B	1	1770 x 19mm*
Front seat supports	C	2	1200 x 12mm*
Rear seat supports	D	2	1250 x 12mm*
Long seat retainers	E	2	1350 x 19mm*
Backrest retainer	F	1	1350 x 12mm*
Short seat retainers	G	2	650 x 12mm*
Canopy supports	H	4	415 x 12mm*

Cutting list for mild steel

Description	Key	Quantity	Dimensions
Braces (black)	J	2	120 x 20 x 5mm†
Gussets (black)	K	2	270 x 20 x 5mm†
Hooks (bright)	L	2	165 x 8mm*
Tie rods (bright)	M	2	750 x 6mm*

* diameter   † thick

Stage 1

Measure and cut with a hacksaw all the gas pipe and black and bright mild steel pieces according to the dimensions shown (see cutting lists); smooth the cut ends with a fine flat file. All the tubular pieces (gas pipe) are held together by bolts passed through holes in the flattened ends. With the exception of the top B, all the tube ends are flattened flush with one side (see 1a); the ends of the top B are flattened so the flat portions are central on the tube (see 1b).

To flatten the tubes a blacksmith's anvil is ideal, although you could use a 50mm thick block of steel or cast iron. The ends of the tubes are heated with a blowtorch until they are red hot, placed on the anvil and beaten flat with a hammer; only the end 50mm of the top B should be placed on the anvil to ensure the flat portions are central on the tube (see 1b). The corners of the flat ends must be rounded off with a flat file when the steel has cooled; this is important for safety

Flatten one end of each upright A, round off the corners with a flat file, place the flat end of each one in a vice and bend the tubes to form the 15 degree angle (see 2). Mark out the centre for the 9mm hole in the flat portion of each upright at the dimensions shown (see 2) and make an indentation in the steel at these points with a centre punch to ensure the drill bit will not slip out of position. Drill the 9mm diameter holes. Mark out, punch and drill the two 6.5mm diameter holes in the same way, making sure they are at right-angles to the flat end in each case (see 2). Flatten both ends of the top B, making sure the flat ends are central on the tube and parallel to each other; round off the corners with a flat file. Mark out, punch and drill the 9mm diameter hole in both

TOOLS AND MATERIALS

gas pipe tubing and mild steel (see cutting lists)
measuring tape, pencil and try square, spanners, hacksaw
fine flat file, fine emery cloth, sliding bevel, protractor
blacksmith's anvil or 50mm thick steel or cast-iron block
blowtorch, hammer, electric drill, 4, 6.5 and 9mm bits
centre punch, vice, self-grip wrench, screwdriver
lubricating oil, M.6 and M.8 dies, die stock
M.6 round head machine screws 25 and 35mm long and nuts
  to fit
M.8 hexagonal head machine screws 25 and 35mm long and
  nuts to fit, four rubber ferrules, two M.8 dome head nuts
matt black enamel or aluminium paint, 25mm paint brush
  (for finish)

For cushions, sling and canopy
1200 × 500 × 100mm medium density foam (seat cushion)
1200 × 400 × 50mm medium density foam (backrest cushion)
2.6m of 25mm wide webbing tape, 5.5m of cotton fringing
two expanding curtain rods to stretch to 1330mm long
scissors, needle and matching button thread
7m of 150cm wide strong fabric (preferably canvas)

Assembly diagram

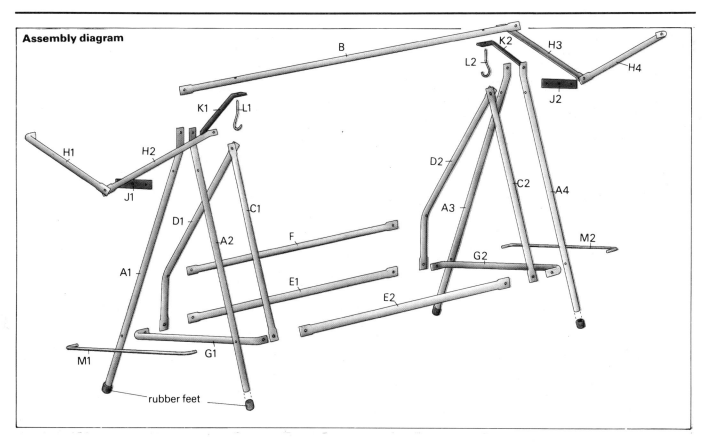

rubber feet

flat ends at the dimensions shown (**see 3**). Mark out, punch and drill the other two 9mm diameter holes in B at the dimensions shown (**see 3**), making sure they are at right-angles to the flat ends. Flatten both ends of both front seat supports C so one flat end is at a right-angle to the other; make one left and one right-hand support and round off the corners with a flat file (**see 4**). Mark out, punch and drill the 6.5mm hole in one flat end and the 9mm diameter hole in the other flat end at the dimensions shown (**see 4**). Flatten one end of both rear seat supports D and round off the corners with a file. Fill them, one at a time, with dry sand and stop the open end of the tube with a bung made from a piece of scrap wood; make certain the sand is packed tightly by ramming it down with a length of scrap dowel or metal rod. Mark out the position of the bend on each tube by making a mark with a centre punch at the dimensions shown (**see 5**); using a blowtorch heat this area until red hot. Place each tube, one at a time, in a vice and check the flat end is in the correct position (**see 5 inset**). Pull the tube to the

correct angle (**see 5**), remove it from the vice and empty out the sand; to ensure the correct angle, it is a good idea to make a hardboard template first. Bend the other rear seat support D in the same way and flatten the open end of both tubes, taking care to make one for the left-hand side of the seat and one for the right (**see 5 and assembly diagram**). Round off the corners of the flattened ends as before. Mark out, punch and drill the 9mm diameter hole and the two 6.5mm holes in both rear seat supports D at the dimensions shown (**see 5**). Flatten both ends of both long seat retainers E and the backrest retainer F so the flattened ends are parallel; round off the corners with a flat file (**see 6**). Mark out, punch and drill the 6.5mm diameter hole in both flat ends of all three tubes at the dimensions shown (**see 6**). Flatten both ends of both short seat retainers G so the flattened ends are parallel and bend the ends to right-angles while the steel is still hot (**see 7**). Round off the corners with a flat file. Mark out, punch and drill the 6.5mm diameter hole in the ends of both tubes at the

dimensions shown (**see 7**). Flatten both ends of all four canopy supports H so the ends are parallel and bend the shorter end of each to a right-angle while the steel is still hot (**see 8**); round off the corners with a flat file. Mark out, punch and drill the 9mm and 4mm diameter holes in the ends of the four tubes at the dimensions shown (**see 8**).

Stage 2

Smooth all surfaces of all the tubular pieces (gas pipe) with some fine emery cloth and give all surfaces two coats of matt black enamel or aluminium paint.

Stage 3

Mark out, punch and drill the 9mm diameter hole and the 6.5mm diameter holes in both braces J at the dimensions shown (**see 9**).
Mark out the bend line 25mm in from each end of both gussets K (**see 10**) and place them in a vice, one at a time, so one of the bend lines is just above the top of the vice jaws. Hammer the gusset just above the vice until you obtain the correct angle; form the angle at the other end in

the same way. Make the second gusset. Mark out, punch and drill the 9mm diameter hole in the ends (**see 10**).
Hold one end of one of the hooks L in a self-grip wrench, clamp a length of scrap gas pipe firmly and horizontally in a vice and, using a blowtorch, heat the hook until red hot; hammer it round the projecting gas pipe to form the curved end (**see 11**). Remove the gas pipe from the vice and bend the hook according to the dimensions shown (**see 11**). Make the second hook in the same way. Lubricate the straight end of both hooks with light oil and, using an M.8 die held in a die stock, cut 50mm of thread (**see 11**); check the die is held squarely to each hook.
Mark out the bend positions 30mm in from each end of both tie rods M with a centre punch (**see 12**). Place one of the rods in a vice so 30mm protrudes from the top of the vice jaws and hammer this end over to a right-angle; there should be no need to heat the rods before bending them. Bend the other end parallel to the first bend and form the second tie rod in the same way. Lubricate the ends

of both rods and, using an
M.6 die, cut 15mm of thread
(**see 12**).
Smooth all surfaces of the
mild steel pieces with fine
emery cloth and apply a
finish as before to all
surfaces except the threaded
portions.

Stage 4

Cut the main piece of fabric
for the seat cushion cover
into one 1230mm square,

1 Flattening gas pipe ends
(dimensions in millimetres)

1a All pipes except top

1b Top pipe

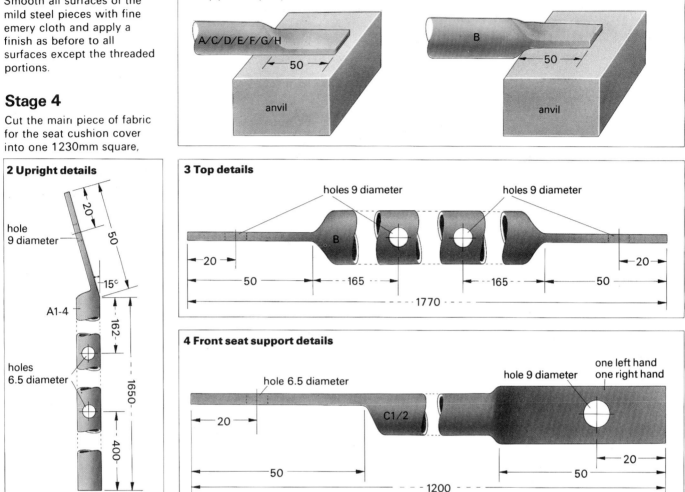

2 Upright details

3 Top details

4 Front seat support details

5 Rear seat support details

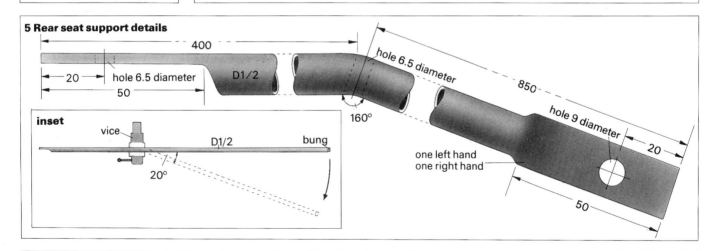

6 Long seat and backrest retainer details

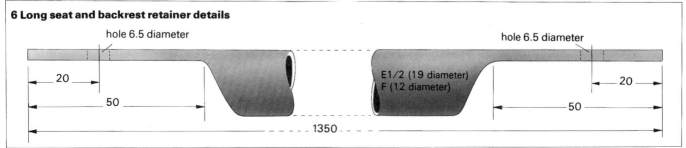

7 Short seat retainer details

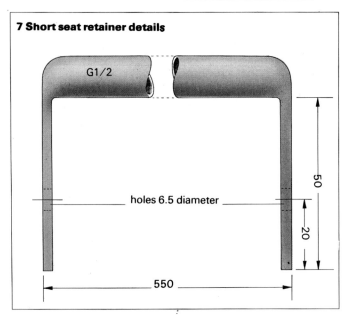

G1/2

holes 6.5 diameter

50

20

550

8 Canopy support details

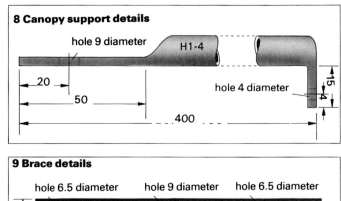

hole 9 diameter

H1-4

hole 4 diameter

20

50

400

15

4

9 Brace details

hole 6.5 diameter   hole 9 diameter   hole 6.5 diameter

20

10

42   42

60   60

10 Gusset details

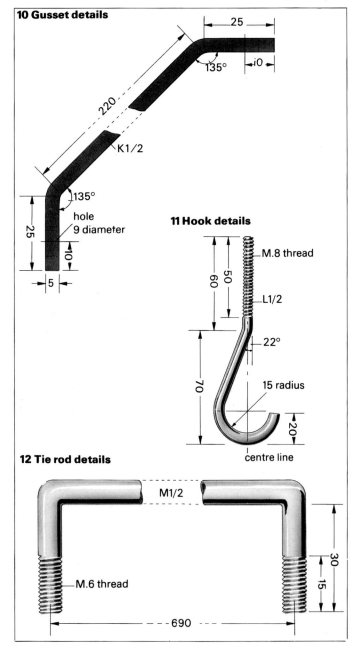

25

135°

10

220

K1/2

135°

25

10

hole
9 diameter

5

11 Hook details

M.8 thread

50

60

L1/2

22°

70

15 radius

20

centre line

12 Tie rod details

M1/2

M.6 thread

30

15

690

then cut two pieces measuring 530 × 130mm for the ends (**see cutting plan for fabric**). Finish off the raw edges of the fabric with zig-zag stitching to prevent them fraying. Making 15mm seams in all cases, stitch the three pieces together in the positions shown (**see 13**); leave three edges of one of the small end pieces unsewn so you can turn the cover right side out and insert the foam.

For the backrest cushion cover cut one piece of fabric measuring 1230 × 930mm, then cut two pieces measuring 430 × 80mm for the ends (**see cutting plan for fabric**). Finish off the raw edges of the fabric with zig-zag stitching to prevent them fraying. Make the backrest cushion cover in the same way as the seat cushion cover (**see 13**), turn both covers right side out and insert the 100mm thick slab of foam into the seat cover and the 50mm thick slab into the backrest cover. Slip-stitch the three unsewn edges on both flaps (**see 13 inset**); these edges can be easily undone should you want to remove and wash the covers. Cut the canvas sling to the dimensions shown (**see cutting plan for fabric**) and stitch 15mm hems all round. Fold the sling over to the wrong side of the fabric and double-stitch along its width at the dimensions shown (**see 14**) using a matching button thread.

For the canopy cut one piece of fabric measuring 1830 × 1430mm and two pieces measuring 830 × 330mm for the ends (**see cutting plan for fabric**). Finish off the raw edges of the fabric with zig-zag stitching to prevent them fraying. Turn over and stitch 15mm hems on both long edges of the main piece and on one long edge of both end pieces. Baste and stitch the ends to the main piece, leaving 15mm seams, so the sewn hems meet in the corners (**see 15**). Cut two lengths of webbing tape (about 1300mm long and 25mm wide) and stitch these to the inside of the canopy at the positions shown (**see 15**); these are to take the expanding curtain rods which clip onto the canopy supports H (**see assembly diagram**). We stitched some cotton fringing all round the bottom edges of the canopy.

Stage 5

Push the rubber ferrules onto the bottom ends of the four uprights A (**see assembly diagram**). Assemble the main frame first (uprights A and top B) using M.8 screws 25mm long for the top corners. Fit the braces J to the outside of the frame with M.6 screws 35mm long and nuts. Fit the tie rods M in the uprights and secure them with M.6 nuts on the inside of the frame.

Twist an M.8 nut right to the bottom of the thread on both hooks L, push the hooks through the gussets K and the top B and secure them, so the hooks are facing inwards, with a dome head M.8 nut at the top of the frame (**see assembly diagram**; cut the thread on the hook to length with a hacksaw. Fit the unattached ends of K1 and K2 to the inside of the braces J with the 35mm long M.8

screws and nuts so the screw heads are on the inside. Fit the canopy supports H over the ends of these screws (**see assembly diagram**) and tighten another M.8 nut against each support; these nuts can be slackened to adjust the angle of the canopy. Alternatively use wing nuts.
Assemble one side of the seat frame (long and short seat retainers E and G, backrest

retainer F and front and rear seat supports C and D), leaving the nuts loose. Slide the sling over E1, E2 and F; assemble the other side of the seat frame, leaving one end of the backrest retainer unattached. Attach the seat supports C and D to the hooks (**see assembly diagram**), fix the free end of the backrest retainer and tighten all nuts, checking the frame is square.

Thread the expanding curtain rods through the channels in the inside of the canopy, turn the canopy the right side out and attach the hooks in the ends of the curtain rods to the holes in the ends of the canopy supports H.

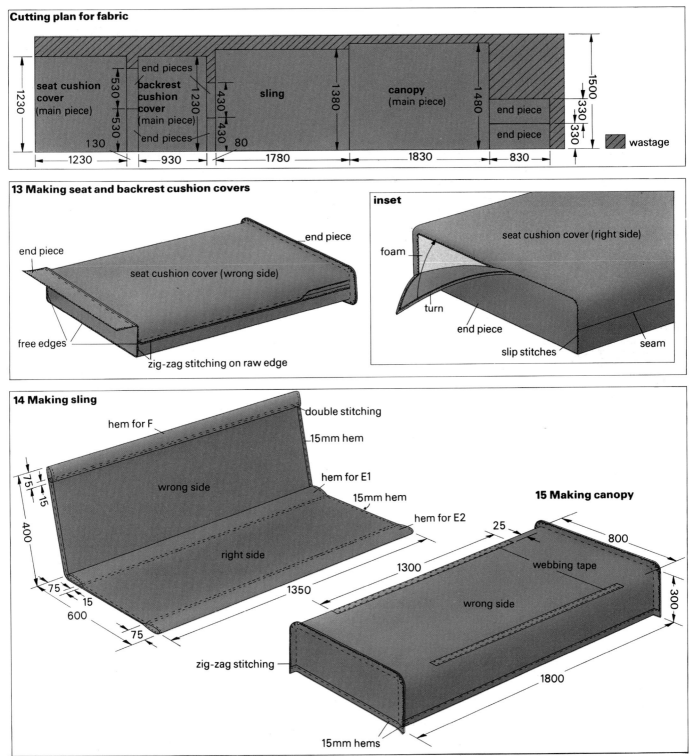

Cutting plan for fabric

seat cushion cover (main piece)

end pieces

backrest cushion cover (main piece)

end pieces

sling

canopy (main piece)

end piece

end piece

1230 · 530 · 530 · 1230 · 430 · 430 · 1380 · 1480 · 1500 · 330 · 330 · 130 · 80

1230 · 930 · 1780 · 1830 · 830

wastage

13 Making seat and backrest cushion covers

end piece

seat cushion cover (wrong side)

end piece

free edges

zig-zag stitching on raw edge

inset

seat cushion cover (right side)

foam

turn

end piece

slip stitches

seam

14 Making sling

hem for F

double stitching

15mm hem

wrong side

hem for E1

15mm hem

hem for E2

right side

75 · 15 · 400 · 75 · 15 · 600 · 75

1350

1300

zig-zag stitching

15 Making canopy

25

800

webbing tape

wrong side

300

1800

15mm hems

PICNIC TABLE

This attractive picnic table folds away like a brief case and can be put up in seconds simply by clipping the legs in position. It is light and easy to carry and there is enough room inside for a few plates, serviettes and cutlery. Just the job for the summer.

Stage 1

Measure and cut with a tenon saw all the pieces of timber to the dimensions shown (**see cutting list**) and label each part with the appropriate code letter.
Using a tenon saw and mitre box (or guide) mitre each end of the frame sides A and ends B, apply woodworking adhesive to the fixing edge of each mitre and assemble each frame clamping with web-clamps until the adhesive has set. Check each frame is square and wipe off all excess adhesive with a clean dampened cloth.
When the adhesive has set,

remove the clamps and reinforce the mitre joints with the 3mm diameter dowels which are inserted into holes drilled at right-angles to each mitre. To do this, mark out the hole centres on the outside face of the frame sides A 22mm in from each end and 22mm in from the top and bottom edges. Drill a 3mm diameter hole right through the mitre joint at each of these points.
Cut the 3mm dowel into eight 36mm lengths, apply adhesive to each one and push them in position. Wipe off excess adhesive with a clean dampened cloth and remove the protruding

TOOLS AND MATERIALS

timber (see cutting list)
measuring tape, pencil and try square
tenon saw, coping or jig saw, mitre box or guide
hammer and nail punch, two web-clamps, vice
screwdriver and countersink bit
medium fine and fine glasspaper
combination square or sliding bevel or protractor
pair of compasses, piece of scrap hardboard (for template)
hand or electric drill, 3, 5, 6 and 12mm bits
15 and 18mm chisels, block plane
water-resistant woodworking adhesive, clean cloth

For assembly

1600mm of 12mm dowel for two 410 and two 366mm lengths
400mm of 3mm dowel for eight 40mm and four 16mm lengths
one 6mm round head bolt 75mm long with wing nut and washers
panel pins 18, 25, 32 and 38mm long
No 8 countersunk rustproof screws 45mm long
No 6 rustproof countersunk screws 32mm long
one 6mm and four 12mm wide Terry clips
two 50mm long brass butt hinges and 38mm long rustproof
    screws to fit
two small brass toggle catches

For finish

wood stain and lint-free rag, clear matt polyurethane
    lacquer or primer, undercoat and top coat
50mm paint brush

Cutting list for softwood & plywood

Description	Key	Quantity	Dimensions
Frame sides	A	4	564 x 44 x 22mm
Frame ends	B	4	486 x 44 x 22mm
Cross slats	C	22	442 x 32 x 9mm
Supporting battens	D	4	520 x 32 x 16mm
Legs	E	8	500 x 32 x 22mm
Handles (plywood)	G	2	486 x 75 x 6mm

Overall dimensions (when folded)
608mm long, 486mm wide, 88mm thick (24 × 19 × 3in).
Project dimensions are in metric only and do not allow for
cutting wastages.

dowel with a chisel.
Mark out the shaping lines on
all four frame sides A and
two of the four frame ends B
according to the dimensions
shown (**see end section**).
Place each frame in a vice
and plane down to these
lines. Smooth all surfaces
with medium fine, then fine,
glasspaper. The two unshaped
frame ends B will be hinged
together to form the centre of

the table.
Mark the slots for the toggle
catches 90mm in from each
end of both shaped frame
ends B (**see plan**), make
two cuts with a tenon saw to
a depth of 5mm (**see 1**) and
spaced according to the width
of your catches and
remove the waste from
between the cut lines with a
chisel. The catches should
fit flush with the timber when

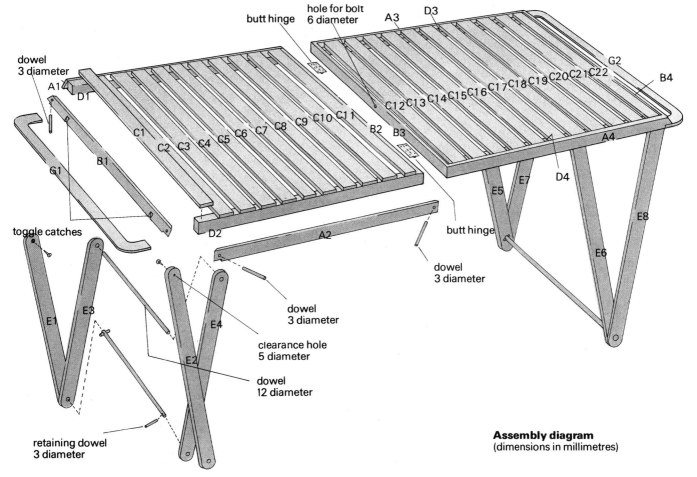

Assembly diagram
(dimensions in millimetres)

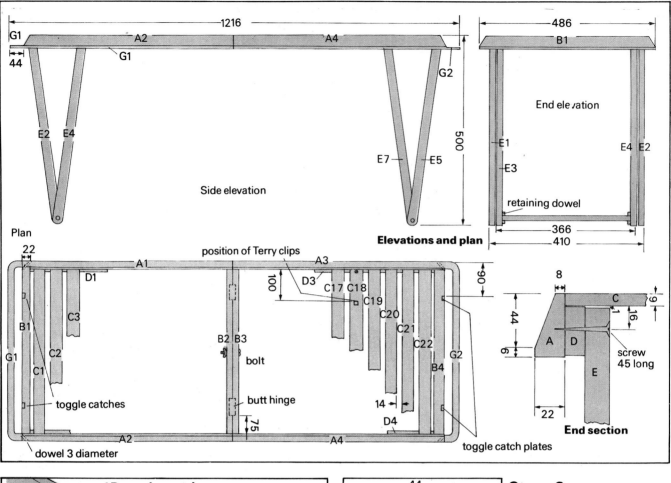

Elevations and plan

Side elevation

End elevation

retaining dowel

Plan

position of Terry clips

bolt

toggle catches

butt hinge

toggle catch plates

dowel 3 diameter

End section

screw 45 long

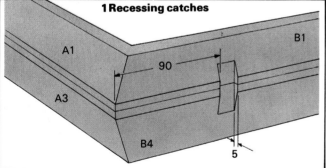

1 Recessing catches

screwed in place so try them for fit and make the slots deeper if necessary.

Stage 2

For the handles, mark on the cutting lines at the dimensions shown (**see 2**). Set your compass to a radius of 44mm, place the compass point at X (**see 2**) and draw the outside curve. Place the point at Y to draw the other outside curve and draw the inside curves by placing the compass point at X and Y, with the radius set at 22mm. Remove the waste with a coping or jig saw and smooth all cut edges with medium fine, then fine, glasspaper.

Use this finished handle as a template to mark out the second handle. This ensures both handles are identical. Make the slots on the underside of the corners of the frame where the handles are to be (**see 2 inset**). These slots must be 22mm square and 6mm deep to house the thickness of the plywood. Remove the waste from the slots with an 18mm chisel, apply a layer of adhesive to all four slots and pin the handles in position using the 25mm long panel pins. Wipe off excess adhesive.

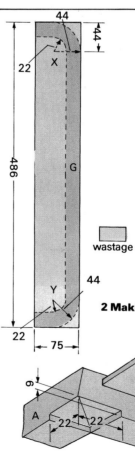

wastage

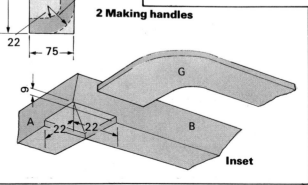

2 Making handles

Inset

Stage 3

Apply adhesive to one 32mm wide face of each supporting batten D and, using the 38mm long panel pins, fix the battens in position 9mm down from the top on the inside face of the frame sides A (**see end section**). Wipe off excess adhesive with a clean dampened cloth.

Apply adhesive to the top edge of all four supporting battens D and to each end of all the cross slats C and pin the slats in position at the dimensions shown (**see plan**), using two 18mm long panel pins for each end of each slat. Punch all pin heads

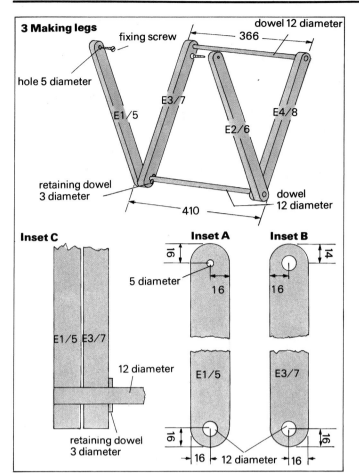

3 Making legs
dowel 12 diameter
366
fixing screw
hole 5 diameter
E1/5
E3/7
E4/8
E2/6
retaining dowel 3 diameter
410
dowel 12 diameter

Inset C
E1/5 E3/7
12 diameter
retaining dowel 3 diameter

Inset A
16
5 diameter
16
E1/5
16
16 12 diameter 16

Inset B
14
16
E3/7
16

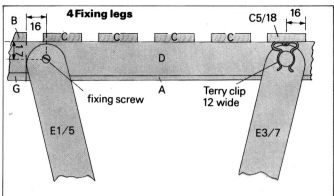

4 Fixing legs
B
16
C
C
C
C
C5/18
16
17
G
D
A
fixing screw
Terry clip 12 wide
E1/5
E3/7

5 Hinge detail and bolt hole
A2
A4
75
D2
D4
butt hinge
C11 B2 C12
B3
bolt

below the surface of the timber with a nail punch. Wipe off excess adhesive. Drill a 4mm diameter clearance hole 8mm in from each end of the fifth slat in from the handle end of both frames and countersink them to take No 6 screws. Mark through these holes with a bradawl and drive the No 6 screws firmly home. These slats will take some of the pressure exerted by the legs when weight is put on the table and they therefore require a stronger fixing.

Stage 4

To make the curve at both ends of each leg E first make a hardboard template. This ensures all 16 curves will be identical. Mark a 32mm square onto a piece of scrap hardboard, place the point of your compass at the centre of this square (where the diagonals cross) and draw a semicircle of 16mm radius. Remove the waste with a coping saw and smooth the cut edge with fine glasspaper. Place this template at each end of each leg and trace

round it with a pencil. Cut off the waste from the ends of the legs with a coping saw and smooth the curves with medium fine, then fine, glasspaper.
Drill a 12mm diameter hole at both ends of four of the legs but only at one end of the other four at the dimensions shown (**see 3a and b**).
With a tenon saw cut the 12mm dowel into two 410mm lengths and two 366mm lengths. To assemble each leg, apply adhesive to the inside of the hole at one end of two of the legs with holes drilled at both ends and insert the 366mm length of dowel (**see 3**). Make sure these legs are parallel by laying them on a perfectly flat surface and pin through them into the dowel with 25mm long panel pins, making sure the ends of the dowel are flush with the outside faces of the legs. Push the 410mm dowel in position (**see 3**) and pin into it through the outer legs only, making sure its ends are flush with the outside faces of the outer legs.

Drill a 3mm diameter hole through the 410mm dowel just inside each inner leg (**see 3c**), cut the 3mm dowel into two 16mm lengths, apply adhesive to each one and push them in position so 2mm protrudes at either side of the dowel. These small retaining dowels prevent the inner leg sliding out of position. Wipe off all excess adhesive and assemble the other leg in the same way.
To fix the legs in position, drill a 5mm diameter clearance hole at the unattached end of all four outer legs (**see 3b**) at the dimensions shown. Countersink these holes to take No 8 screws and fix the legs in place (loosely enough for them to pivot easily) at the dimensions shown (**see 4**) with No 8 screws 45mm long.

Stage 5

Fill all holes, cracks and abrasions with plastic wood and rub all surfaces smooth with medium fine, then fine, glasspaper.
For a finish we applied a

dark green stain with a lint-free rag and four coats of clear matt polyurethane lacquer for weather protection. Allow plenty of time for each coat to dry before applying the next.
To paint the table apply a coat of primer, an undercoat and at least two top coats, allowing time for each to dry before applying the next.
On the underside of the fifth slat from the handle end of each frame screw two 12mm Terry clips in position with the 6mm long rustproof screws. These clips should be about 100mm in from each end of the cross slats C5 and 18 (**see 4**); they hold the legs in position when the table is in use.
To fix the two frames together, mark and cut a recess for the hinges 75mm in from each end of the unshaped frame ends B (**see 5**). Make these recesses the same depth as the thickness of the hinge leaves and screw the hinges firmly in position with the 38mm long countersunk rustproof screws.
Drill a 6mm diameter hole in the centre of each hinged frame end B (**see 5**) so, when the table is in use, a bolt can be inserted for extra strength and stability. Screw the 6mm wide Terry clip in position as before to the underside of one of the cross slats near the middle; this houses the stabilizing bolt so you do not lose it when the table is not being used.
Screw the body of each catch in position inside the slots in one frame end B using 25mm long screws to fit and screw the catch-plates inside the slots in the other frame end B in the same way.

TILE-TOPPED TABLE

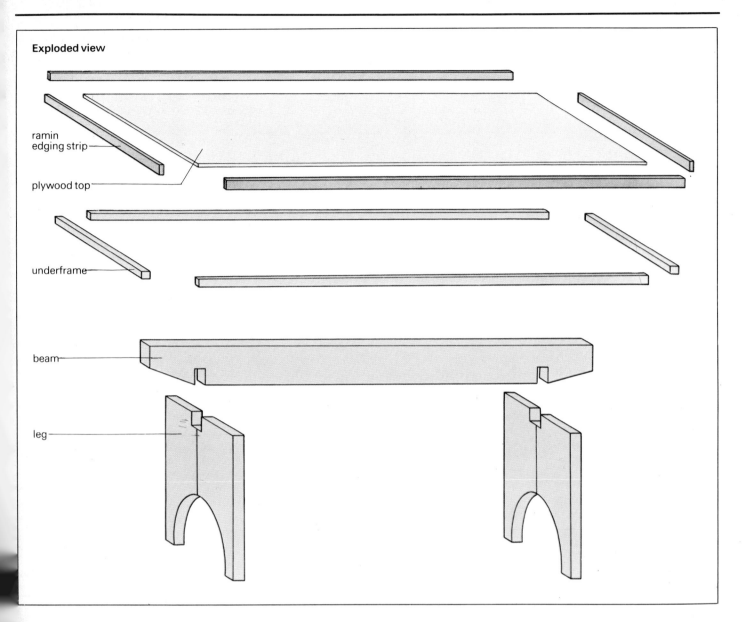

Exploded view

ramin
edging strip

plywood top

underframe

beam

leg

This tile-topped table is very simple to make and is one that you will use constantly during the summer months. Handy for drinks or an al fresco buffet party, it is equally useful indoors, too.

Tools

steel measuring tape
set square and pencil
hand saw; tenon saw
coping saw or jig saw; hammer
fine glasspaper; nail punch

Materials

m (6 ft) of 146 × 33mm (5¾ × 1¼ in) softwood *for legs*
220mm (48 in) of 95 × 45mm (3¾ × 1¾ in) softwood *for beam*
220 × 460mm (48 × 18 in) sheet of 6mm ¼ in) white plywood *for top*
wo 1120mm (44 in) lengths and two 60mm (18 in) lengths of 22 × 16mm (⅞ × in) softwood batten *for underframe*

two 1120mm (44 in) lengths and two 460mm (18 in) lengths of 35 × 5mm (1⅜ × 3/16 in) ramin strip *for edging strip*
forty 108mm (4½ in) square ceramic glazed tiles
ceramic tile adhesive
ceramic tile grouting compound
13mm (½ in) veneer pins
20mm (¾ in) panel pins
250ml can polyurethane clear gloss varnish

Construction

The legs are constructed first, then the beam is attached. The top and underframe are joined together and then attached to the base. Finally the tiles are fixed in place.

For the base

Cut two lengths, 711mm (28 in), of the leg timber. On each length cut two notches 48 × 22mm (1⅞ × ⅞ in) at opposite ends (see diagram **1a**). Glue the two lengths

together with wood adhesive (diagram **1b**) making sure that the notches match exactly. Keep them cramped together for at least one hour, then leave them lying flat for 24 hours while the bond cures. (If you can obtain 292mm (11½ in) wide timber then this gluing process is not necessary. The slots can then be cut out with the coping or jig saw.)

For the next step, find the centre of the piece and mark a circle with 115mm (4½ in) radius and a halfway transverse line running through the centre (see diagram **1c**). Cut right through the transverse line, then cut the marked semicircles out of the two halves (see diagram **1d**). You now have the two leg sections.

Cut the beam timber to shape as shown in diagram **2**. Glasspaper the beam and both leg sections to a fine finish and fit them together using wood adhesive. **Be sure the top of the beam is flush with the top of the leg sections. Leave to dry standing, with weights on the beam.**

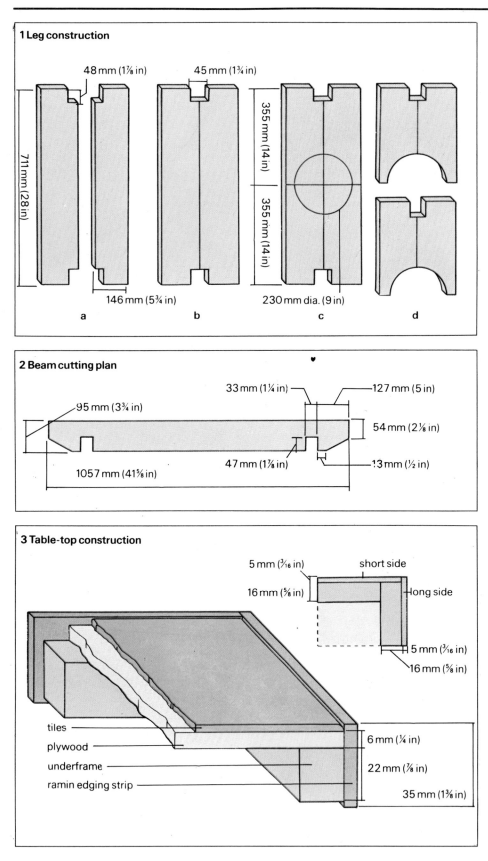

1 Leg construction

48 mm (1⅞ in)

45 mm (1¾ in)

711 mm (28 in)

355 mm (14 in)

355 mm (14 in)

146 mm (5¾ in)

230 mm dia. (9 in)

a   b   c   d

2 Beam cutting plan

95 mm (3¾ in)

33 mm (1¼ in)   127 mm (5 in)

54 mm (2⅛ in)

1057 mm (41⅝ in)

47 mm (1⅞ in)   13 mm (½ in)

3 Table-top construction

5 mm (³⁄₁₆ in)   short side

16 mm (⅝ in)   long side

5 mm (³⁄₁₆ in)

16 mm (⅝ in)

tiles

plywood

underframe

ramin edging strip

6 mm (¼ in)

22 mm (⅞ in)

35 mm (1⅜ in)

Page 119: exploded view of the table This page: diagrams of leg construction, beam cutting plan and table-top construction. Note that the depth of the beam (95mm) is equal to the sum of the leg and beam notches

For the top

Cut the plywood to 1089 × 436mm (42⅞ × 17³⁄₁₆ in) and glasspaper it to a reasonable finish, taking care not to round edges or corners. Cut the two longer pieces of batten to the same length as the plywood.

Pin and glue them to one face of the plywood flush with its long edges, with their narrower sides to the plywood. Cut the two shorter pieces to fit the plywood's shorter edges between the long battens and pin and glue them in place (see diagram **3**).

Now pin and glue the top to the leg and beam structure, using the 20mm (¾ in) panel pins. The top must be carefully centred on the structure, both lengthways and crossways. The best way to do this is to stand the structure *upside down* on the *upper* surface of the top, measure it carefully to centre it, then lightly trace the outline of the structure with a pencil on the plywood. Next, with a set square, extend the lines to the edges of the top and vertically down the frame battens. Apply glue to the top surfaces of the structure, then fix the top onto it by lining the structure up with the pencil marks on the frame. The pencilled outline on the plywood is also a guide for nailing.

Cut two pieces of ramin strip the same lengths as the shorter sides of the top and pin and glue them to the underframe ends, using veneer pins. They should not run flush with the plywood but should project above it by the thickness of a tile – so use a tile as a guide when fixing the strips. Next cut two 1098mm (43¼ in) lengths of the ramin and pin and glue these to the long sides of the frame so that they cover the ends of the shorter pieces (diagram **3**). Alternatively, the corners can be mitred.

Lightly punch in the veneer pins and fill the cavities with plastic wood, then glasspaper the edging strip to obtain a really fine finish.

Assembling and finishing

Next give the whole structure three or four coats of varnish, lightly rubbing down with fine glasspaper before the final coat. Allow each coat to dry thoroughly before applying the next.

When the varnish is finally dry, fix the tiles in place with the tile adhesive and leave to dry for at least 24 hours. Then grout the spaces between the tiles and between the tiles and the edging strip.

Note: the timber sizes given here are actual sizes, not 'nominal'. Even so, there can be variations in widths and thicknesses of timber that are supposed to be the same and these can affect measurements. In the case of this table, that could be critical only where the cross-halving joints attach the beam to the leg sections. Check carefully that the width of the slot equals the *thickness* of the *other* timber and that the depth of all slots is *half* the depth of the beam timber.

MAKE A WINDOW AWNING

The virtue of a window awning to the gardener is the shade it affords potted plants and cut flowers resting on the windowsill during the hot, sunny days of summer.
The awning pictured above is both attractive and easy to make.

Tools
steel rule
set square
chisel
tenon saw
bradawl
screwdriver
hand or electric drill
4mm ($\frac{3}{16}$ in) bit, *for wood*
6·5mm ($\frac{1}{4}$ in) masonry bit
hammer
wood rasp
paint brush

Materials
timber *see cutting list*
40 oval nails, 40mm ($1\frac{1}{2}$ in)
6 brass or zinc-plated backflaps, 33mm ($1\frac{1}{4}$ in)
36 brass or zinc-plated screws, 12mm ($\frac{1}{2}$ in), *for backflaps*
7 zinc-plated, countersunk woodscrews, 40mm ($1\frac{1}{2}$ in) × No 8
5 zinc-plated, countersunk woodscrews, 50mm (2 in) × No 8
50 upholstery nails, *plastic-headed, according to colour of fabric*
6m (18 ft) nylon cord
11 plated screw eyes
1 cleat hook, 100mm (4 in)
4m (13 ft) non-stretch webbing, 25mm (1 in) wide
wood stopping or plastic wood
waterproof wood glue
glasspaper and mastic sealer

primer, undercoat and gloss paint
fabric, *for cover*
tacks or staples
5 masonry fixing plugs

Timber cutting list

	Qty	Section	Length
For outer casing			
a	1	19 × 150mm ($\frac{3}{4}$ × 6 in)	210cm (6 ft 10$\frac{3}{4}$ in)
b	1	19 × 150mm ($\frac{3}{4}$ × 6 in)	207cm (6 ft 9$\frac{1}{2}$ in)
c	2	19 × 150mm ($\frac{3}{4}$ × 6 in)	90cm (2 ft 11$\frac{1}{2}$ in)
d	2	19 × 100mm ($\frac{3}{4}$ × 4 in)	75·5cm (2 ft 5$\frac{3}{4}$ in)
For awning frame			
e	4	25 × 40mm (1 × 1$\frac{1}{2}$ in)	197cm (6 ft 5$\frac{1}{2}$ in)
f	8	25 × 40mm (1 × 1$\frac{1}{2}$ in)	76cm (2 ft 6 in)

121

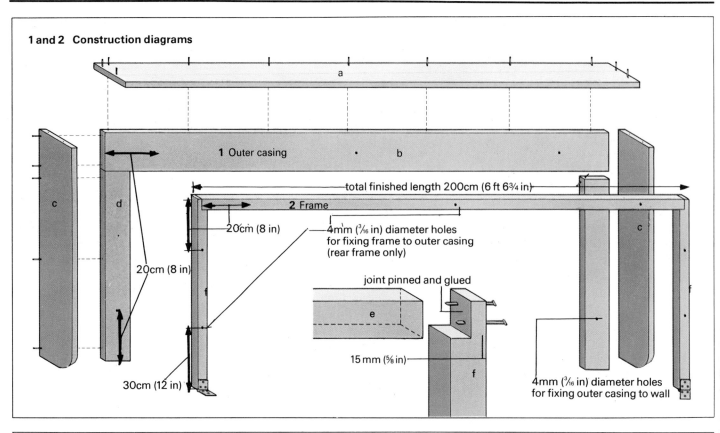

1 and 2 Construction diagrams

1 Outer casing

a

b

c

d

c

total finished length 200cm (6 ft 6¾ in)

2 Frame

20cm (8 in)

20cm (8 in)

4mm (³⁄₁₆ in) diameter holes
for fixing frame to outer casing
(rear frame only)

joint pinned and glued

e

f

f

15 mm (⅝ in)

30cm (12 in)

4mm (³⁄₁₆ in) diameter holes
for fixing outer casing to wall

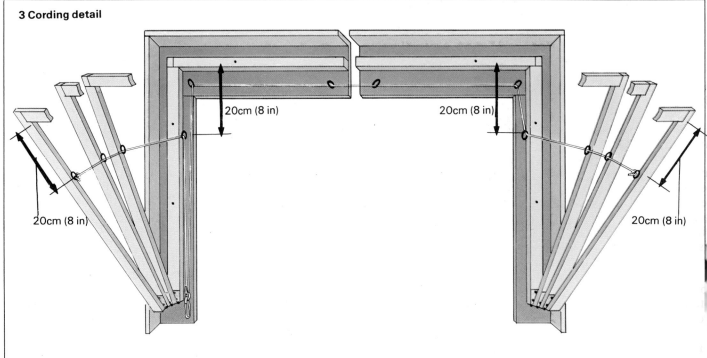

3 Cording detail

20cm (8 in)

20cm (8 in)

20cm (8 in)

20cm (8 in)

20cm (8 in)

All the materials required for the con-struction of this awning are standard items available from any good do-it-yourself shop. The timber sections are nominal ones, and prepared timber should be used throughout. Since the final planed thickness of timber varies from supplier to supplier, it is advisable to double-check all measurements to ensure they are accurate: for example, the length

of piece **b** in the outer casing should be the length of piece **a** minus the variable thickness of the two pieces **c**.

The awning has been designed for construction in two basic sections. The first – the outer casing – is permanently fixed to the wall, and acts as a protective shell for the second section, the hinged, material-covered awning. The awning can therefore be removed quite simply

Top: construction diagrams show outer casing (1) and individual frame of hinged awning (2), and include inset close-up of corner joint of frame
Above (3): nylon cord used to close awning is threaded through screw eyes fixed to inside edges of frames and to casi
Above right: once whole unit has been hinged, webbing is fixed in position
Right (4): cutting details for fabric cover

during winter months for storage in a dry place, thus prolonging the life of the covering material. Although designed to fit above a window 1·78m (5 ft 10 in) wide, the basic size can be adapted to any width by increasing or decreasing the length of the horizontal members, parts **a**, **b** and **e**.

Constructing the outer casing

First cut all the timber for the outer casing to length, remembering to allow for varying thickness, and then round the two side pieces **c** at the bottom as shown in diagram **1**. The base of a litre can of paint, used as a template, provides a suitable curve. Most of the excess wood can be cut off with the tenon saw, and the final shaping is done with the wood rasp.

Drill holes in pieces **b** and **d**, using the 4mm ($\frac{3}{16}$ in) bit; in due course, these holes will be used to fix the casing to the wall. Next assemble the entire unit, using waterproof wood glue on all joints, and 40mm ($1\frac{1}{2}$ in) oval nails. The join between the top edge of **d** and the bottom edge of **b** can be secured by driving a nail diagonally through **d** into **b**. The casing should now be left for several hours, lying flat, to enable the glue to set. Once it has done so, punch all the nails below the surface of the timber, and fill the holes with a wood topping or plastic wood. Smooth all the wood with glasspaper, and apply a primer, followed by an undercoat, paying particular attention to the back surface, which is going to be against the wall.

Fix the casing to the wall using 50mm (2 in) No 8, plated screws with your choice of masonry fixing plugs. If the wall is in an exposed position and liable to have a lot of rainwater running down it, then it is advisable to seal the join between the wall and the top of the casing with a waterproof mastic sealer to prevent water being trapped behind the casing, since this could cause the timber to rot in time. Finally, give the casing its top coat.

Constructing the hinged awning

Although looking slightly more complicated than the outer casing, the hinged awning requires no special skills. Cut the four pieces, **e**, and eight pieces, **f**, to length. The rebate (see diagram **2** inset) is made by cutting across the grain of the timber at a point determined by the actual planed width of cross-piece **e**, probably 33 or 34mm (about $1\frac{1}{4}$ in), to a depth of half the width of piece **f** – in other words, 16 or 17mm ($\frac{5}{8}$ in). Remove the excess wood with a chisel.

Using waterproof wood glue and 40mm ($1\frac{1}{2}$ in) oval nails, assemble the four separate frames, ensuring that they are all completely square. When the glue has set,

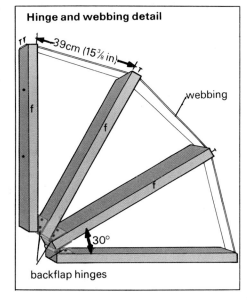

Hinge and webbing detail

39cm (15$\frac{3}{8}$ in)

webbing

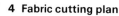

30°

backflap hinges

punch the nail heads just below the surface, fill the holes with wood stopping or plastic wood, and glasspaper the joints. The frame that is to be the back needs seven 4mm ($\frac{3}{16}$ in) holes drilled through it (see diagram **2**) to enable it to be fixed to the outer casing in due course. Apply a primer, undercoat and topcoat to each frame. When the paint is dry, link the four frames together using brass or plated backflaps with 12mm ($\frac{1}{2}$ in) woodscrews.

As the whole unit will now be fully hinged and therefore likely to swing open easily, it is advisable to fix the 25mm (1 in) webbing into position to restrict the movement of each frame. Do this by tacking one end of a length onto the top of each end of the back frame and one in the middle. Open the first hinged section to an angle of 30 degrees and secure the webbing on the upper surface, again using tacks or staples; repeat the operation for the other two frames.

At this stage, the entire unit should be placed *in situ* on the outer casing, and seven 40mm ($1\frac{1}{2}$ in) No 8, plated and countersunk woodscrews inserted into the holes already drilled in the rear frame. Check that the webbing allows the frame to open to 90 degrees and that the horizontal struts are perfectly level. If they are not, adjust the webbing.

While the frame is still in position, fix screw eyes to the inside edges of both ends of the three movable frames, and onto the outer casing (see diagram **3**). These will act as guides for the nylon cord that is used for closing the awning when it is not needed for shading.

Making the cover

Remove the frame, and with the help of someone handy in the art of sewing, make a cover. Use a strong material like canvas,

and design the cover to fit the hinged frame (see diagram **4**). Fix it in position with upholstery nails, or alternatively attach fabric ties to the cover and knot them around the wooden frame.

Final assembly

Replace the covered awning on the outer casing, as before. Secure one end of a 6m (18 ft) length of nylon cord to the screw eye on the right-hand, outer, hinged frame. Thread this through the other screw eyes, positioned as in diagram **3**, ending at the screw eye on the outer left-hand frame. Fix a cleat hook at the base of the outer frame and secure the nylon cord around this: the awning can be held either firmly shut, or partially open, but keep it closed during wet or windy spells of weather.

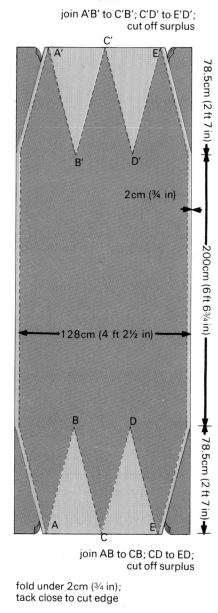

4 Fabric cutting plan

join A'B' to C'B'; C'D' to E'D'; cut off surplus

78.5cm (2 ft 7 in)

2cm (¾ in)

200cm (6 ft 6¾ in)

128cm (4 ft 2½ in)

78.5cm (2 ft 7 in)

join AB to CB; CD to ED; cut off surplus

fold under 2cm (¾ in); tack close to cut edge

CANVAS AWNING

TOOLS AND MATERIALS

measuring tape and pencil
tenon saw, medium fine and fine glasspaper
hand or electric drill, 9 and 32mm bits
vice, bradawl
500mm of 60mm square softwood batten (for corner joints)
13m of 32mm dowel for two dowels 2400 long and four
   dowels 2000mm long
250mm of 9mm dowel for four dowels 60mm long
creosote and old paint brush
five 3m lengths of strong nylon cord or rope (for guy ropes)
six tent pegs

For canvas canopy

7.40m of 112cm wide canvas
2.2m length of cotton fringing
matching thread, dressmaker's pins and needles
sharp scissors
14 brass eyelets, 3m of matching seam tape
latex-based adhesive (for fixing fringing)

Our canvas awning acts both as a wind-break and a sunshade. The frame slots together – no parts are fixed – making it easy to put up and quick to dismantle at the end of the day.
The canvas canopy has four pockets – two large ones to take magazines and newspapers and two smaller ones for breakables such as sun-glasses.

Stage 1

Using a tenon saw cut the 32mm diameter dowel into two 2400mm lengths for the cross supports and four 2000mm lengths for the uprights. Place one of the upright dowels in a vice and form a point at one end of it by making four cuts with a tenon saw (**see 1**). Repeat this procedure at one end of each of the other three upright dowels. Rub all the dowels smooth with medium fine, then fine, glasspaper.
For the retaining pegs place the 9mm diameter dowel in a vice, cut it into four 60mm lengths and rub all surfaces smooth as before.

Stage 2

For the corner joints cut the 60mm square batten with a tenon saw into four 120mm lengths. Drill a 32mm diameter hole through one of these cut pieces at the dimensions shown (**see 2**) placing a piece of scrap wood under the drilling area to prevent the timber on the bottom face breaking away as you drill through.
Drill a 32mm diameter hole 50mm deep into the underside to take one of the uprights. Fit a rubber collar or wrap adhesive tape round the bit to ensure the correct depth (**see 2**). Rub all surfaces smooth with medium fine, then fine, glasspaper, slightly rounding off all sharp corners and edges. Make the other three corner joints in the same way.
Place the corner joints at each end of the cross supports so the dowels protrude 30mm (**see 2**) and drill a 9mm hole in each corner joint and through the cross support dowel at the dimensions shown to a depth of 50mm with rubber collar or tape. These holes will house the retaining pegs when the awning is erected (**see assembly diagram**). To make the timber weather-proof remove the dowel and apply two coats of creosote with an old paint brush to all surfaces, making sure to cover the insides of the holes in the four corner joints.

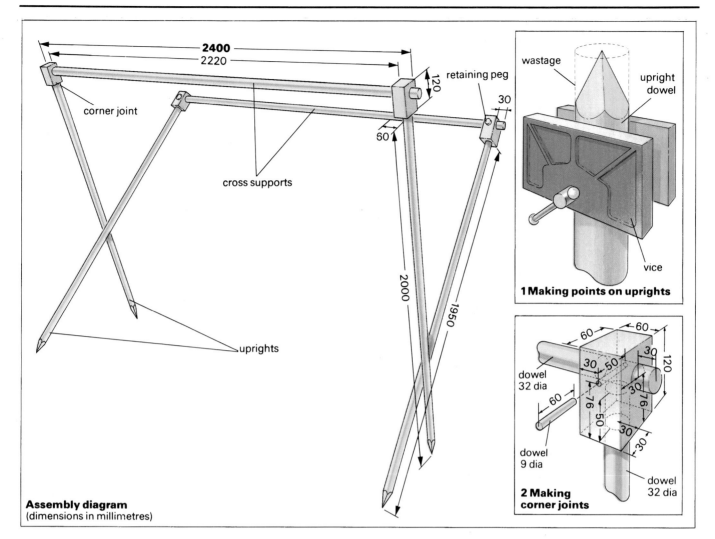

2400
2220
retaining peg
120
30
60
corner joint
cross supports
2000
1950
uprights

1 Making points on uprights

wastage
upright dowel
vice

2 Making corner joints

dowel 32 dia
60
60
30
50
30
120
30
76
30
76
50
30
30
dowel 9 dia
dowel 32 dia

Assembly diagram
(dimensions in millimetres)

Stage 3

Measure and cut off 20cm across the width of the fabric. Cut two 28cm widths out of this for the two large pockets and two 11cm squares for the two small pockets (**see cutting plan for fabric**). To make each pocket, turn in 15mm to the wrong side of the fabric on three sides then pin and baste in place. On the remaining cut edge turn down 5mm to the wrong side, then a further 10mm. Pin, baste and stitch across this edge. The pockets will be stitched in position later (**see Stage 4**).

Cut the remaining length of fabric in half across its width (two 360cm lengths) and, with the right sides of the fabric uppermost, lay them side by side lapping the centre selvedges over one another by 60mm (**see 3**). Pin, baste and stitch the two pieces together making the stitch lines close to each selvedge edge (**see 3**).

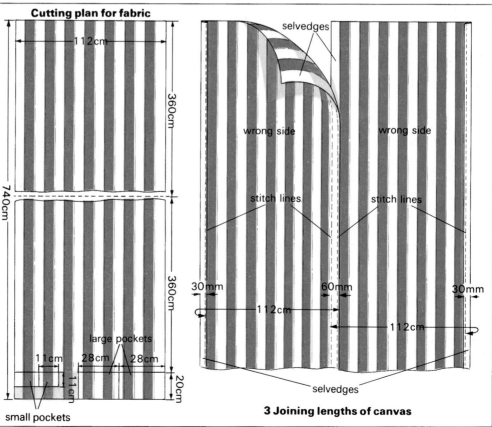

Cutting plan for fabric

112cm
360cm
360cm
740cm
11cm
28cm
28cm
large pockets
11cm
20cm
small pockets

selvedges
wrong side
wrong side
stitch lines
stitch lines
30mm
60mm
30mm
112cm
112cm
selvedges

3 Joining lengths of canvas

125

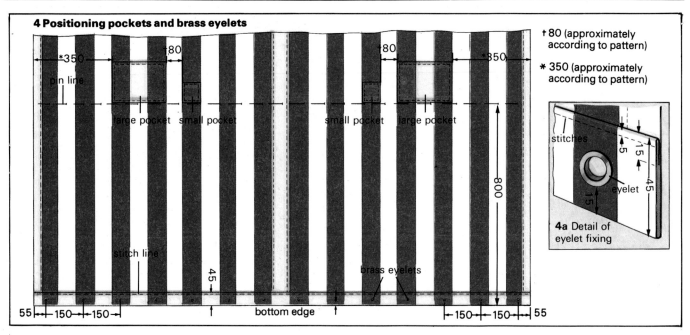

4 Positioning pockets and brass eyelets

pin line

*350   †80   large pocket   small pocket   small pocket   large pocket   80   *350

† 80 (approximately according to pattern)

* 350 (approximately according to pattern)

800

stitch line

45

brass eyelets

55 ⊢150⊣150⊣   bottom edge   ⊢150⊣150⊣ 55

stitches

15   5

eyelet

45

15

4a Detail of eyelet fixing

Turn in 30mm to the wrong side of the fabric along the two outside edges (parallel to the centre seam) and pin and stitch in place (**see 3**). Across one of the shorter sides (top) turn 5mm to the wrong side then a further 10mm. Pin, baste and stitch the hems down. With a latex-based adhesive stick the length of cotton fringing to the wrong side of the fabric. On the other short side (bottom) turn 15mm to the wrong side then a further 45mm (**see 4**). Pin, baste and stitch in place. Fix in the brass eyelets (following manufacturers' instructions) 15mm up from the hemmed edge and at 150mm intervals across the width of the fabric (see **4a**).

One guy rope is threaded through the eyelets to keep the bottom of the canvas close to the ground.

To make the cylindrical sleeve for the back cross support, erect the timber frame (**see assembly diagram**) using four guy ropes tied to the ends of both cross supports (**see photograph**), then lay the fabric over the frame so the back edge touches the ground.

Using pins, mark where the fabric touches the top centre of the back cross support dowel. Remove the fabric from the timber frame and, with the right sides of the fabric together, fold it across its width so the pins lie along the fold lines (**see 5a**).

Remove these pins and baste and stitch across the width of the fabric 55mm down from the fold line (**see 5a**). Dismantle the frame and slide the cross support dowel into this sleeve (**see 5b**).

Stage 4

To position the pockets, mark a line 800mm up from the bottom back edge (with brass eyelets) of the fabric with pins. Place the bottom edges of the large pockets on this line approximately 350mm in from each edge, making sure the stripes (or pattern) on the material align. Place the small pockets about 80mm in from the large pockets (**see 4**). Pin, baste and stitch them in position round both side edges and the bottom edge, leaving the top open. Erect the timber frame again, lay the fabric over it and let the fringed front edge fall over the front cross support. On the wrong side of the fabric, mark close to either side of the cross support with pins across the width of the fabric. Remove the fabric from the frame and at 150mm intervals stitch a 100mm length of seam tape along both pin lines (**see 6a**). The top of the canvas canopy can then be tied to the front cross support (**see 6b**).

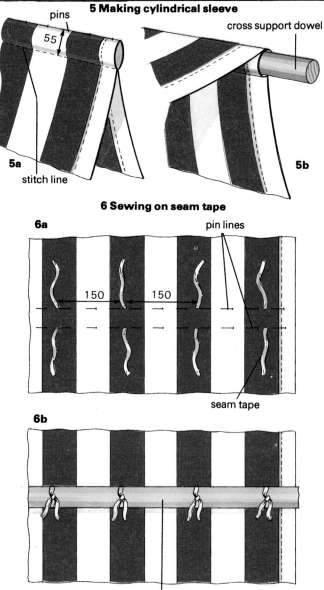

5 Making cylindrical sleeve

pins   55   cross support dowel

5a stitch line   **5b**

6 Sewing on seam tape

6a   pin lines

150   150

seam tape

6b

cross support dowel

Cutting list for softwood & plywood

Description	Key	Quantity	Dimensions
Main frame sides	A	2	1530 x 98 x 22mm
Seating frame sides	B	2	1480 x 98 x 22mm
Back support arms	C	2	700 x 98 x 22mm
Canopy sides	D	2	1300 x 98 x 22mm
Notch covers (plywood)	E	2	350 x 98 x 16mm

Overall dimensions (folded)
1880mm long (minimum), 750mm wide (70 × 30in).
Project dimensions are in metric only and do not allow for cutting wastages.

Assembly diagram

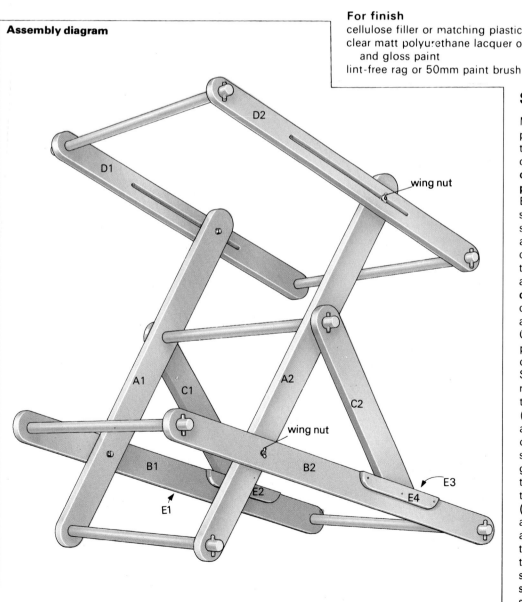

TOOLS AND MATERIALS

timber (see cutting list)
measuring tape, pencil and try square
panel, tenon and coping saws
pair of compasses, piece of scrap hardboard
vice, hand or electric drill, and 2, 5, 12 and 38mm bits
medium fine and fine glasspaper
hole saw drill attachment (if used)
bradawl, screwdriver, countersink bit
mitre box or guide (as needed)
12mm chisel, block plane, hammer, half-round file
3m of 84cm wide deck-chair canvas and 1.2m cotton fringing
sewing thread (to match canvas colour)
dressmaker's scissors, needle and pins, domestic iron
water-resistant woodworking adhesive, clean cloth

For assembly
4500mm of 38mm dowel for six dowels 750mm long
1800mm of 12mm dowel for 12 dowels 64mm long and 12 dowels 80mm long
No 8 countersunk rustproof screws 25mm long
four 12mm diameter rustproof bolts 60mm long and eight flat washers and four wing nuts to fit bolts
galvanized or brass tacks 6mm long

For finish
cellulose filler or matching plastic wood
clear matt polyurethane lacquer or primer, undercoat and gloss paint
lint-free rag or 50mm paint brush

Stage 1

Measure and cut with a panel saw all the pieces of timber squarely to size to the dimensions shown (see cutting list and cutting plan).
Both ends of the main frame sides A, the seating frame sides B, the canopy sides D and the plywood notch covers E and only one end of the back support arms C are curved (see assembly diagram). To form these curves you must first make a hardboard template.
Cut a 98mm square out of a piece of hardboard and mark on the diagonals (see 1). Set your compass to a 49mm radius and place the point in the centre of the square (where the diagonals cross) and draw on the curve. Cut off the waste with a coping saw and smooth with fine glasspaper. Using this template mark the curves on the various pieces of timber (see assembly diagram) and cut off all the waste with a coping saw. Before cutting the notch covers, score along the cutting lines on both sides of the timber with a sharp knife to prevent the surface veneer breaking away when sawing.

Side section
(dimensions in millimetres)

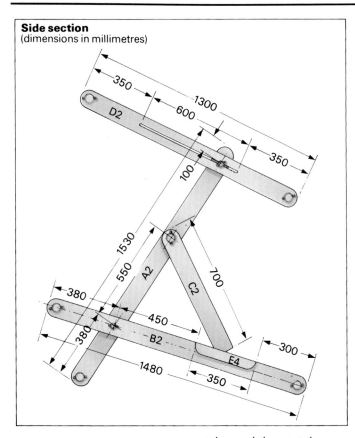

Cutting plan

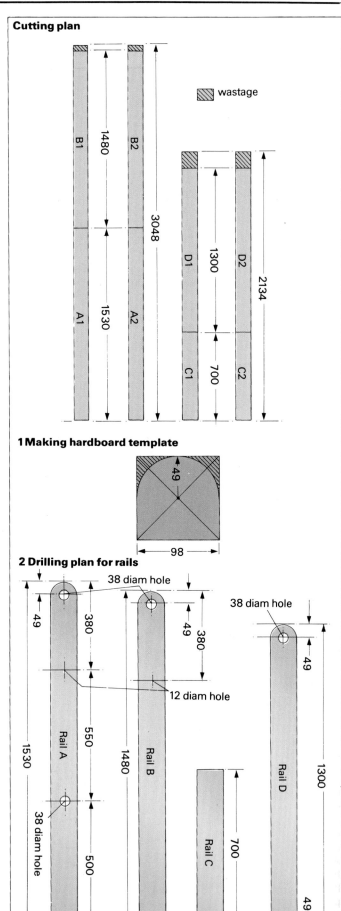

wastage

1 Making hardboard template

2 Drilling plan for rails

Stage 2

With a tenon saw cut the 38mm diameter dowel into six 750mm lengths, and the 12mm diameter dowel into twelve 64mm and twelve 80mm lengths. With medium fine glasspaper chamfer both ends of all the dowels. Drill two 38mm diameter holes on both main frame sides A for the dowels and two 12mm holes for the bolts at the dimensions shown (see 2a). Then drill holes in B, C and D at the dimensions shown (see 2b, c, d). Smooth the holes in C with medium fine, then fine, glasspaper or with a half-round file.
When drilling, place a piece of scrap wood under the drilling area to prevent the surface wood on the bottom face breaking away as the bit drills through.
Drill 12mm diameter holes 24mm in from each end of five of the 38mm dowels and 46mm in from both ends of the remaining one. This one will be used to fix the bottom ends of the two main frame sides A so label the dowel accordingly.
Place one of the seating frame sides B in a vice, mark on the cutting lines for the

notches and then cut them out with a tenon saw to the dimensions shown (see 3). Cut the notches in the other seating frame side B.
With a panel saw cut the two notch covers E in half (to make four pieces) by cutting centrally along their length, again scoring the cutting lines. Drill three 5mm clearance holes in each piece at the dimensions shown (see 3) and countersink them to take No 8 screws. Hold one of these notch covers in the required position (see 3) so its top edge is flush with the top edge of the seating frame side B and, with a bradawl, mark through these clearance holes onto B. Drill 2mm pilot holes at these points, apply a layer of woodworking adhesive to the fixing edge of the notch cover and screw it firmly in position with 25mm long screws. Wipe off excess adhesive with a clean dampened cloth. Fix the remaining three notch covers in the same way.
To make the slots for the bolts in the canopy sides D drill a series of 12mm holes at the dimensions shown (see 4), placing a piece of scrap wood under the drilling area as before, and cut out the remaining waste with a

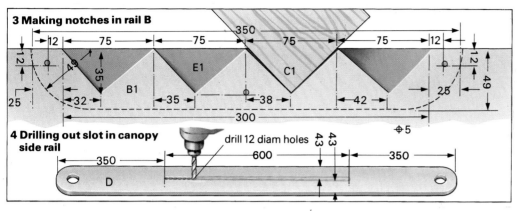

3 Making notches in rail B

4 Drilling out slot in canopy side rail

drill 12 diam holes

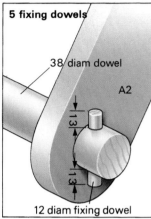

5 fixing dowels

38 diam dowel

A2

12 diam fixing dowel

12mm chisel. Alternatively, drill a 12mm hole at either end of the slot and cut out the waste with a pad saw. Smooth the inside of the slot with a half-round file or a piece of medium fine glasspaper wrapped round a length of dowel of no more than 9mm diameter.

Stage 3

Fill all holes, cracks and abrasions with cellulose filler or plastic wood. Matching plastic wood is better if you are applying a natural finish. Rub all surfaces smooth with medium fine, then fine, glasspaper, rounding off all sharp corners and edges. Apply a finish before assembling the chair. We applied four coats of matt lacquer for a durable, natural finish. Be sure to apply at least three coats so the deck-chair can be left outdoors even if it rains. Allow each coat to dry before applying the next. If painting, apply a coat of primer, two undercoats and then gloss, leaving each coat to dry.

Stage 4

Apply adhesive to the inside edges of the 38mm holes in the canopy sides D and to four of the 64mm long 12mm dowels. Push two 38mm dowels in position in D1 and D2 (**see assembly diagram**) and secure them with the 64mm long 12mm dowels so they protrude 13mm at either side (**see 5**). Wipe off excess adhesive. Check the joints are square, and that D1 and D2 are close against the 12mm dowels, place the structure on a flat surface and leave for the adhesive to set thoroughly. Fix two 38mm dowels in the seating frame sides B in the same way and leave on a flat surface as before for the adhesive to set thoroughly. When the adhesive has set hard, fix the main frame sides A to the seating frame sides B with the 12mm bolts, placing a washer between the bolt head (and the wing nut) and the timber (**see assembly diagram**).
Apply adhesive to the 38mm holes in main frame sides A and position A1 and A2 so they are not parallel. Slide the previously marked 38mm dowel into the bottom hole in A1 and another 38mm dowel into the other hole in A1 so they protrude 90mm. Then position A2 parallel to A1 and push the dowels back through into A2 to the required position. Wipe off excess adhesive.
Push the back support arms C over the top dowel (**see assembly diagram**), making sure there is no adhesive on the dowel as C must pivot freely for adjusting height. Apply adhesive to four 64mm long 12mm dowels and push these in position as before.

Stage 5

When all the adhesive has set, drill a 12mm hole, 80mm deep, in the underside (so as not to be easily seen) of rails A, B and D through the 38mm dowels so that small (12mm diameter) stabilizing dowels can be inserted (**see 6**). Again, don't drill through the back support arms C as they must be able to move freely. Apply adhesive to the 80mm long stabilizing dowels (two at a time) and push them firmly into position in these holes. Wipe off excess adhesive and trim any protruding dowels with a block plane. Patch up these areas with whatever finish you used for the chair.

Stage 6

For the seat cut a piece of deck-chair canvas 1.6m long and 66cm wide. Turn 1cm of the canvas to the underside on both long edges and press the folds with a domestic iron. Turn these a further 2cm, pin in position then baste and stitch them down. Turn under 2cm to the underside across both width edges. With the right side of the canvas uppermost, and the length of it lying away from you, fix the canvas with tacks to the back side of the front dowel, placing the tacks at 25mm intervals.
Bring the canvas round under the front dowel and loop it round the back dowel, taking it round far enough so the tacks will not show (**see 7**).
For the canopy cut the canvas to 1.4m long and 66cm wide. Turn all hems as before and place the canvas over the canopy frame, marking on the required position of the cotton fringing. Remove the canvas and stitch on the fringing. Fix the canvas to the back and front dowels of the canopy frame as before, pulling it taught enough between them to prevent it flapping.
Screw the canopy frame in position with the wing nuts and bolts, placing a washer between the wing nuts (and bolt heads) and the timber.

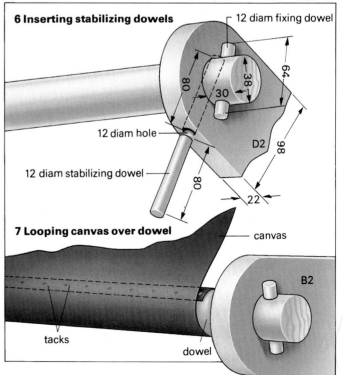

6 Inserting stabilizing dowels

12 diam fixing dowel

12 diam hole

12 diam stabilizing dowel

7 Looping canvas over dowel

canvas

tacks

dowel

BUILDING A BRICK BARBECUE
in your garden

The overall design of our barbecue garden can be varied to suit the site you choose. Use our ideas and follow the constructional details for building the major features.

For the 'floor' of this barbecue garden we chose brick or pre-cast paving and methods for laying these were given on pages 58–60.

Concrete block wall

The high wall running out from the house is a different matter, however, being built from hollow concrete blocks, a versatile material that could be used in the garden far more than it is. Concrete blocks come in a number of different sizes, the two most common being $115 \times 455 \times 230$ mm ($4\frac{1}{2} \times 18 \times 9$ in), or $230 \times 455 \times 230$ mm ($9 \times 18 \times 9$ in). They are constructed to withstand great pressure and are available in a rough or smooth finish, either of which can be given a finishing coat of stone paint.

Their size allows work to take shape quickly but it does mean that they are heavy, particularly in the larger size that you will need to use for a wall of anything over 1·2m (4 ft) high. Walls 230mm (9 in) thick, made either of block or brick, are visually and structurally most sound for garden work. Thinner walls of 115mm ($4\frac{1}{2}$ in) inevitably need buttresses and these detract from the appearance of the whole.

The wall here is 2·3m ($7\frac{1}{2}$ ft) high and for this you will need a good concrete 'footing' or foundation that will be twice as wide as the wall itself. The depth of the concrete will depend on the nature of the ground. If you are building on solid rock, virtually no footing is needed, but if the ground is marshy you will need an ample depth. On reasonable ground, as a general rule, a 75cm ($2\frac{1}{2}$ ft) trench, 45cm (18 in) wide is quite enough. This can be filled with 60cm (24 in) of concrete and allows the first course of blocks to be laid just below ground level.

You should use a simple stretcher bond, that is, lay all the blocks lengthways and stagger the joints, checking the levels as work progresses. Once five or six courses have been built, you will need a

simple scaffold or stage from which to work. Two people make the job a lot easier, with one laying blocks and the other mixing mortar and passing up the blocks as they are needed.

Joist hangers for overhead beams

As the wall nears completion you have to consider the insertion of 'joist hangers' that will hold the white overhead beams in place. These are triangular-shaped 'shoes', open at one end and with a strap that can be bedded between the top row of blocks and the brick on edge that acts as a coping. On some walls you will notice a double row of tiles just below the coping; this is known as 'creasing' and acts as a damp course that prevents water from penetrating into the top of the wall.

Low brick wall

The second, lower 1m ($3\frac{1}{2}$ ft) high wall is built of brick and will act as a host for the seat and barbecue.

On page 11 we show the basic method of joining bricks called stretcher bonding, with every brick laid lengthwise so that the joints fall in the centre of a brick in the course below. For this wall we suggest Flemish bond, where two bricks are laid lengthwise and one across the width of the course. The methods for laying were given on pages 58–60. It is essential to check your levels while working and make sure you point the joints (see page 11) at the end of each bricklaying session. With this wall you have to turn through 90 degrees behind the barbecue and, in order to marry the two angles together, you will need to cut a 'closer' brick to ensure the bond is correct (see diagram). The coping here will be brick, on edge again, but it is normal to omit the tile creasing from walls of this height.

Above right: section of joist hanger embedded in concrete block wall between top block and coping
Right: section of barbecue wall with brick laid in Flemish bond and with a 'closer' cut to accommodate the 90° turn
Far right: section of brick barbecue area showing store cupboard, adjustable cooking grill and high, sheltering wall

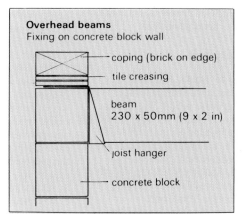

Overhead beams
Fixing on concrete block wall

- coping (brick on edge)
- tile creasing
- beam 230 x 50mm (9 x 2 in)
- joist hanger
- concrete block

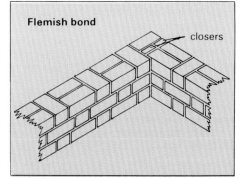

Flemish bond

closers

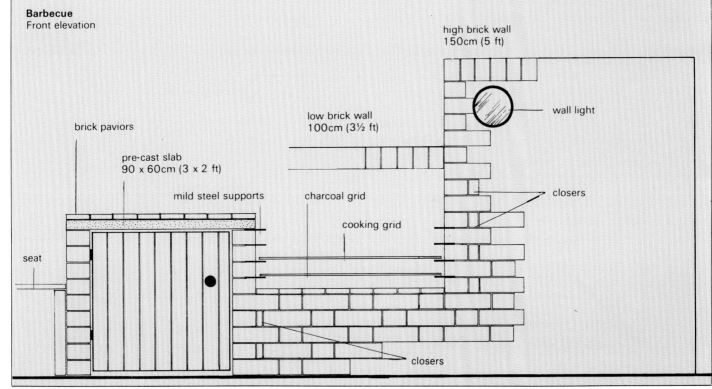

Barbecue
Front elevation

high brick wall
150cm (5 ft)

brick paviors

low brick wall
100cm (3½ ft)

pre-cast slab
90 x 60cm (3 x 2 ft)

wall light

mild steel supports

charcoal grid

closers

cooking grid

seat

closers

closers

Brick barbecue and high wall

The barbecue and the final 1·5m (5 ft) wall are built together. The barbecue is made up of two units: the store and the actual cooker. Construct the store with a single shelf and top it with a working surface. A simple 900×600mm (3×2 ft) pre-cast concrete paving slab can act as a bed for the final finish of glazed paving bricks, or 'paviors'. Make the door from tongue and groove boards, but remember that the hinges, screws and catch should be of brass or a non-ferrous metal, to stop rust.

Below grill level, the barbecue is a solid structure and the cavity formed by the four surrounding walls should be filled with rubble and hardcore, and surfaced with glazed paving bricks. As the walls rise on either side, remember that at the sixth and subsequent courses you have to allow for the supports to hold the adjustable cooking grid. If you want a higher cooking level you must take this

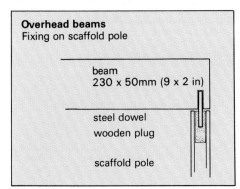

Overhead beams
Fixing on scaffold pole

beam
230 x 50mm (9 x 2 in)

steel dowel
wooden plug

scaffold pole

into consideration. Continue building the 1·5m (5 ft) wall in a Flemish bond with 'closers' as illustrated in diagram 2.

Barbecue grid

Modern foot-scrapers make remarkably effective grids and these can be held easily on several levels by 6mm ($\frac{1}{4}$ in) mild steel strips bedded into the joints of the brickwork. Alternatively, a garage or local engineer will often make up a grid of any size or specification for a reasonable charge. If you are burning charcoal, a second grid or tray can be used on the lowest position, but the beauty of a brick-built barbecue is that it will accept logs that can be burned directly on the brick top; they also give the cooked food a delicious flavour.

Garden seat

Once the barbecue is finished you are ready to build the seat to the left of the store. This can have an open or closed front, the latter being a little more complicated and expensive. The top consists of six lengths of 200×20mm ($7\frac{3}{4} \times \frac{7}{8}$ in) boards which you screw into 50×50mm (2×2 in) frames (see seat diagrams). In turn, the frames are plugged and screwed into the brick and concrete walls and paving. A neatly-

Left: down support married into beam
Below and below right: L-shaped garden seat of six boards screwed into frames, secured, in turn, to walls and paving

mitred butt joint will be necessary where the boards meet in the corner formed by the high concrete wall and the low brick one. Remember to chamfer the edges of all exposed wood surfaces, that is, round them off using a plane, and then finish them with a fine grade of sandpaper. The seat can either be painted white (primer, undercoat and top coat), or stained with a wood preservative, such as Cuprinol.

Overhead beams and down supports

The final feature is the white overhead beam structure that will fit into the joist hangers already inserted into the high concrete block wall. The timbers should be lengths of 230×50mm (9×2 in) and planed all round. Do not be tempted to use smaller beams as they will only look flimsy. Climbers will soften their outline.

There is a choice of down supports: either a 50mm (2 in) square steel section, or a simple scaffold pole, dowelled at the top to accept the beams. The supports are of different lengths, the longest being bedded into a secure concrete foundation that will be surrounded by planting. Use the same method as given for erecting the pergola poles on page 85. The shorter pole is fixed into the top of the lower brick wall and can be neatly married in with the coping. This is achieved by cementing it into a 5cm (2 in) hole in the middle of the brick. Paint the supports black and maintain them, along with the beams, by giving them a rub down and a fresh coat of paint every two years.

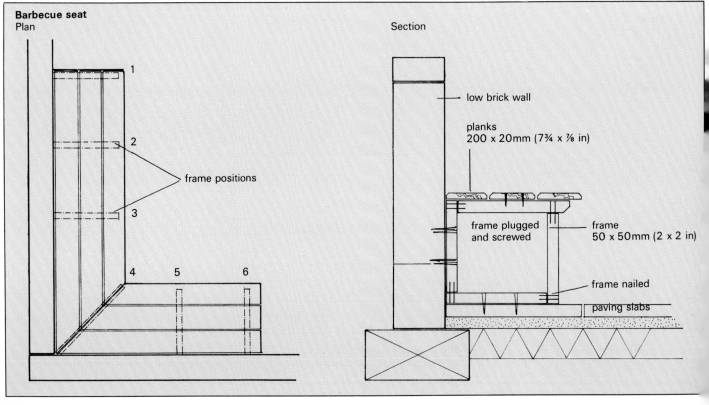

Barbecue seat
Plan

1
2
3

frame positions

4 5 6

Section

low brick wall

planks
200 x 20mm (7¾ x ⅞ in)

frame plugged
and screwed

frame
50 x 50mm (2 x 2 in)

frame nailed

paving slabs

MAKE A SANDPIT

Sand is an invaluable plaything for most children and a sandpit can become a very useful piece of garden equipment. All too often, however, it is poorly constructed and badly sited – an eyesore and a feature of your garden that never realizes its full potential.

Incidental features in garden design are often overlooked, and their finishing details, the most crucial and obvious aspects of any job, need to be closely attended to.

Siting your sandpit

Sandpits are inherently messy so it is sensible to site them in an area where the mess can be kept down to a minimum. Also, it is important that children, especially young ones, can be kept easily in view. This reduces your choice of position to somewhere close to the house, preferably an easily-swept area of paving that will keep feet free from mud.

At this point you might say that you would rather have an uncluttered 'patio', but it is possible to build a sandpit that is practical as well as attractive, and serves both children and adults alike.

A sandpit can make an attractive addition to any garden, provided you approach its design and location with sense and imagination. Here (see plan and section opposite) a herb bed bounded by a hedge of well-trimmed box adjoins the raised sandpit

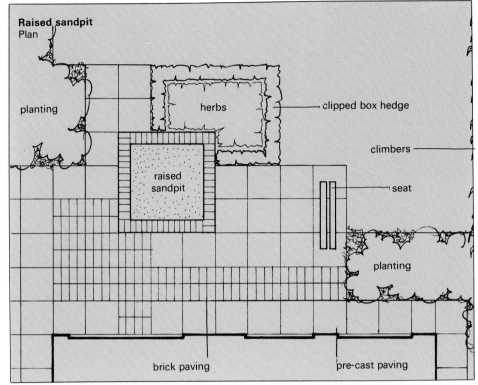

Raised sandpit
Plan

planting

herbs

clipped box hedge

climbers

raised sandpit

seat

planting

brick paving

pre-cast paving

SANDBOAT

This fun idea for a sandpit in the shape of a boat, which involves simple techniques, will keep the children amused for hours.

Stage 1

Measure and cut with a panel saw all the pieces of timber (except the four seat supports F) to the dimensions shown (**see cutting list and** cutting plan).

To cut the seat supports F place the timber rail in a vice or mitre box and make the 45 degree angle cuts with a tenon saw at the dimensions shown (**see cutting plan**).

TOOLS AND MATERIALS

timber (see cutting list)
measuring tape, pencil, try square
panel saw, tenon saw, vice, mitre box (or guide)
hand or electric drill, 2, 5 and 25mm bits
screwdriver, bradawl, countersink bit
hammer, nail punch, block plane, mallet (if used)
water-resistant woodworking adhesive, clean cloth
sharp knife or chisel, medium fine and fine glasspaper
No 10 rustproof countersunk screws 50 and 63mm long
oval nails 50mm long
1829mm of 25mm dowel (for mast)
exterior grade cellulose filler or plastic wood
clear gloss polyurethane lacquer (for mast)
primer, undercoat and gloss top coat paint (for finish)
50 and 100mm paint brushes

Overall dimensions
2439mm long, 1220mm wide, 225mm high (86 × 48 × 9in).
Project dimensions are in metric only and do not allow for
cutting wastages.

Assembly diagram

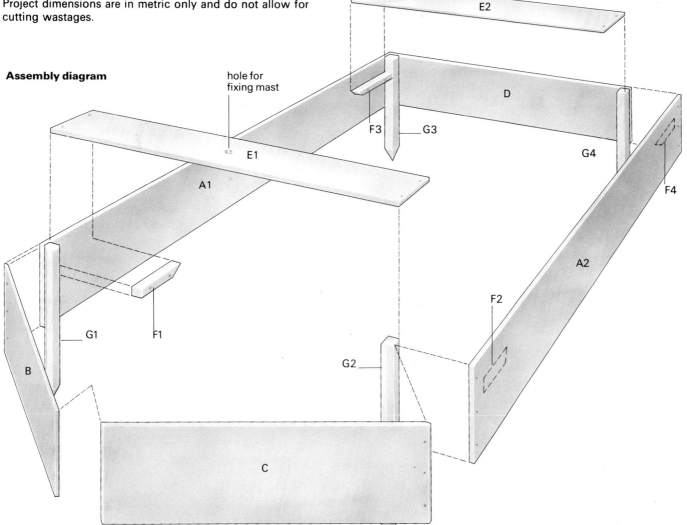

Make four cuts with a tenon
saw at the bottom of all four
uprights G to shape the
points for fixing the sandpit
firmly into the ground (**see
1a**). Mark the chamfer on the
square end of the uprights G1
and G2 to the dimensions
shown (**see 1b**) and remove
the waste with a block plane.

Stage 2

Drill three 5mm diameter
clearance holes 44mm in
from one end of both sides
A, placing them 25mm in
from the edges of each plank
and one in the middle (**see
side elevation**).
Drill three 5mm clearance
holes 12mm in from the other
end of both sides A and
countersink all the holes to
take No 10 screws.
Drill three 5mm clearance
holes 22mm in from either

end of the back D, placing
these 30mm in from the
edges and one off centre
between them. Countersink
them to take No 10 screws.
Apply adhesive to both ends
of the back D and fix the
back ends of both sides A
(the clearance holes are
44mm in from the back ends)
squarely to the back D with
the 50mm long oval nails,
avoiding the clearance holes.
Hold the uprights G3 and G4
in position in the joints
between the back and the
two sides so the top edges
are flush and mark with a
bradawl through the
clearance holes in A and D
onto the uprights. Drill 2mm
pilot holes at these points
and glue and screw G3 and
G4 firmly in position with the
50mm long screws. Wipe off
excess adhesive with a clean
dampened cloth.

Stage 3

Hold the uprights G1 and G2
against the other end of the
sides A so the back edge of
the chamfer on each upright
is flush with the end of each
side A. Mark with a bradawl
through the clearance holes
in the sides onto the uprights
and drill 2mm pilot holes at
these points. Glue and screw
both uprights in position
with 50mm screws and wipe
off all excess adhesive.
Drill three 5mm clearance
holes, 35mm in from
one end of both bow sections
B and C and countersink
them to take No 10 screws.
Mark the 45 degree mitre on
the drilled end of B and C
(**see plan inset**) and
carefully remove the waste
from each with a block
plane to form the mitre.
Glue and nail the square end

of the right bow section B
squarely to the square end of
the left bow section C with
the 50mm long oval nails
(**see plan**). Wipe off excess
adhesive.
Hold the assembled bow
section in the required
position against the uprights
G1 and G2 so the top edges
are flush (**see plan and side
elevation**), making sure the
mitred ends of B and C are
pressed hard against the
uprights G and the sides A.
The outside edges of the
mitred ends of B and C will
protrude, but don't trim this
off until you have assembled
the sandpit.
Mark with a bradawl through
the clearance holes in B and
C onto both uprights G and
drill 2mm pilot holes at these
points. Apply adhesive to the
chamfered edge of G1 and
G2 and fix the bow section

Cutting plan for softwood

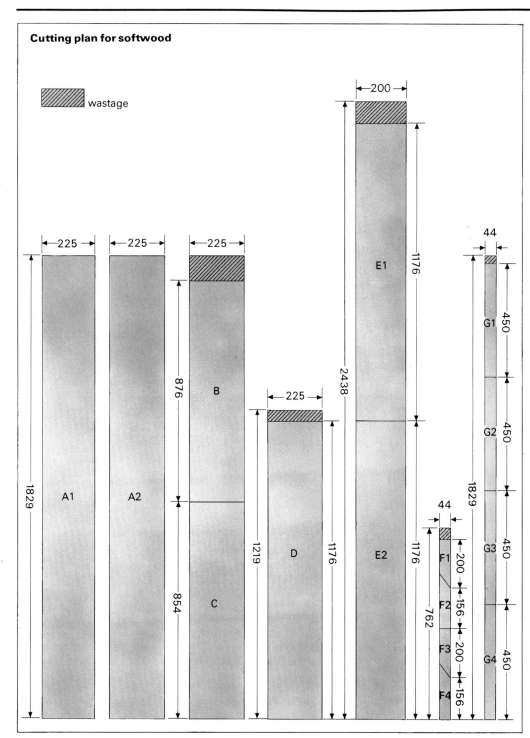

wastage

Description	Key	Quantity	Dimensions
Sides	A	2	1829 x 225 x 22mm
Right bow section	B	1	876 x 225 x 22mm
Left bow section	C	1	854 x 225 x 22mm
Back	D	1	1176 x 225 x 22mm
Seats	E	2	1176 x 200 x 22mm
Seat supports	F	4	200 x 44 x 44mm
Uprights	G	4	450 x 44 x 44mm

in position with 50mm screws. Wipe off all excess adhesive. Drill a 5mm clearance hole 50mm in from each end of the four seat supports F and countersink them to take No 10 screws. Hold the seat supports in the required position against the sides A 80mm down from the top edges of the sides A and with the square ends of the seat supports touching the uprights G (**see side elevation and plan**). Mark with a bradawl through the clearance holes in the

seat supports onto the sides A and drill 2mm pilot holes at these points. Apply adhesive to the fixing edges of the seat supports and glue and screw them firmly in position with the 63mm long screws. Wipe off excess adhesive.

Drill two 5mm clearance holes 22mm in from each end and 35mm in from each edge of both seats E and countersink them to take No 10 screws. Place the seats in the required position on the seat supports (**see plan**) and mark with a bradawl through the clearance holes in the seats onto the seat supports. Remove the seats and drill 2mm pilot holes at these points, apply adhesive to the top faces of the four seat supports and fix the seats firmly down with the 50mm long screws. Wipe off excess adhesive. Remove the waste wood at the two joins between the assembled bow section and the sides A with a block plane. Apply two coats of gloss polyurethane lacquer to the 1829mm length of 25mm dowel to make the mast weatherproof.

Drill a 25mm diameter hole in the centre of the front seat E1, make a point at one end of the 25mm dowel with a knife or chisel and insert this dowel through the hole in the seat. When the sandpit is in position, drive the mast at least 150mm into the ground.

Stage 4

Fill all holes, cracks and abrasions with exterior grade cellulose filler or plastic wood and rub all surfaces smooth with medium fine, then fine, glasspaper.

Apply a coat of primer, an undercoat and at least three top coats of gloss paint for a durable, weatherproof finish. Allow each coat to dry before applying the next. Place the sandpit in a level part of your garden and hammer each upright G a little at a time into the ground, using a mallet or hammer and a block of wood, until the bottom edges of the sides A are at ground level. Fill the boat with about $\frac{1}{4}$cu m (or $\frac{1}{4}$cu yd) of silver sand. Don't use builder's sand since this will stain clothes.

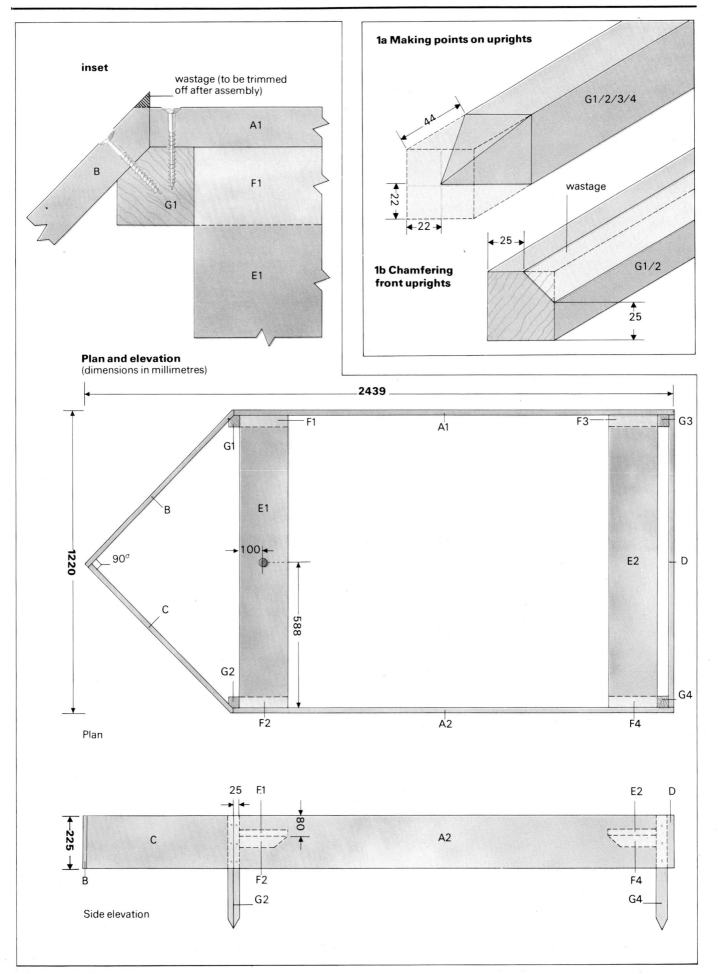

inset

wastage (to be trimmed off after assembly)

A1

B

G1

F1

E1

1a Making points on uprights

G1/2/3/4

44

22

22

wastage

25

G1/2

1b Chamfering front uprights

25

Plan and elevation
(dimensions in millimetres)

2439

F1   A1   F3   G3

G1

B

E1

90°

100

E2   D

588

C

G2

F2   A2   F4

G4

Plan

25   F1

E2   D

80

C   A2

B   F2

F4

G2   G4

Side elevation

225

SEE-SAW

This see-saw has two height settings to allow for growing children and, although we gave it a tough outdoor finish, it can be lifted out of the ground and stored away in bad weather.

TOOLS AND MATERIALS

timber (see cutting list)
measuring tape, pencil, try square, spirit level
panel, tenon and coping saws, block and smoothing planes
round and fine flat files, medium fine and fine glasspaper
hand or electric drill, 2, 5, 6 and 19mm bits, centre punch
screwdriver, bradawl, countersink bit
hammer, nail punch, two G-clamps, garden spade
water-resistant woodworking adhesive, clean cloth
cement and ballast, hardcore

For assembly

No 10 rustproof countersunk screws 38 and 65mm long
No 8 rustproof round head screws 19mm long
panel pins 25mm long
210mm of 20mm gas pipe (for pivot tube)
two conduit saddles (to fix pivot tube)
320mm of 19mm mild steel rod (for pivot bar)

For finish

exterior grade cellulose filler or plastic wood
primer, undercoat and gloss paint, 100mm paint brush
creosote and creosote brush or old paint brush

Stage 1

Measure and cut all the pieces of timber with a panel saw to the dimensions shown (**see cutting lists**). Cut off the corners of the seat plank A with a tenon saw at the dimensions shown (**see 1**) and chamfer the top and bottom edges of the plank with a smoothing plane.

Mark out and drill the 5mm diameter clearance holes in the seat plank A at the dimensions shown (**see 1**) and countersink them to take No 10 screws on the top face of the plank except the four holes for fixing the handles; these must be countersunk on the bottom face.
Cut off the two bottom corners of both reinforcers B

138

Cutting list for softwood & exterior grade plywood

Description	Key	Quantity	Dimensions
Seat plank	A	1	2500 x 200 x 22mm
Reinforcers	B	2	2500 x 73 x 22mm
Uprights	C	2	1000 x 149 x 44mm
Gussets	D	2	300 x 149 x 22mm
Locking piece	E	1	200 x 44 x 22mm
Handles	F	2	200 x 73 x 22mm
Box sides (plywood)	G	4	450 x 170 x 9mm
Box ends (plywood)	H	4	450 x 45 x 9mm
Base (plywood)	J	1	450 x 200 x 9mm

with a tenon saw at the dimensions shown (**see 2**). Mark and cut out the centre notch in both reinforcers with a coping saw to the dimensions shown (**see 2 and inset**); the pivot tube must be a tight fit so be sure to cut on the waste side of the line; check for fit and, if necessary, remove more wood with a round file. Position the seat plank A on the two reinforcers B (**see assembly diagram**) so the clearance holes in A line up along the centre of each reinforcer B. Mark with a bradawl through the clearance holes, remove A and drill 2mm pilot holes at these points.
Apply water-resistant woodworking adhesive to the

top edge of one of the reinforcers B and fix it firmly in position with the 65mm long No 10 screws. Wipe off excess adhesive with a clean dampened cloth. Fix the second reinforcer in the same way.

Stage 2

Position the pivot tube in the centre notches in the reinforcers B so 5mm of the tube protrudes at either side of the seat plank A. Fix the tube in position with the two metal conduit saddles (**see assembly diagram**) fixing these onto A to the outside of the reinforcers with the round head screws.
Mark out the shaping lines on one of the handles F to the

Assembly diagram

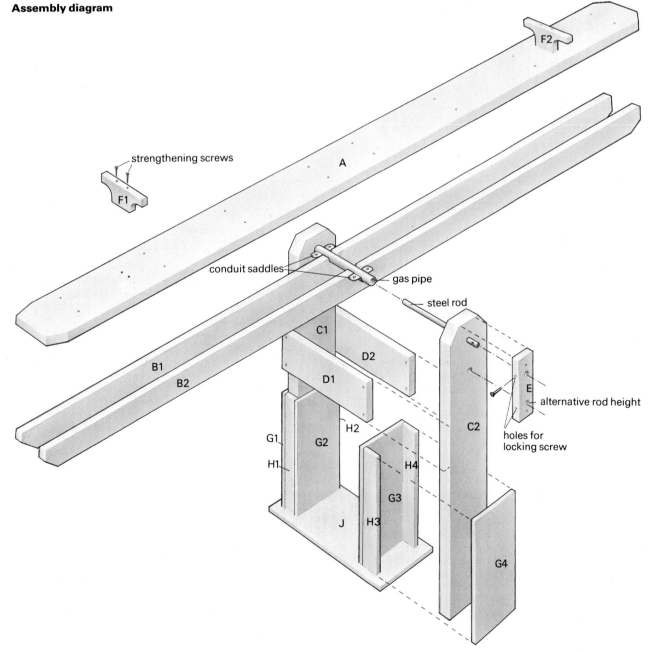

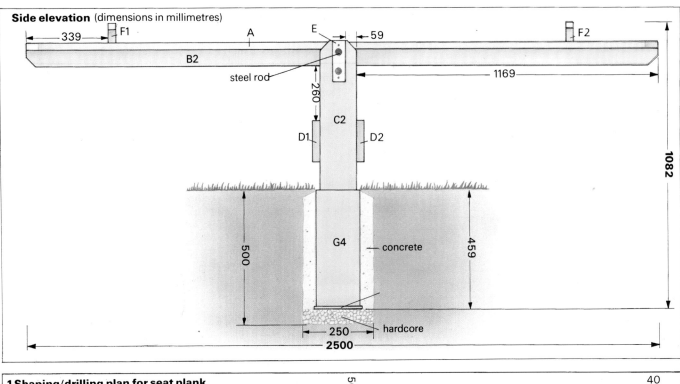

Side elevation (dimensions in millimetres)

339 — F1

A   E   59

B2

steel rod

260

C2

D1   D2

G4 — concrete

500

459

250

hardcore

1082

1169

2500

1 Shaping/drilling plan for seat plank

50

350   350   350   350   350   350   40

40   40

40   80

40   80   A

40   40

40   120   40

120   40

350   350

clearance holes
5 diameter

2 Shaping plan for reinforcers

26   26

40   B1/2   centre notch   40

40   1250   40

inset

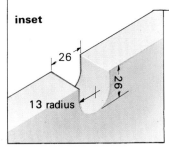

26

26

13 radius

dimensions shown (**see 3**) and cut off the waste with a coping saw. Smooth the curves at either side of the main shaft of the handle with a round file and round off the handle grips with a block plane and medium fine glasspaper. Drill two 5mm diameter clearance holes in the top of the handle at the dimensions shown (**see 3**) for the strengthening screws. Countersink these holes to take No 10 screws then drive the 65mm screws firmly home. These screws only

strengthen the handles; they do not fix anything.
Hold the handle in the required position over the clearance holes on the seat plank A and mark with a bradawl through the clearance holes onto the handle. Apply adhesive to the fixing edges of the handle and fix it firmly in position with the 65mm long countersunk screws. Wipe off excess adhesive. Shape and fix the second handle in the same way.
Fill all holes, cracks and abrasions with exterior grade cellulose filler or plastic wood and rub all surfaces smooth with medium fine, then fine, glasspaper. Apply a coat of primer, an undercoat and three top coats – we chose gloss yellow. Allow plenty of time for each coat to dry before applying the next.

Stage 3

Mark out and cut off the two top corners of both uprights C with a tenon saw to the dimensions shown (**see 4**) and chamfer all edges of C with a smoothing plane.
Mark out and drill the 19mm diameter holes in the locking piece E at the dimensions shown (**see 5**); drill the two 5mm diameter clearance holes and countersink them to take No 10 screws; finally drill two 5mm diameter holes, 27mm deep, in one edge of E through to the 19mm clearance holes and countersink them to take the locking screw.
Hold the locking piece E against the outer face of one of the uprights C so the top edges are flush (**see side elevation**) and mark with

a bradawl through the 5mm clearance holes in E onto C. Drill 2mm pilot holes at these points, apply adhesive to the fixing face of E and fix it firmly in position with the 38mm long No 10 countersunk screws. Wipe off excess adhesive.
Make sure both uprights are exactly the same size then clamp them together with two G-clamps so all edges are flush and the locking piece E is uppermost. Drill 19mm diameter holes through the previously drilled 19mm diameter holes in E (which can now act as a guide to ensure accuracy) through both uprights. This guarantees all the holes will line up perfectly when the see-saw is assembled. Place a piece of scrap wood under the drilling area to prevent wood breaking away as the

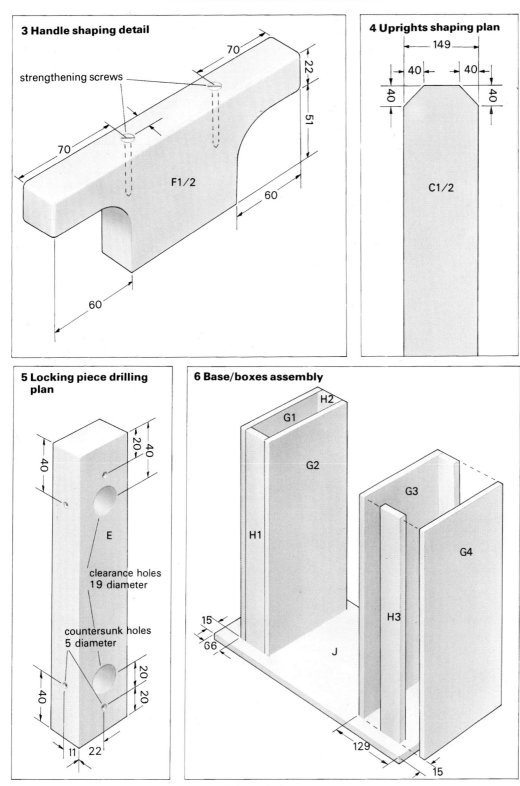

3 Handle shaping detail

strengthening screws

70

70

22

51

60

60

F1/2

4 Uprights shaping plan

149

40 40

40 40

C1/2

5 Locking piece drilling plan

40 20

40

E

clearance holes 19 diameter

countersunk holes 5 diameter

20 20

40

11 22

6 Base/boxes assembly

H2

G1

G2

H1

G3

G4

H3

15

66

J

129

15

Stage 4

Apply adhesive to both side edges of two box ends H and fix two of the box sides G in position with panel pins, making sure all edges are flush. Wipe off excess adhesive and assemble the second box in the same way. Apply adhesive to the bottom edges of both of these boxes and fix the base J in position with 25mm long panel pins in the position shown (**see 6**). When the adhesive has set hard apply two coats of creosote to the boxes and the base.

Stage 5

To set up the see-saw, find a flat area in your garden, cut the turf away carefully and dig a hole about 500mm by 250mm and about 500mm deep. Compress hardcore into the bottom of the hole, mix up concrete and pour some of this over the hardcore so the hole is only about 450mm deep. Lower the boxes in position on top of the wet concrete and check they are level in all directions by using a spirit level. Pour concrete all round the boxes (but not inside) using small pieces of hardcore to help fill the space. When you have filled the hole to within about 50mm from the top of the boxes, make the concrete slope down towards the outside of the hole (**see side elevation**). Allow at least 36 hours for the concrete to set then top up with soil and put back the turf so all that can be seen is the hole at the top of each box. Hold the seat plank A in position so the pivot tube is between the holes at the required height at the top of the two uprights C. Smear some car grease on the pivot bar and slide this through the hole in C1, through the pivot tube and the hole in C2 into the locking piece E so the small hole at the end of the pivot bar lines up with the hole in the side edge of E. Secure the pivot bar by pushing the 38mm locking screw through the clearance holes in E and the bar and screwing into the other side of E.

drill bit bursts through. Drill a 5mm diameter clearance hole 22mm in from each corner of both gussets D and countersink them to take No 10 screws. Hold one of the gussets in the required position against the two uprights C (**see side elevation**) so the ends of the gusset are flush with the outside faces of the uprights. Mark with a

bradawl through the clearance holes onto the uprights. Drill 2mm pilot holes at these points, apply adhesive to the fixing areas of the gusset (not more than 44mm in from each end) and fix it in position with 65mm screws. Wipe off excess adhesive. Fix the other gusset in the same way. Fill all holes and paint as before. File the ends of the pivot bar

square with a fine flat file, mark the position of the hole for the locking screw 11mm in from one end of the bar and make an indentation at this point with a centre punch. This prevents the drill bit sliding out of position; if you do not have a centre punch, a large nail will do. Drill a 6mm diameter hole through the bar at this point.

ROCKER

This unusual rocker will give your children hours of excitement. It is sturdily designed to take two or four children and can be used indoors or outdoors on an even surface.

Stage 1

Draw a grid of 100mm squares onto the hardboard offcut using a sharp pencil and metal straight-edge (**see 1**). Secure to the hardboard with panel pins a length of flexible hardwood batten, about 3mm thick, so it follows one of the curves of the main template; trace the curve onto the hardboard when you are certain the batten is accurately positioned (**see 1, cutting plan A and side elevation**). Remove the batten, use it to trace the other curve as before then

mark out the 50mm radius curve at the narrow end of the marked template. Cut out the template with a jig or pad saw and smooth the cut edges with fine glasspaper.
Place this main template on one of the sheets of plywood and trace round it onto the plywood at the four positions shown (**see cutting plan A**).
Remove the left section of the main template, cutting between the points X (**see 1**) to form the top template and half of the joint template.
Trace round the top template onto the same sheet of

TOOLS AND MATERIALS

two 2438 × 1219mm sheets of 9mm thick exterior grade
  plywood (see cutting plans)
1m of 16mm diameter dowel (for handles)
5m of 25mm diameter dowel (for bracing and footrest
  dowels)
1219 × 600mm of 3mm hardboard (for templates)
1930mm of 86 × 44mm softwood (for beam)
800mm of 44 × 22mm softwood (for handles)
200mm of 44 × 44mm softwood (for retaining blocks)
measuring tape, pencil and try square, mortise gauge
protractor and sliding bevel, metal straight-edge
pair of compasses, 19mm chisel, spirit level, bradawl
jig or pad saw, coping saw, fine-tooth panel saw
hammer and nail punch, mallet, two G-clamps, screwdriver
spokeshave, block plane, smoothing plane
electric drill, 2, 4, 5, 16 and 25mm bits, countersink bit
medium fine, fine and flour glasspaper
water-resistant woodworking adhesive and clean cloth

For assembly

panel pins 15, 32 and 50mm long
No 6 rustproof countersunk screws 19 and 32mm long
No 8 rustproof countersunk screws 32 and 50mm long
No 10 rustproof countersunk screws 50mm long
No 10 brass cup washers
matching plastic wood or cellulose filler, non-toxic gloss
  polyurethane lacquer or paint, 25 and 50mm paint brushes
  (for finish)

plywood as before at the four positions shown (**see cutting plan A**) and round the joint template at the two positions shown; you must turn the joint template over to form a mirror image to mark the whole of the required shape. Cut out all these shapes from the plywood using a jig or pad saw.

Apply water-resistant woodworking adhesive to one face of the main rocker pieces and fix the top and joint rocker pieces to them with the 15mm long panel pins so all curved edges are flush (**see 2a**); only two rocker halves need joint pieces. Wipe off all excess adhesive with a clean dampened cloth. Punch all pin heads below the surface of the plywood with a nail punch. Apply adhesive to the fixing surfaces of all the rocker halves and pin each joint together to form two

complete rockers (**see 2b**). Wipe off excess adhesive. When the adhesive has set hard, clamp both rockers together (without adhesive) and trim all edges with a spokeshave to ensure the rockers are exactly the same shape and size.

Stage 2

Mark the shape of the body side template onto the hardboard offcut using a flexible hardwood batten to mark the curve as before (**see 1, cutting plan B and side elevation**). Draw the 80mm radius curve with compasses, cut out the template with a jig or pad saw and smooth the cut edges with fine glasspaper. Place this template on the second sheet of plywood and mark out one of the body sides, turning the template over to form a mirror image for the second half of the side

Assembly diagram

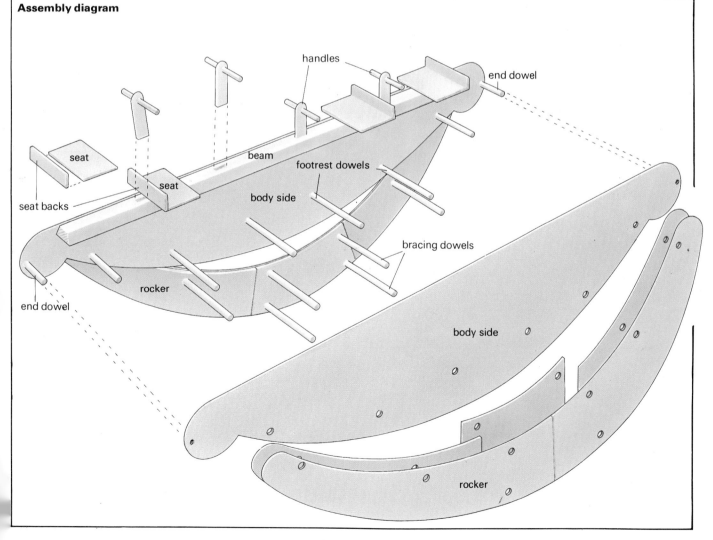

seat

seat

seat backs

handles

end dowel

beam

footrest dowels

body side

bracing dowels

rocker

end dowel

body side

rocker

Plan and elevation
(dimensions in millimetres)

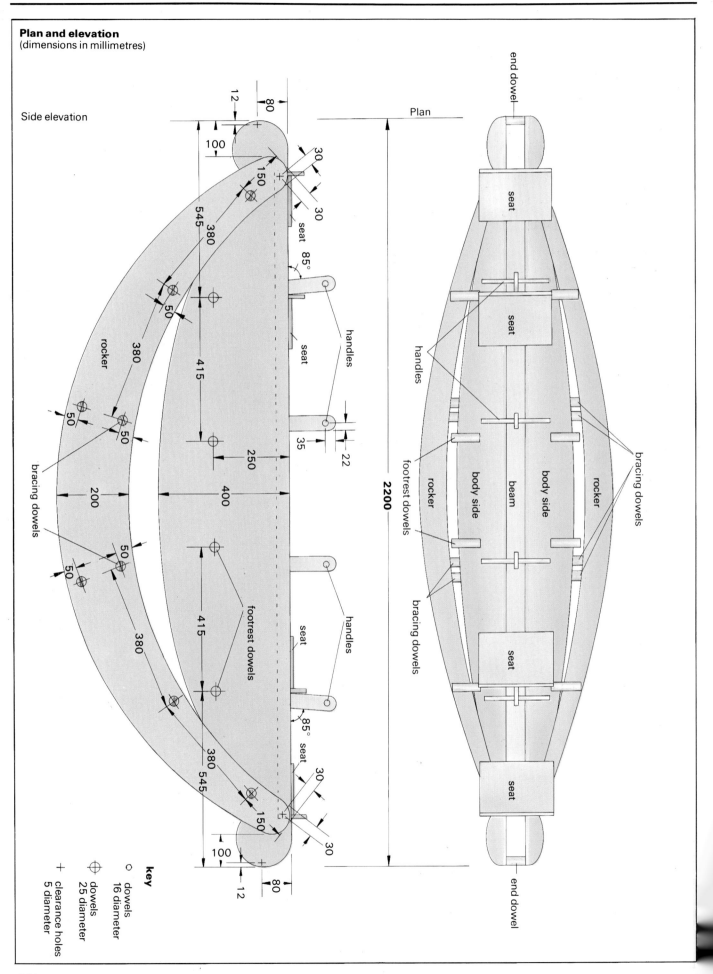

Side elevation

Plan

2200

12
80
100
30
30
150
545
380
seat
85°
380
rocker
50
415
handles
50
50
seat
bracing dowels
200
35
22
400
250
footrest dowels
415
50
50
seat
380
380
545
handles
85°
seat
150
30
100
30
80
12

end dowel

seat

seat

handles

footrest dowels

rocker
body side
beam
body side
rocker

bracing dowels

bracing dowels

seat

seat

end dowel

key
○ dowels
16 diameter
⊕ dowels
25 diameter
+ clearance holes
5 diameter

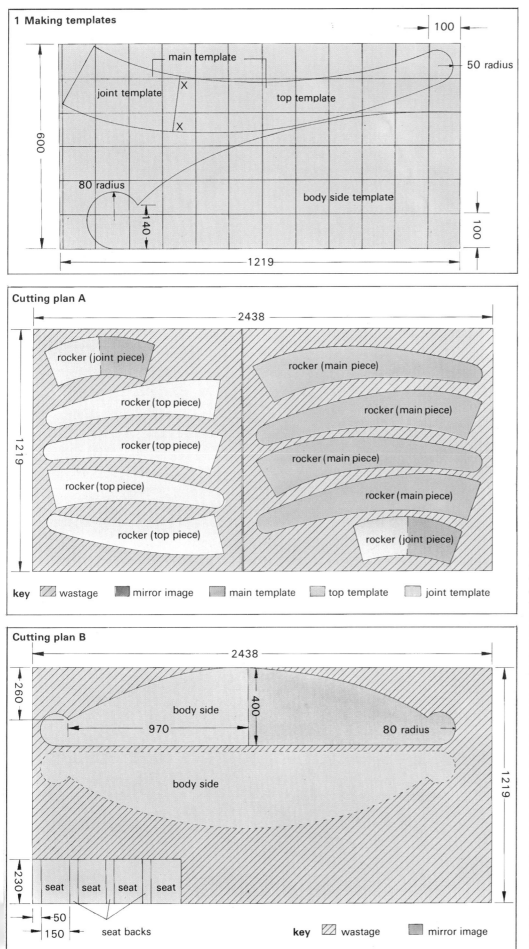

1 Making templates

main template

joint template

top template

50 radius

600

X

X

80 radius

140

100

1219

100

Cutting plan A

2438

1219

rocker (joint piece)

rocker (top piece)

rocker (top piece)

rocker (top piece)

rocker (top piece)

rocker (main piece)

rocker (main piece)

rocker (main piece)

rocker (main piece)

rocker (joint piece)

key ▨ wastage ▨ mirror image ▨ main template ▨ top template ▨ joint template

Cutting plan B

2438

260

body side

970

400

80 radius

1219

body side

230

seat | seat | seat | seat

50

150

seat backs

key ▨ wastage ▨ mirror image

to ensure it is symmetrical (**see cutting plan B**). Cut out this body side with a jig or pad saw and use this piece as a template to mark out the second body side. Cut out the second body side as before, clamp the two pieces together (without adhesive) and trim all edges using a spokeshave for the curves and a block plane for the straight edges.

Stage 3

Cut the length of 86 × 44mm softwood to 1930mm long. Using a mortise gauge, mark out in the beam the two parallel mortises for the outer handles and the two tapered mortises for the inner handles according to the dimensions shown (**see 3a and 3b**); chop out the waste from each one with a 19mm chisel, drilling out the bulk of the waste first. Mark out the 75 degree angles onto the beam using a protractor and sliding bevel (**see 3c**). Cut off the waste with a circular saw or a panel saw and plane down the cut edges to the dimensions shown (**see 3c**) using a smoothing plane. Cut the 44 × 22mm softwood into four 190mm lengths for the handles, mark out the 22mm radius curve at one end of each cut length and cut off the waste with a coping saw. Drill a 16mm diameter hole 35mm in from the curved ends and drill a 5mm diameter clearance hole in the top of each handle into these holes. Countersink the clearance holes to take No 8 screws. Cut the 16mm diameter dowel into four 200mm lengths and glue and fix these in the holes in the handles; secure them by driving 50mm long No 8 countersunk screws through the clearance holes into the dowels so the dowels protrude by an equal amount each side. Wipe off excess adhesive.

Cut eight wedges to the dimensions shown (**see 4**), apply adhesive to the insides of the mortises and to the wedges, push the handles inside the mortises and ram the wedges firmly home with a mallet; the wedges go from the top and bottom of the beam to form the angled outer handles and from the top only for the straight inner handles (**see 4**). Plane off the protruding bottom ends of the handles and wedges with a block plane and remove the protruding wedges at the top of the beam with a chisel.

Stage 4

Cut with a fine-tooth panel saw all the seats and seat backs from the second sheet of plywood according to the dimensions shown (**see cutting plan B**); smooth the cut edges with medium fine, then fine, glasspaper, slightly rounding off all corners and edges.

Drill four 5mm diameter clearance holes in the seat backs at the dimensions shown (**see 5**) and countersink them to take No 8 screws. Hold the seat backs in the required position against the seats and mark with a bradawl through the clearance holes. Drill 2mm pilot holes at these points, apply adhesive to the back edges of the seats and fix the backs firmly in position with the 32mm long No 8 screws. Apply adhesive to the two planed faces of the beam and fix the body sides firmly in position with the 50mm long panel pins making certain there is an equal gap between each end of the beam and the ends of the body sides (**see side elevation**). Wipe off excess adhesive and trim the protruding top edges of the body sides flush with the top of the beam.

Mark out the required position of each complete seat onto the top of the beam according to the positions shown (**see plan and side elevation**) and apply adhesive to the fixing areas. Fix the seats firmly in position with the 32mm long panel pins so there is an equal overhang at each side of the beam. Wipe off excess adhesive.

Drill 5mm diameter clearance holes at both top ends of both rockers and body sides at the dimensions shown (**see side elevation**); countersink the holes in the rockers for No 10 screws. Apply adhesive to the area of the body sides which will be in contact with the rockers and fix the rockers firmly and centrally in position with the 50mm long No 10 screws (**see side elevation**); we used brass screws and cup washers for a decorative finish. Tighten a G-clamp round each of these joints until the adhesive has set. Wipe off all excess adhesive.

Stage 5

Drill all the 25mm diameter dowel holes in the rockers

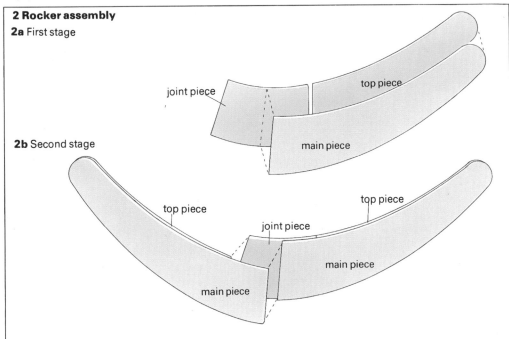

2 Rocker assembly

2a First stage

joint piece

top piece

main piece

2b Second stage

top piece

top piece

joint piece

main piece

main piece

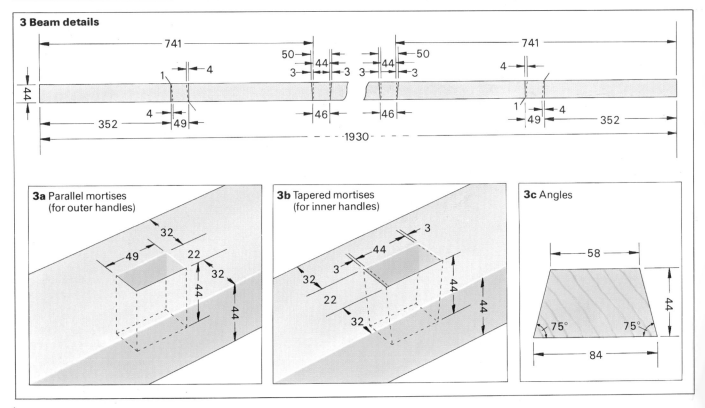

3 Beam details

741 · 50 · 44 · 3 · 44 · 50 · 741 · 4 · 44 · 1 · 4 · 3 · 3 · 3 · 4 · 352 · 4 · 49 · 46 · 46 · 1 · 49 · 352 · 1930

3a Parallel mortises (for outer handles)

32 · 49 · 22 · 32 · 44 · 44

3b Tapered mortises (for inner handles)

3 · 44 · 3 · 32 · 3 · 22 · 44 · 44 · 32 · 44

3c Angles

58 · 44 · 75° · 75° · 84

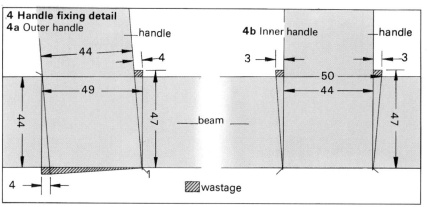

4 Handle fixing detail
4a Outer handle
handle

44
4
49
44
47
4

4b Inner handle
handle
3
50
44
47
3

beam

▨ wastage

5 Seat detail
+ clearance holes
5 diameter

seat back
50
230
seat
25
150
5
60
60
60
25

and the body sides according to the dimensions shown (**see side elevation**). Check all the time your drill is horizontal; it is best to tape a small spirit level to the top of the drill for this.

To fix the bracing dowels, slide the bought length of 25mm diameter dowel into each pair of holes and mark off where to cut it to ensure you cut exactly the right length. Cut the dowels, keeping slightly to the waste side of the marked line in every case, and cut a slot 20mm deep and about 3mm wide in both ends of all the cut dowels. Cut 16 wedges to the dimensions shown (**see 6**), glue the dowels in position, apply adhesive to the wedges and ram these firmly home inside the slots in the ends of the dowels with a mallet for a really strong fixing. When the adhesive has set hard, plane off the protruding ends of the dowels.

Cut two lengths of the 25mm diameter dowel to make the end dowels which fit between the body sides to brace the ends; these also act as handles so two people can carry the rocker without difficulty (**see plan**). Apply

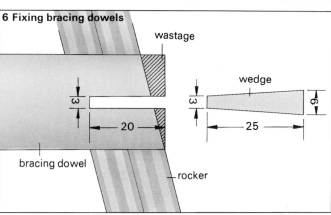

6 Fixing bracing dowels
wastage
wedge
3
3
6
20
25
bracing dowel
rocker

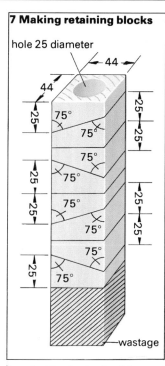

7 Making retaining blocks
hole 25 diameter
44
44
25
25
25
75°
75°
75°
25
75°
25
75°
25
75°
25
75°
25
75°
75°
wastage

adhesive to the ends of these dowels and fix them firmly in position with the 32mm long No 8 screws, using brass cup washers for a decorative finish.

Cut the remaining length of 25mm diameter dowel into four 400mm lengths for the footrests. These are held rigidly in position by retaining blocks screwed to the inside faces of the body sides. To make these blocks, drill a 25mm diameter hole centrally through the length of 44mm square softwood, drilling from each end towards the centre (**see 7**). Mark out the 75 degree cutting lines and cut off eight blocks from the same length of timber. Drill 4mm diameter clearance

holes 5mm in from the top and bottom edges of the retaining blocks (**see 8**) and countersink them to take No 6 screws. Slide the footrest dowels through one of the body sides and position the retaining blocks onto them so the angled faces of the two retaining blocks on each dowel face outwards towards the body sides (**see 8**). Slide the footrest dowels through the other body side, apply adhesive to the areas of the dowels which will be inside the holes in the body sides and adjust the dowels so they protrude equally at both sides. Apply adhesive to the angled faces of the retaining blocks and to the area of each dowel

just inside the body sides and fix the retaining blocks firmly to the body sides with the 19 and 32mm long No 6 screws. Pin through the sides of the retaining blocks into the dowels for a really strong fixing and wipe off all excess adhesive.

Stage 6

Fill any holes, cracks and abrasions with matching plastic wood or cellulose filler and rub all surfaces smooth with fine, then flour, glasspaper. For the finish, you could apply a coloured gloss polyurethane lacquer or gloss paint. We used an emulsion paint thinned with water so the wood grain would still be visible underneath and sealed this with three coats of gloss polyurethane lacquer for a weather-resistant finish to protect the rocker outside.

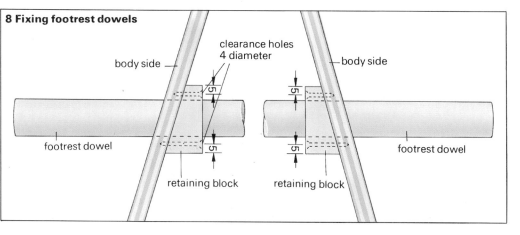

8 Fixing footrest dowels
clearance holes
4 diameter
body side
body side
5
5
5
5
footrest dowel
footrest dowel
retaining block
retaining block

Decorative features

*Every keen gardener likes to add features to make a garden
distinctive. For nature lovers we suggest bird habitats or a
water garden; or outdoor lighting for your barbecue may be
the distinction you prefer. For the less ambitious a new
planter or hanging basket can pretty up a dull corner.*

SINK GARDENS

There are two ways in which a sink garden can be made. The easiest and most popular method is to use an old porcelain sink. The other way is to use a mould and form the sink completely out of hypertufa.

Making a 'stone' sink

You will need two very strong cardboard, or wooden, boxes, one at least 5cm (2 in) smaller all round than the other, for your mould. The inner box should be about 30cm (12 in) deep (certainly no shallower) as this is an ideal depth for the plants.

You will need to make drainage holes in the bottom of the sink. In preparation for this, insert two pieces of wooden dowelling, about 2–3cm (1 in) in diameter and 10cm (4 in) long through the bottom of the inner box. In the base of the larger box place a layer of hypertufa, 5cm (2 in) deep. Use the basic recipe of (by volume) 2 parts coarse sand, 1 part horticultural or granulated peat and 1 part cement. Place the inner box in position inside the larger one, leaving an even space all round. Push the pegs down firmly into the base layer of hypertufa. (After the box moulds are finally removed, the pegs can easily be knocked through the drainage holes with a hammer.)

While the base layer is still moist, fill the cavity between the sides of the two boxes with hypertufa. Tamp the mixture down well with a piece of wood or an old broom handle to make sure there are no air pockets as these could weaken the sink.

Cover everything with moist sacking or some similar material for three or four days. After this period you should be able to remove the outer box by cutting it away and roughen the surface of the sink with a stiff brush to produce a more natural-looking effect. About 7–10 days later take away the inner box and also remove the wooden pegs.

Preparing the sink for use

Wash your home-made sink thoroughly before planting, otherwise chemicals in the cement may affect the plants. Either wash down and then soak the whole sink for several days or, for quicker results, use a solution of potassium permanganate crystals, dissolving 14gm ($\frac{1}{2}$ oz) of crystals in 13lit (3 gal) of water. Block up the drainage holes, fill the sink with this

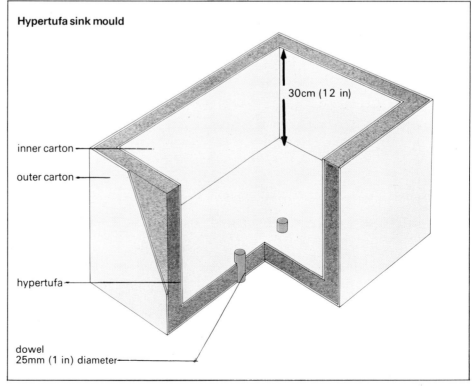

Hypertufa sink mould

30cm (12 in)

inner carton

outer carton

hypertufa

dowel
25mm (1 in) diameter

solution and allow it to remain in the sink for at least 24 hours. Finally, carefully scrub the inside with a stiff brush before draining off the solution.

Stand the sink on a few bricks to raise it about 15cm (6 in) above the paving so that surplus water can drain easily from the holes in the base.

The bottom of the sink should have a layer, about 5cm (2 in) deep, of drainage material such as clinker, stones, broken bricks or broken clay flowerpots. To prevent compost from blocking this drainage material, place a shallow layer of coarse peat, leaf mould or broken-up turfs over it. A suitable compost for alpines is J.I. No 1 to which some extra coarse sand or grit has been added to ensure good drainage. Alpines do like a really 'open', well-drained and well-aerated compost.

Try to obtain a few pieces of real tufa rock and place them in a natural-looking way on the surface of the compost, sinking them to about half their depth. If you cannot obtain natural tufa then make a few rocks with hypertufa. Blend the basic hypertufa mixture into a stiff but pliable mixture and mould it with your hands into small rocks. Allow to dry for a fortnight, soak in a solution of potassium permanganate for 24 hours and then they will be ready for use.

Planting the sink

The sink is now ready for you to start planting. There is quite a large range of suitable plants, so try to avoid those that are very vigorous in habit, otherwise they will soon outgrow the sink.

The positioning of plants will depend on your skill at producing natural-looking arrangements. Generally speaking, however, follow the simple and fairly obvious guidelines of placing trailing plants at the edges of the sink so that they cascade over the sides, with 'mat-formers' and cushion- and hummock-forming plants between the rocks. Adding one or two groups of dwarf conifers will give height to your garden.

Alpines are supplied in pots and the most suitable planting time is from late spring to mid summer (April–June). Use a small hand trowel for planting and make the plant holes large enough to take the soil ball when the plants are knocked out of their pots. Firm in the plants well with your fingers.

When you have finished planting spread a layer of small stone chippings over the compost. This creates a natural-looking appearance and will also prevent the surface of the compost from drying out rapidly. Then water in the plants and

remember to keep your sink watered regularly during dry weather, as it will tend to dry out quickly.

Choosing the plants

The following selection of plants can be thoroughly recommended for sink gardens. Starting with the trailing kinds there is: *Campanula carpatica* (bellflower), 15cm (6 in) high, with blue or white flowers in summer; *Gypsophila repens* Rosea (baby's breath), 15cm (6 in) high, has pink flowers in summer; *Phlox subulata* (moss phlox), 4–8cm (2–3 in) high, has pink, mauve or purple flowers in early and mid summer (May and June).

Of the hummock- and cushion-forming plants you could choose from: *Aethionema* Warley Rose, 10cm (4 in) high, with pink flowers from mid summer to early autumn (June–August); *Armeria caespitosa* (thrift), 5cm (2 in) high, with pink flowers in early summer; *Dianthus neglectus* (alpine pink), 10cm (4 in) high has pink flowers in mid summer (June); *Erodium chamaedryoides* Roseum (stork's bill), 2–3cm (1 in) high, with pink flowers in early summer (May); *Gentiana verna* (spring gentian), 8cm (3 in) high, with blue flowers in early summer (May);

Page 149 (top): hypertufa sink with gentian, saxifrage, cyclamen and some sedums, amid cleverly-placed rocks
Page 149 (below): how to make a sink
Below: colourful cushion plants look just as effective on the rocks as they do spreading between them

Geranium cinereum (cranesbill), 15cm (6 in), with pink flowers in late summer to early autumn (July–August); *Hypericum olympicum* (St John's wort), 15cm (6 in) high, with yellow flowers in summer; *Saxifraga apiculata* (saxifrage), 8cm (3 in) high, with pink flowers in mid to late spring (March–April); *Sedum spathulifolium* Capa Blanca, 8cm (3 in) high, with purple and white leaves and yellow flowers in early to mid summer (May–June); and any of the sempervivums (houseleeks) with fleshy leaves in various colours, 2–5cm (1–2 in) high.

Creeping or mat-forming plants include: *Raoulia australis* with silver foliage in summer; *Thymus drucei* (thyme) with pink, red or white flowers in summer; *Morisia monantha* forms rosettes of leaves 2–3cm (1 in) high and in spring produces yellow flowers.

A good dwarf conifer is the bluish-green, columnar *Juniperus communis* Compressa (juniper). It grows only about 2–3cm (1 in) per year. Plant in groups of three for a pleasing effect. Most other dwarf conifers are eventually too large for sink gardens.

Finally, miniature bulbs could be planted between the other plants, the planting time being autumn. Try the tiny yellow daffodils *Narcissus cyclamineus* and *N. bulbocodium* (hoop petticoat), and the blue *Scilla sibirica* (squill); all flower in spring. The crimson miniature *Cyclamen europaeum*, that flowers in early autumn (August), is also worth trying; plant this one in the spring.

MAKE A WINDOW BOX

A window box is not hard to make and will add colour and interest to the front of any house or flat. If you have no garden or patio, then an indoor window box may be your only way of enjoying a continuous display of plants – flowering, or evergreen (as shown here), and proving your green fingers to friends and neighbours.

Materials (for outdoor type)
timber (see cutting plan)
560mm (22 in) of 50 × 56mm (2 × 2 in) planed timber, *for feet*
approx thirty 30mm (1½ in) panel pins
waterproof wood glue, medium-size tin
twenty-four 50mm (2 in) No 8 brass or plated countersunk wood screws
waterproof wood filler, small tin
glasspaper
250ml (½ pt) primer paint, *for first coat*
250ml (½ pt) undercoat, *for second coat*
250ml (½ pt) top coat paint
or 500ml (1 pt) varnish (2–3 coats)
or 1 litre (2 pt) wood preservative

Materials (for indoor type)
timber (see cutting plan)
360mm (14 in) of 30 × 30mm (1½ × 1½ in) planed timber, *for feet*
approx thirty 30mm (1½ in) panel pins
woodworking glue, PVA type
wood filler; glasspaper, paint or varnish (*as for outdoor structure*)

Tools
measuring tape and pencil; tri square, panel saw; hammer; medium screwdriver; woodworking plane; pincers; hand or electric drill with 3mm ($\frac{3}{16}$ in) drill bit and 25mm (1 in) bit; bradawl (*for cutting screw thread pilot holes*); screwhead countersink bit; pin punch and Surform rasp type plane, *for indoor structure*

Our window box design has been arranged so that the method of construction (see diagram 1) can be applied to a wide range of materials and uses.

Indoor type

Where the box is to be used indoors and not exposed to damp earth or weather, then the construction material can be comparatively light and need not be weatherproof. If you prefer, you can stand plants in their pots inside the box, rather than fill the box with earth.

Plain chipboard This material provides an economical box which is constructed using panel pins and glue. After sanding smooth all joints and exposed ends, apply a finish either by painting or adding a heavy duty self-adhesive plastic covering. Take the covering over the top and 3–5cm (1–2 in) down the inside, and the same turn under the base where the feet, part D, will help to hold it in place. Drain-holes are not required but the inside should be fitted with a one-piece plastic sheet or aluminium kitchen foil liner to prevent any dampness penetrating the chipboard. Other methods and styles of finishing your indoor window box are shown on the next page.

Veneered chipboard For an elegant, real wood finish a ready-veneered chipboard material such as Conti-board can be used. Construction is the same except that all exposed cut edges should be veneered with matching edge trim before final assembly. This material is simple to apply using a standard electric iron, full instructions being supplied with the edge trim pack.

Carefully punch the heads of the panel pins you are going to use and fill the holes with matching plastic wood. A clear lacquer or varnish is suitable for the exterior finish, with the interior being lined as already described for plain chipboard.

Outdoor type

Where the box is to be used outdoors a heavier waterproof unit will be necessary. Plants in pots can also be stood inside the box if you do not want to fill it with earth.

Solid timber Standard softwood is suitable provided adequate weather protection is built in. A better quality material stocked by most timber yards is parana pine, but this, too, must be well weather-protected.

Page 151: constrasting evergreen planting in our completed window box has a repeat pattern of lavender, conifer and hebe at the back and shorter acuba, trailing ivy and euonymus in front

Plywood Use marine plywood, or water-and-boil-proof grade plywood, which is designed to withstand exposure to the weather. With outdoor boxes drain-holes must be provided (see diagram 1) to prevent water build-up. The holes should be about 25mm (1 in) in diameter. Location of the holes (in part B) is not critical provided that they are not covered by the feet (part D).

Cutting to fit

The cutting plan (diagram 2) allows for a box measuring externally 915mm (3 ft) long × 290mm (11 in) wide × 230 mm (9 in) deep. Sizes may, however, be adjusted to suit individual need or preference and a revised cutting list drawn up on the lines of that shown, so that construction remains as for diagram 1.

The alternative cutting plan (diagram 3) is for a lightweight indoor box measuring 610mm (2 ft) long × 180mm (7⅛ in) wide × 150mm (5⅞ in) deep.

Veneered/plain chipboard plywood Here one or two strips of material, preferably ready-cut out or at least cut to the desired width, should be purchased. Cutting of the various parts is then much more simple (see diagram 3) than cutting from a square sheet of material.

Solid timber Here a standard width plank should be purchased and the parts again cut as for diagram 2 by simply sawing across the length.

Assembly for indoor type

For a lightweight indoor box 30mm (1½ in), panel pins and glue may be used for assembly.

As the finished thickness of timber varies considerably, the cut length of part B must be determined taking this variation into account. Deduct from the length of parts C the thickness of the two ends, parts A, and then cut B to this size. Cut parts A to size and assemble to part B, then add the sides, part C.

Next cut the feet, parts D, from 30mm (1½ in) square timber to the over all width of the box and pin and glue in position from inside. Then punch all nails using a purpose-made steel pin punch, and fill the holes flush with plastic wood.

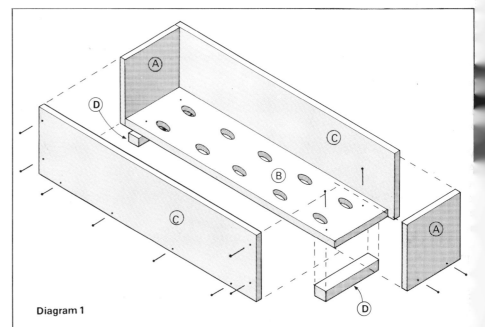

Diagram 1

Diagram 2 Cutting plan (Outdoor type) 25mm (1in) thick material

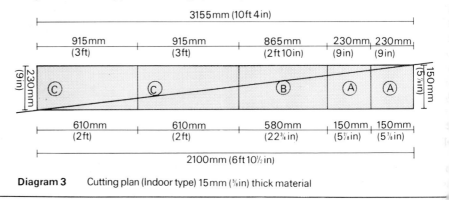

Diagram 3 Cutting plan (Indoor type) 15mm (⅝in) thick material

Assembly for outdoor type

The outdoor unit should be assembled (see diagram **1** and **2**) using waterproof glue and either brass or plated 50mm (2 in) × No 8 countersunk wood screws.

The size of part B must be determined in the same way as described for indoor assembly. Then glue parts A and temporarily pin to part B. Drill pilot and countersunk holes for the screws, and remove the temporary pins after the screws have been driven home.

Add parts C in a similar manner and cut the feet, parts D from 50mm (2 in) square timber, and screw in position from inside the box. Fill all screwheads and other imperfections with waterproof filler and plane and sand smooth the whole assembly. It is worth remembering that if your window ledge slopes downward, you can put leftover pieces of timber to good use as wedges to keep the box upright.

Painting

For complete weatherproofing you must paint the box carefully all round, paying particular attention to the end grain and inside the drainage holes. Any gaps in the paint will allow water penetration and lead to rapid deterioration of the timber and surrounding paint. Ideally you should give the box an initial coat of wood primer, followed by two undercoats and a final top coat. Allow each coat to dry thoroughly before applying the next one.

Wood preservative

Apply clear or coloured wood preservative, brushing all over the box. At least two coats should be applied and the box left to 'weather' for two to four weeks before putting in your plants.

If you want to use the box immediately, apply a horticultural-type preservative which will not harm the plants.

EVERGREEN PLANTING

For a permanent planting, a well-chosen mixture of evergreen plants provides a pleasing effect and requires the minimum attention. A selection from our list, which has been specially chosen for window boxes includes a wide range of foliage colour. If they are looked after properly the following plants could provide a display for up to four years: *Aucuba japonica viridis* (spotted laurel), *Euonymus japonicus*, lavandula (lavender), hebe and most varieties of hedera (ivy) – especially the variegated forms.

Several of the compact slow-growing conifers are also ideal for boxes; but when these grow too tall they should be replanted elsewhere rather than pruned.

IDEAS FOR DECORATION

After painting your box according to our instructions on this page, you could add a simple border stripe in a contrasting colour. Use strips of masking tape as guidelines. If you want something more elaborate, you can use the masking tape to mark out a design of horizontal, vertical or criss-cross stripes.

Stencil motif

Paint your own motifs, or spray paint a stencil pattern to make a bold design around the box. Fasten stencil in place with masking tape and when dry finish with clear lacquer if necessary. Simple designs using one or two colours look best so as not to compete with your plants.

Tile decoration

Choose traditional or modern designs and space tiles evenly along the sides and front of your box, using the correct tile adhesive. Or stick on self-adhesive plastic tiles but these may not withstand frost.

Collage

Try your hand at designing a collage of shells, mosaic, glass or broken pottery pieces. Set them into a quick-hardening plasticized cement mortar-mix such as Marley Smoothtex. Apply the cement as a 6–13mm ($\frac{1}{4}$–$\frac{1}{2}$ in) layer and leave till tacky – about 10 minutes. Stick on your shells etc. and leave to set for a couple of hours. It is easier to work with the box front up, to give a horizontal working surface.

CONCRETE PLANTER

This planter is ideal for use outside the home and needs no maintenance; you can make as many as you want with the same mould.

TOOLS AND MATERIALS

timber (see cutting list)
measuring tape, pencil and try square
fine-tooth panel saw, tenon saw, block plane
medium fine and fine glasspaper
hand or electric drill
3 and 5mm bits, 12mm masonry bit
screwdriver, bradawl, countersink bit
hammer and nail punch
water-resistant woodworking adhesive, clean cloth
exterior grade cellulose filler
5m of 19 × 6mm hardwood batten
No 10 countersunk screws 50mm long
panel pins 12 and 25mm long
0.5 litre of clean (new) engine oil
fine ready-mix concrete (about 40kg for one planter)
watering-can and stiff brush, steel float
expanded polystyrene (for drainage plugs)

Stage 1

Measure and cut all the pieces of plywood with a fine-tooth panel saw according to the dimensions shown (**see cutting list**). Smooth all cut edges with medium fine, then fine, glasspaper.

Drill all the 5mm diameter clearance holes in the two mould box sides B at the dimensions shown (**see 1**) and countersink them to take No 10 screws. Hold the sides B, one at a time, in the required position against the base A (**see assembly diagram**) and mark with a

bradawl through the clearance holes in B1 and B2 onto A. Drill 3mm pilot holes at these points and fix the sides firmly in position with the 50mm long No 10 screws; don't use adhesive for the fixing or you will not be able to take the mould box apart.

Hold the mould box ends C, one at a time, in the required position between the sides and on top of the base (**see**

assembly diagram) and mark with a bradawl through the clearance holes in B1 and B2 onto C1 and C2. Remove the ends C, drill 3mm pilot holes at these points and fix them firmly in position with the 50mm long No 10 screws.

Stage 2

Chamfer all the edges of the mould plug base D with a sharp block-plane according to the dimensions shown (**see 2**). Mark out and cut the mould plug sides E and ends F to the required shape (**see 3a and 3b**) and smooth the cut edges with medium fine, then fine, glasspaper. Drill all the 5mm diameter clearance holes in the two sides E at the dimensions shown (**see 3a**) and countersink them to take No 10 screws.

Apply water-resistant woodworking adhesive to both long edges of the mould plug base D and fix the sides E in position with the 50mm long No 10 screws. Wipe off excess adhesive with a clean dampened cloth. Don't remove the waste from the bottom edges of the sides until you have finished making the mould plug.

Hold the two ends F in the required position between the two sides E (**see assembly diagram**) and mark with a bradawl through the clearance holes drilled in E1 and E2 onto F1 and F2. Drill 3mm

Cutting list for exterior grade plywood

Description	Key	Quantity	Dimensions
Mould box base	A	1	645 x 230 x 16mm
Mould box sides	B	2	645 x 246 x 16mm
Mould box ends	C	2	230 x 230 x 16mm
Mould plug base	D	1	453 x 102 x 16mm
Mould plug sides	E	2	563 x 206 x 16mm
Mould plug ends	F	2	192 x 148 x 16mm
Support battens	G	2	322 x 30 x 16mm
Support stops	H	4	40 x 30 x 16mm

Assembly diagram

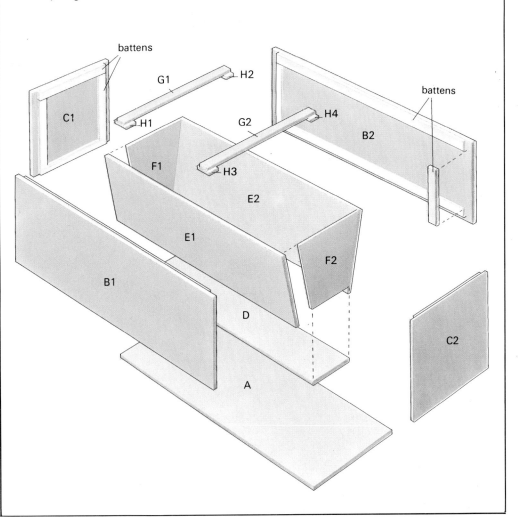

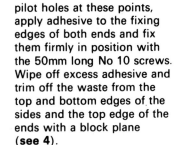

pilot holes at these points, apply adhesive to the fixing edges of both ends and fix them firmly in position with the 50mm long No 10 screws. Wipe off excess adhesive and trim off the waste from the top and bottom edges of the sides and the top edge of the ends with a block plane (**see 4**).

Fill any holes, cracks and abrasions with exterior grade cellulose filler and rub smooth the inside face of the mould box and the outside face of the mould plug with medium fine, then fine, glasspaper. These faces must be perfectly smooth since they will be in contact with the concrete.

Cut the hardwood batten with a tenon saw into four 613mm lengths, four 218mm lengths and eight 192mm lengths. Glue and pin these in the required position to the inside faces of the mould box (**see assembly diagram**) using the 12mm long panel pins. Punch all pin heads below the surface of the timber with a nail punch, wipe off excess adhesive and fill the remaining holes with exterior grade cellulose filler. Using medium fine glasspaper, round off the edges of these battens so they do not grip the concrete, which would

Plan and sections
(dimensions in millimetres)

Plan

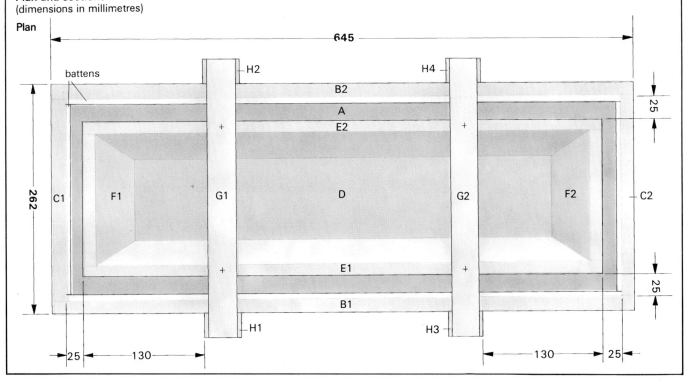

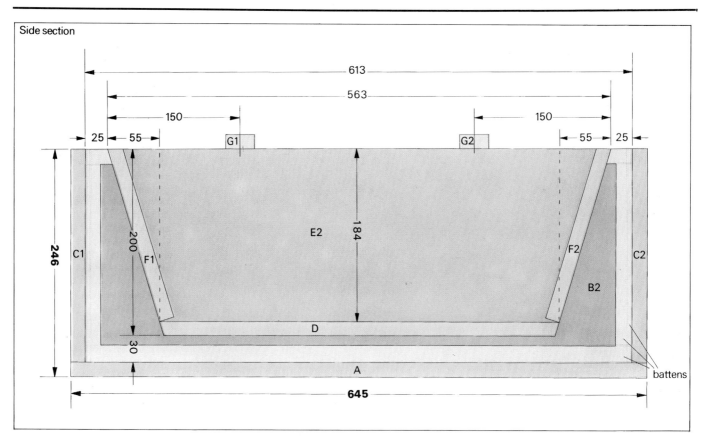

Side section

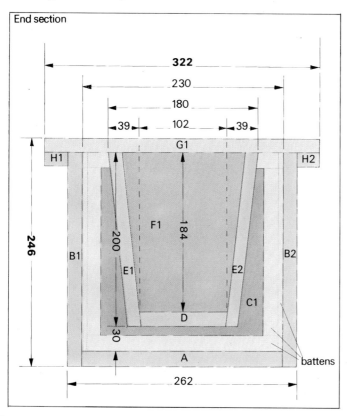

End section

make it difficult to remove the mould box when the concrete has set.
Glue and pin the support stops H at both ends of both support battens G with 25mm long panel pins so the end edges are flush and the side edges of the stops overhang the battens by 5mm at each side (see 5). Wipe off excess adhesive. Drill two 5mm diameter clearance holes in both support battens at the dimensions shown (see 5) and countersink them to take No 10 screws. Place the support battens in the required position over the mould plug and mark with a bradawl through the clearance holes in the support battens G onto the mould plug sides E. Drill 3mm pilot holes at these points before fixing the supports to the mould plug with the 50mm long No 10 screws.

Stage 3

A few days before using the mould, wet the mould plug to make the timber swell. This is to prevent it swelling any further when in contact with the wet concrete, since this would make it almost impossible to withdraw when the concrete has set.
Before mixing and casting the concrete, give the surfaces of both the mould box and mould plug, which will be in contact with the concrete, a generous coat of clean (new) engine oil.
Leave this for several hours for the plywood to absorb the oil, then apply a second coat and a third just before pouring the concrete into the mould. The oil prevents the concrete bonding to the surface of the mould, but be sure to wipe off all excess oil from the plywood otherwise it could stain the surface of the concrete.
Add water to about 40kg of fine ready-mix concrete with a maximum coarse aggregate size of 10mm. If you intend to make a number of planters, it is cheaper to buy the sand and cement separately.
Remove the mould plug from the mould box and pour some concrete (a little at a time) into the bottom of the box to a final depth of 30mm, tamping it thoroughly to prevent air bubbles forming which would spoil the appearance of the planter and weaken the concrete.
Cut two blocks of expanded polystyrene about 30 × 15 × 15mm and push these centrally into the concrete 100mm in from each end; these will be drilled out later to form drainage holes. Position the mould plug centrally inside the box and anchor it by hammering 25mm long panel pins through the support battens G into the top edges of the mould box. Fill the box with concrete (not the inside of the plug) adding it gradually and tamping it firmly down to ensure there are no air bubbles. When the mould is full, smooth the top of the concrete with a steel float

and leave to set. Don't leave the concrete to set outdoors if there is likely to be a frost; frost is concrete's biggest enemy.

After about four hours test to see whether the concrete has hardened by pressing a finger on the top surface. On a hot, dry day the concrete will harden quickly; on a cold, damp day it could take a long time; don't try to remove the mould from the concrete before the concrete has hardened. Tap lightly all round the inside of the mould plug to loosen the hold between the plug and the concrete and pull on the support battens to remove the plug. With a little patience and persuasion the plug will lift straight out. Unscrew the mould box sides from the ends and base and remove all the plywood; this can be stored away until it is to be used again.

Immediately after releasing the planter from the mould, the surface of the concrete can be washed to expose the coarse aggregate and produce a pebbledash effect. Sprinkle water all over the concrete with a watering can fitted with a fine rose and brush it off with a stiff brush until the aggregate is exposed. Find the positions of the expanded polystyrene blocks and drill them out with a masonry drill to give you the drainage holes.

For the next week be sure to keep the concrete damp by sprinkling it with water from time to time and wrapping it in polythene; but you must remember to keep it protected from frost.

Before filling the planter with soil, line the bottom of it with small pebbles to ensure there is sufficient drainage and the drainage holes do not become blocked. If you do not do this, the soil could become waterlogged and affect the plants.

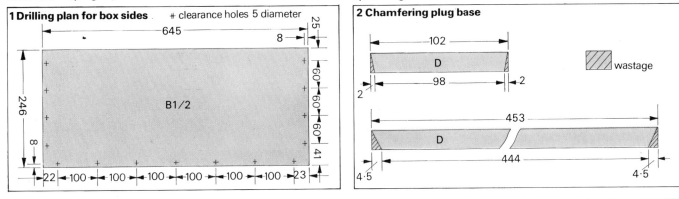

1 Drilling plan for box sides   + clearance holes 5 diameter

2 Chamfering plug base

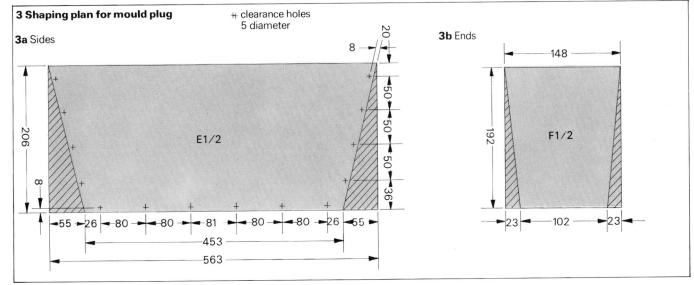

3 Shaping plan for mould plug   + clearance holes 5 diameter

3a Sides

3b Ends

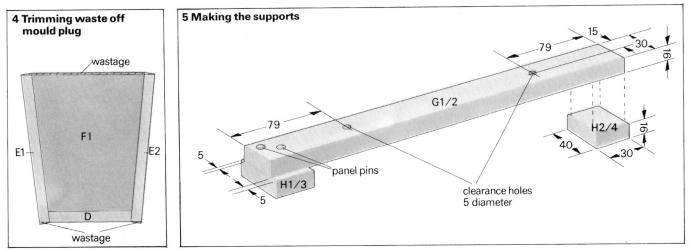

4 Trimming waste off mould plug

5 Making the supports

MAKE A HANGING BASKET
for your patio

This type of hanging basket was originally designed for spike orchids so that their flowers could grow through the wooden slats. Although still much used by orchid growers, the basket will accommodate any trailing plant, but don't choose one that will be constricted by the hanging chains. The trailing ivy we show here, petunias or pelargoniums would all be a good choice.

Tools

set square
tenon saw
rule
hand or electric drill with 6mm (¼ in) bit
hammer
pliers

Materials

4·6m (15 ft) of 12 × 12mm (½ × ½ in) square-section ramin
2m (2 yd) brass-finish flat-link safety chain
one 25mm (1 in) and four 13mm (½ in) key rings or split curtain rings, preferably brass finish
wood glue
four 25mm (1 in) panel pins
plastic wood
yacht varnish or linseed oil
15cm (6 in) flower pot
angle bracket

Construction

Using the tenon saw, cut twenty 200mm (8 in) lengths and two 150mm (6 in) lengths from the ramin. Mark the positions of the holes (A) on each of the 200mm-long pieces (see diagram 1) and drill. Bring all the wood to a smooth finish with fine glasspaper.

Pin and glue the 150mm-long pieces between two of the 200mm ones, to form the base (see diagram 2). Punch panel pins below the surface of the wood, fill in with plastic wood and bring to a smooth finish with fine glasspaper.

Give all the pieces two coats of yacht varnish, or rub in linseed oil.

Cut the chain into four equal lengths and thread a length through the drilled holes at each corner (see diagram 3), making sure the links are narrow end up. Attach a small ring to the chain at each corner under the base layer and the large ring to the top ends of all four chains, bringing them together.

Finally, fix the wall bracket (make sure it is strong enough to take the weight of the plant and basket) in the desired position and hang the basket up by the ring. It takes a 15cm (6 in) flowerpot, plus drip tray if required

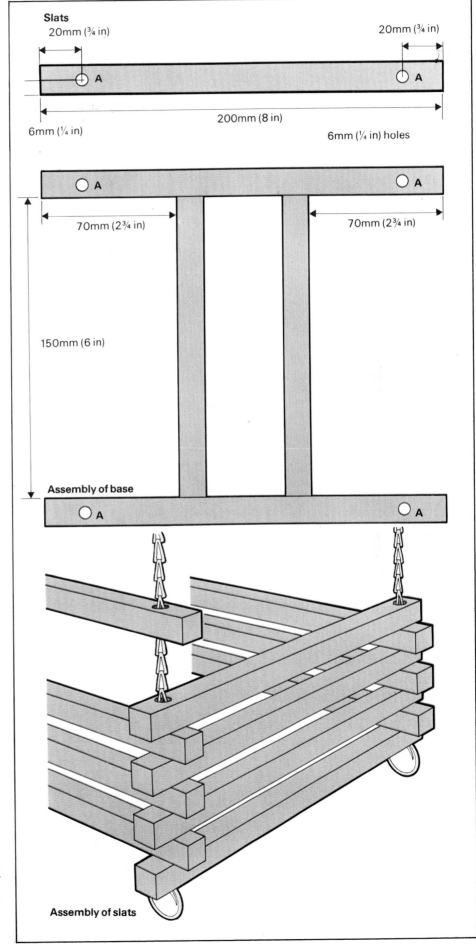

Slats
20mm (¾ in)   20mm (¾ in)
A   A
200mm (8 in)
6mm (¼ in)
6mm (¼ in) holes

A   A
70mm (2¾ in)   70mm (2¾ in)

150mm (6 in)

Assembly of base

A   A

Assembly of slats

BIRD HABITATS

BLUE TIT HOUSE

Blue tits require quiet, open locations about 2m above the ground and facing south. Males claim and defend their territory and will fight any blue tits nesting within 200m. It is, therefore, worth making only one blue tit house unless you have a very big garden. Blue tits are easily driven from their home by more aggressive birds; the 3.5cm entrance hole will exclude starlings and the perch on the inside of the house discourages sparrows.

Cutting, drilling and shaping

Cut all the timber to the sizes and shapes shown (see diagram), using a fine-tooth panel saw. Smooth all the cut edges with medium glasspaper.

Drill the two 3mm holes in the back, the 6mm and the 3.5cm hole in the front and the two 6mm drain holes in the floor.

Using a block plane, bevel the top edge of the roof to fit the back and the bottom edge of the holding slat to fit the roof.

Assembly

Glue and fix the two sides to the floor, using 38mm long panel pins and ensuring the bottom, back and front edges are flush. Use a water-resistant woodworking adhesive for all fixings. Glue and pin the

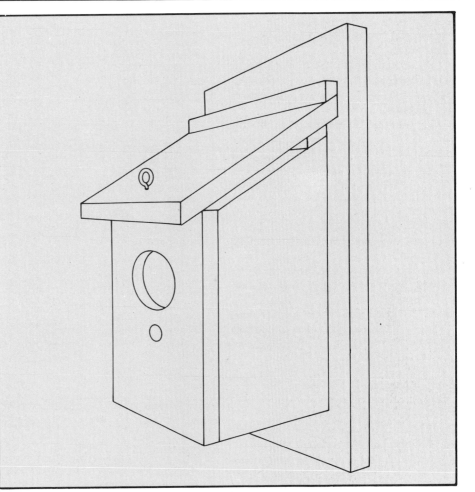

Tools and materials

1.5m of 205 × 20mm softwood
measuring tape, pencil and try square
fine-tooth panel saw
medium glasspaper, block plane
electric drill, 6mm and 35mm bits
38mm long panel pins
5cm of 6mm diameter dowel
one large brass screw eye
water-resistant woodworking adhesive
wood preservative, old paint brush

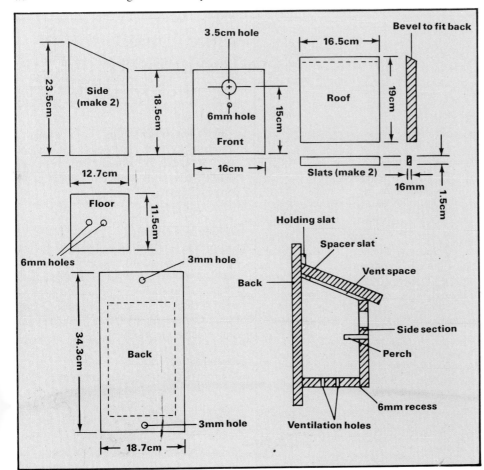

Above: Blue tits are easily driven from their nests by more agressive birds, but the 3.5cm hole in the front will prevent the entry of most types; the perch inside discourages sparrows. The roof of the house can be opened by unscrewing the eye that fixes it to the front; this will enable you to clean out the house once a year

Left: Cutting and drilling plans for the softwood with which to make the blue tit house and a cross-sectional detail

front in position on the sides and floor, making sure it is the right way up and all edges are flush.

Cut a 5cm length from some 6mm diameter dowel and glue it inside the small hole in the front to form the perch **(see diagram)**.

Glue and pin the spacer slat to the top ends of the sides and ensure the joints remain square. Put the roof in place and pin the holding slat tightly against it but not to it. Insert a large screw eye centrally through the bottom end of the roof into the front. Once a year, remove this eye to clean the inside of the bird house. Leave the house in a safe place for the adhesive to set hard.

For the finish, apply three generous coats of wood preservative to all outside surfaces with an old paint brush and leave the bird house outside with a cover over it for at least ten days for the wood preservative to dry out completely.

Right: Having cut and drilled all your pieces of softwood correctly, the blue tit house can be assembled, according to the diagram; remember the left-hand side of the house has been omitted for clarity. The construction can be glued and pinned together after you have checked the parts fit together properly

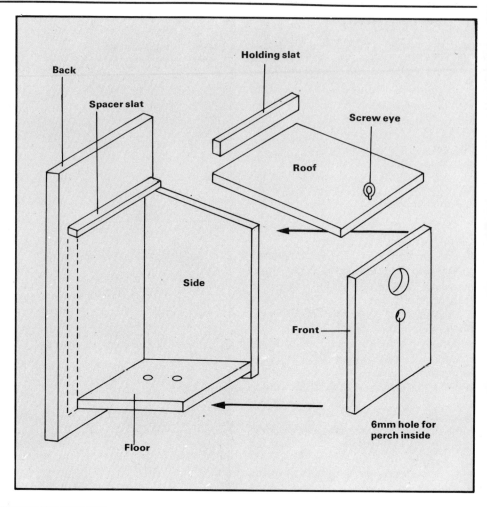

WREN HOUSE

The perky little wren has adapted very well to suburban life and, although it loves to live in a hole in an old tree, it seems to appreciate a well-made house like this one.

The 2.2cm entrance hole excludes larger birds and the house should be fixed at least 3m above the ground—ideally to a wall—out of danger from prowling cats.

Cutting and drilling

Cut all the timber to the sizes and shapes shown **(see diagram)**, using a fine-tooth panel saw. Smooth all the cut edges with medium glasspaper.

Drill the 6mm hole and the 2.2cm entrance hole in the front then drill the 1cm hole in the back.

Assembly

Glue and fix the two sides to the back with the 38mm long panel pins so the outside edges are flush **(see diagram)**; use a water-resistant woodworking adhesive for all fixings. Glue and pin the floor in position so there is an equal gap at each side for drainage and ventilation. Glue and pin

Below left: The wren house is decorative as well as functional and can be situated in the garden or on the side of the house, as long as it is well clear of the ground; the small hole will deter other birds Right: Cutting and drilling plans for the softwood with which to make your wren house and an assembly diagram showing you how the component parts fit together by means of adhesive and pins; the left-hand side of the house has been omitted from the diagram for clarity. Check first all the parts fit together correctly

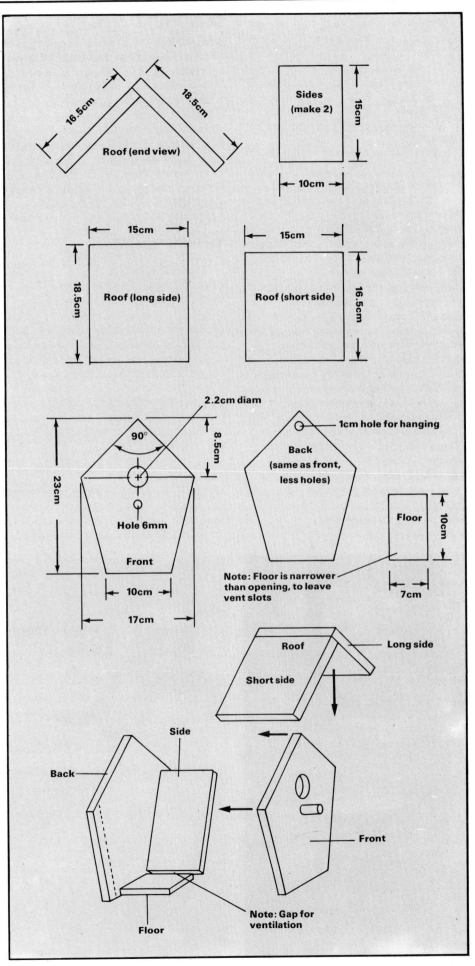

the front in position on the sides and floor, making sure all joints remain square.

Glue and pin the short side of the roof in position so the back edges and the top corners are flush, leaving an overhang at the side and front of the house. Pin the long side of the roof in position, butting it against the short side to leave an over-hang at the side and front of the house as before; don't use adhesive to fix the long side of the roof so you can remove it every year and clean the inside.

Cut a 5cm length from some 6mm diameter dowel and glue this inside the small hole in the front to form the perch **(see diagram)**. When all the adhesive has set hard, apply three coats of wood preservative to all outside surfaces in the same way as for the blue tit house.

Tools and materials
1.2m of 205 × 20mm softwood
measuring tape, pencil and try square
fine-tooth panel saw
medium glasspaper
electric drill, 6, 10 and 22mm bits
38mm long panel pins
5cm of 6mm diameter dowel
water-resistant woodworking adhesive
wood preservative, old paint brush

CONCRETE BIRDBATH

The simplest way to make a birdbath is to use a dustbin lid as a mould, fill it with concrete and either scoop out a shallow central portion as the concrete begins to harden or press the bottom of a dustbin into the concrete and round off the edges with a trowel. We made ours by pressing a dustbin into the concrete in the mould since this is the quickest and easiest way to obtain good results. We used a 50cm diameter dustbin lid which had an overall depth of 7.5cm.

Preparing the mould

Place the dustbin lid upside down in a dustbin filled with water to about two-thirds of capacity to prevent it collapsing under the weight of the concrete.

Cover the indentations in the lid (for the handle and locking tabs) with some rubberized asbestos roofing material, scrap aluminium sheet or stiff plastic and secure the cut pieces with masking tape.

Line the inside of the mould with a sheet of thin polythene to make it easier to remove the hardened concrete from the mould; the polythene peels off easily when the concrete has set.

Filling the mould

We used about two-thirds of a 4.5kg bag of fine ready-mix concrete. If you intend to make a number of birdbaths (they are great presents for friends with gardens), it is cheaper to buy the sand and cement separately.

Mixing concrete Mix the concrete thoroughly with a shovel in a large bowl or bucket or in an old wheelbarrow. Add enough water to make a stiff mix.

Making bottom layer Shovel the mixed concrete into the mould to a depth of 2cm, tamping it down thoroughly to prevent air bubbles forming which would spoil the appearance of the birdbath and weaken the concrete. Using a pair of wire-cutters (pliers will suffice), cut a circle out of the wire mesh or chicken wire about 3cm smaller in diameter than the area filled with concrete. Lay the mesh onto the concrete for reinforcement.

Making top layer Shovel in another 1.5cm of concrete, tamping it down thoroughly as before. Place the bottom of a second dustbin (or similar large container) in the centre of the concrete in the mould, shovel in more concrete round the outside and tamp it firmly down.

Smooth the outside area with a trowel or steel float to form the rim of the birdbath and leave for the concrete to harden. Don't leave the concrete to set outdoors if there is likely to be a frost; frost is concrete's biggest enemy.

Finishing off

After about four hours, test to see whether the concrete has hardened by pressing a finger on the top surface. On a hot, dry day the concrete will harden

Below: The concrete birdbath shown here has a fluted interior and rounded edging to give it some decoration and improve its appearance in the garden
1 To make your birdbath you will need an asbestos patch, dustbins, a cover, concrete mix, a basin, a trowel, wire mesh, wire-cutters and masking tape. If you decide to mix your concrete, use cement, sand and aggregate with a maximum size of 10mm in the proportions of 1:2:4. Alternatively use cement and all-in aggregate in the proportions 1:6
2 Fill two-thirds of a plastic dustbin with water so it holds its shape and will not collapse; place the lid upside down in the dustbin and tape up any indentations and holes around the rim
3 To make it easier to remove the concrete when set, line the inside of the mould with a thin polythene sheet
4 Mix the concrete thoroughly

5 *Put your concrete mix into the mould and spread it evenly to form a 2cm thick bottom layer*

6 *Cut a piece of wire mesh to shape and press it down into the wet concrete; this will reinforce the bottom of the bath*

7 *Having added another 1.5cm of wet concrete over the wire, carefully centre the bottom of another dustbin in the mould*

8 *With the second dustbin in place, fill in the sides with more concrete*

9 *Smooth round the sides of the birdbath with a trowel or steel float*

quickly; on a cold, damp day it could take a long time; don't try to remove the concrete from the mould before the concrete has hardened.

Lift the dustbin out of the centre of the concrete in the mould, turn the dustbin lid carefully over on a smooth, flat surface and tap it lightly until it pulls away from the concrete, then remove the polythene.

For the next week be sure to keep the concrete damp by sprinkling it with water from time to time and wrapping it in polythene; remember to keep it protected from frost.

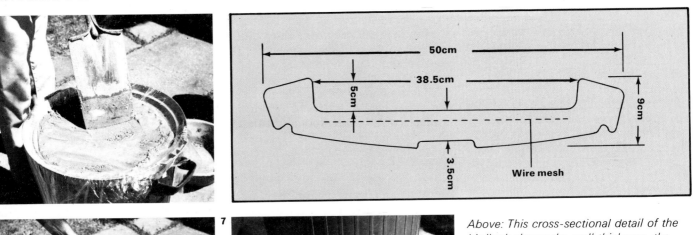

Above: This cross-sectional detail of the birdbath shows the wall thickness, the position of the reinforcing wire mesh and the depth of the area for water

Tools and materials
one 4.5kg bag of ready-mix concrete, or separate sand and cement
dustbin lid (for mould), shovel, trowel or steel float
rubberized asbestos roofing material or aluminium sheet or stiff plastic
masking tape and thin polythene
wire mesh or chicken wire, pair of wire-cutters or pliers, measuring tape

OUTDOOR LIGHTING

Perhaps the most fascinating aspect of exterior lighting is that you can extend the enjoyment of living 'outdoors' well into the late summer evenings.

But lighting can also be put to a more severe or practical purpose – to provide light for walks or steps, or simply to illuminate the terrace or patio. Installed in the greenhouse or in the vegetable garden it enables you to put in those extra few hours caring for plants and crops.

Outdoor lighting kits
Outdoor lighting in a garden has been considerably simplified by the availability of special kits containing all the necessary parts to ensure a neat and quick system. The need to have absolute safety where electricity is concerned is covered by the use of a low-voltage arrangement whereby the mains electricity from the power source is transformed down to the safe voltage of 12 volts. Any outside (waterproof) sockets will require a separate fuse in your fuse box. All materials used for outdoor lighting must be weather-resistant and lamp housings carefully sealed. If, on the other hand, it is intended to use mains voltage throughout the layout – say for decorative lanterns or street lamps – then it is always advisable to call in the services of a qualified electrician to undertake all electrical connections. It is also advisable to check with the local electricity authority to make sure that your fittings comply with their regulations.

A typical garden lighting kit comprises one or more lamp units plus fixing brackets or ground spikes, as well as a generous amount of special cable. In some cases tinted lens covers are available for coloured lighting effects.

The low-voltage system means that there is no need to dig out special trenches for cables and there is, therefore, a substantial saving in time and effort. The cable can be left on the surface of the soil or lightly covered with soil. It can be taken round obstacles quite easily, and as most of the cables are coloured green, they blend well with plants.

The special ground spikes enable lamps to be used at ground level and the lamp-holder adjusted to throw the light at a particular feature. To illuminate a terrace, you use the wall-mounting brackets provided with the kit.

The transformer, that must be under cover, is powerful enough to take up to six lamps so, starting with a two-lamp kit, the gardener can add more lights later on up to the maximum of six. Wiring up the lamps is a simple operation. In some versions, the cable is placed across the rear of the lamp-housing and the cover screwed into place. Special 'teeth' bite into the cable as this is done, thus making the electrical contact. A more conventional system has the cable ends screwing into terminal blocks or connectors within the lamp.

Another system, that operates off mains electricity and so does not use a transformer, has double-insulated lamp-holders moulded in synthetic rubber. It also has lamps on a support leg with base plate and ground spike. Double-insulated cable is used here with a special moulded two-pin plug and extension cables are available with connections so that more lamps can be added to the layout. The cables should be buried 45–60cm (18–24 in) under the soil.

The floodlamps are 100 watt and lamps in red, blue, green, yellow or clear are available. The clear floodlamps can also be used at 150 watts. This particular outfit is the only one that is safe enough for the lamps – and only the lamps – to be used underwater.

Water garden outfits
Some of the most beautiful lighting effects can be achieved with special water garden lighting outfits. Here the lamps are carefully sealed so that they can be either floated on the water's surface, or weighted to provide underwater effects. Lights are usually sold in pairs connected to about 1·8m (6 ft) of cable with a further 3·3m (11 ft) or so of cable connected to one of the units for connection to a low-voltage transformer that should be situated outside the water feature. The lights here are available in colour combinations of amber/blue; red/clear and red/green, providing a versatile range of contrasting shades.

An interesting and very handy device is a flexible 13mm ($\frac{1}{2}$ in) rubber tubing ring with perforations. It is attached to the water pump in a pool and when placed on one of the floating lights, produces a delicate 'ring' fountain effect through which the lamp's beams shine.

What to illuminate?
The first thing to do is to take a careful look at your garden and select those features attractive enough for illumination. Compare the focal points in your garden, such as any ornament, a screen wall, specimen tree or shrub – even the driveway if flanked by colourful borders – and light up some but not all of them. Don't get carried away with too many colour clashes; a scheme using just blue and white lighting is often the most effective. If you have a water feature, this can of course be illuminated to good effect, especially a fountain.

Once you have decided on which features to illuminate, the lights should be placed approximately in position and then connected to the wiring. The next stage is the most important of all – adjusting the throw of the light to achieve the best effect. This will be, to a certain extent, a matter of trial and error. Try to 'enclose' a specimen tree, for example, in a cone or beam of light. For this, you need to place the light near the base of the tree with the lamp angled straight up into the foliage. If you want to illuminate a low feature such as a border or wall you should 'spread' the light.

For a long wall you will require a series of lamps, angling the lamp-heads so that, in the case of a patterned screen wall, for example, the light and shadow created emphasize the attractive patterns, giving a three-dimensional effect. A lamp or two hidden away in the flower borders can produce a dramatic effect, picking out the leaf patterns and casting a warm glow over the colourful flowers.

Lighting adds to the pleasure and entertainment of a garden, making it possible to eat outdoors after dark or give party barbecues, and indulge in midnight bathing if you own a swimming pool. Long after dusk you can also continue playing such popular garden games as bowls, croquet, clock golf – and hide-and-seek for the younger members of the family.

One note of warning though: respect your neighbours and make quite sure that no stray lighting falls onto their property, especially the bedroom windows. Also be careful when illuminating the front garden to see that your lights are not a hazard to passing motorists or cyclists.

Top right: when cable is laid across rear of lamp-housing and cover screwed on, special 'teeth' bite into cable, making electrical contact
Centre: as for push-in system, except cable is looped into terminal block from which leads are connected to lamp-holder
Right: as wire is already connected to lamp-housing, spike on lamp is simply stuck into earth and system plugged in

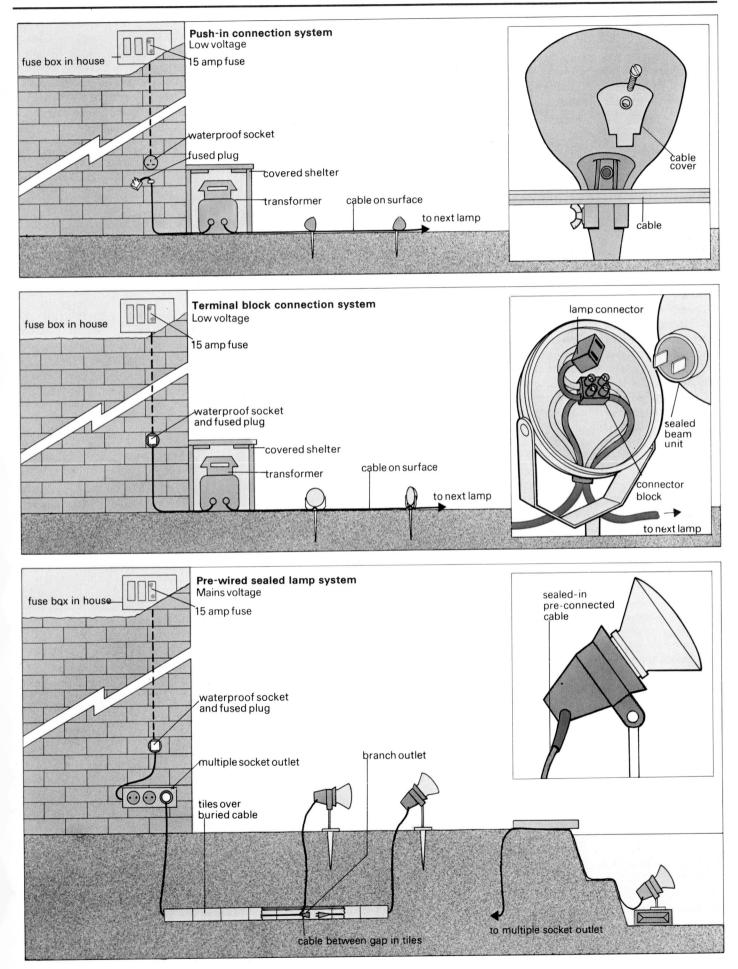

Push-in connection system
Low voltage

fuse box in house

15 amp fuse

waterproof socket

fused plug

covered shelter

transformer

cable on surface

to next lamp

cable cover

cable

Terminal block connection system
Low voltage

fuse box in house

15 amp fuse

waterproof socket
and fused plug

covered shelter

transformer

cable on surface

to next lamp

lamp connector

sealed beam unit

connector block

to next lamp

Pre-wired sealed lamp system
Mains voltage

fuse box in house

15 amp fuse

waterproof socket
and fused plug

multiple socket outlet

tiles over buried cable

branch outlet

sealed-in pre-connected cable

cable between gap in tiles

to multiple socket outlet

WATER GARDENS

When it comes to creating a focal point of interest in a garden there is nothing to beat a pond. It draws the rest of the garden round it, diffusing an aura of calm and rest, and provides a never-ending source of pleasure and enjoyment. Even non-gardening members of the family will be captivated by its charms, whether the sight of gleaming fish or the distant murmuring of a fountain or waterfall. On page 171 we tell you how to make your own garden pond, using either plastics or concrete, and detail the materials now available.

To make and maintain a garden pond is much simpler than generally realized. A hole must be excavated, certainly, but thereafter modern materials make construction a quick and easy job requiring no hard labour. If the basic rules of design and planting are followed there will be no need for frequent changes of water, or for a total annual clearout. A pond can stay clean, healthy and attractive for years with no more than a little annual tidying up, provided you make sensible decisions initially about size, shape and position. Remember that however much the pond may please you, your family and friends, it must first and foremost satisfy the needs of the plants and fish living in it.

Old wives' tales

Don't be influenced by any old wives' tales. There's one that says a pond must be 1·2–1·5m (4–5 ft) deep in one part to make fish safe in winter: this, as will be seen later, is nonsense. Another says that a pond must be in the shade because sunlight makes the water turn green. The problem of green water exists, but is not solved by putting the pond under a tree.

The sectional shape of a pond will affect the occupants' health. The first two shapes below are poor, with low volume-to-surface-area ratios. The third shape includes a marginal shelf and spawning area, and has a much better volume-to-surface-area ratio

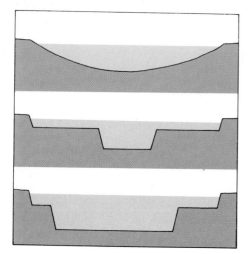

Correct siting

The best site for a pond is the most open you can find. *Nymphaea* (water lily) will flower only sparingly in the shade, and even such tolerant shallow-water plants as *Caltha palustris* (marsh marigold or kingcup), *Iris pseudacorus* (flag iris) and *Mimulus moschatus* (musk) will not give of their best without strong light.

Fish have definite dislikes too, becoming sickly and diseased in water polluted by decaying leaves and twigs. So clearly the last place for a pond is beneath a tree. Both plants and fish will be happier in an open position attracting the maximum amount of sunshine.

If you're considering a fountain pump or underwater lighting remember that you will need to lay a cable for an underwater socket outlet. Bear in mind, too, that you will need a hose for the initial filling and for topping up later.

The best shape and size

The site you decide on will influence the surface shape of the pond. The foot of a rock garden or alongside a curving border calls for informal, natural curves, while on a patio a formal circle or rectangle could be appropriate. But formal or informal, keep the shape as open and simple as possible. When sketching your plan on paper resist the temptation to make it more interesting by the addition of wiggly outlines, serpentine canals, elaborate crosses, pinched waists and quite pointless bridges. Although such designs may look attractive on paper remember that you will not be looking down on your pond from the air. Apart from proving severely cramping to plant growth, narrow arms and canals will become visual nothings when viewed from ground level across the garden.

The need is not for fancy shapes but the broadest stretch of water possible: water to catch light reflections, water to contain the spray of a fountain, water for the free-spreading growth of plants. Squares, egg shapes and broad ovals are all good, and circles—or something very similar—best of all, being visible across their full width from all observation points. The golden